Criminalisation of Politics

Criminalisation of Politics

Caste, Land and the State

Avinash Kumar

RAWAT PUBLICATIONS
Jaipur • New Delhi • Bangalore • Hyderabad • Guwahati • Kolkata

ISBN 978-81-316-0673-5

Published by
Prem Rawat for **Rawat Publications**
Satyam Apts, Sector 3, Jawahar Nagar, Jaipur 302 004 (India)
Phone: 0141 265 1748 / 7006 Fax: 0141 265 1748
E-mail: info@rawatbooks.com
Website: www.rawatbooks.com

New Delhi Office
4858/24, Ansari Road, Daryaganj, New Delhi 110 002
Phone: 011 2326 3290

Also at *Bangalore, Hyderabad, Guwahati* and *Kolkata*

Typeset by Rawat Computers, Jaipur
Printed at Chaman Enterprises, New Delhi

Contents

List of Tables, Figures and Appendices

Tables

Figures

Appendices

Preface

While much has been said about the phenomenon of "criminalisation of politics" in the media in the recent past, it has not attracted adequate scholarly attention. Irrespective of the new contexts in which criminalisation of politics is generally located, the phenomenon is not new for Indian democracy. This is a proper academic attempt to understand the phenomenon, whose roots, the study explains, lies in the very process of democratisation.

To specify, this study does not see the phenomenon of 'criminalisation of politics' merely in narrow terms of electoral politics, but a phenomenon which challenges the very survival of the democratic polity and threatens the social fabric of Indian society, which is so heterogeneous, so plural in its making. It doesn't consider mere entry of criminals into legislatives, rather inquires deeply into, the erosion of democratic institutional mechanism that first led to the crisis of governance and later to the *illegitimacy of the state* itself. Even the deepening of electoral democracy could not erode or halt this decay. The study brings into light how individuals, under the false impression of settling scores of religion and caste, have tried to settle their scores at the expense of the larger democratic system. Using evidence from a variety of sources, it although begins with a modest attempt of examining the relationship of crime and punishment at the highest level in politics, detailed evidence has been collected from the state of Bihar. Life in Bihar has a longstanding reputation of being dependent on the whims of the landed upper/dominant castes. This study suggests that criminalisation of politics in Bihar has its roots in the State's failure to respond to the changing socio-economic and political needs, primarily because of the land-caste link.

Bringing out the salience of the relationship between caste, land and the state in Bihar, the study locates the process of criminalisation of politics in the manner in which it was played out since the politics of the abolition of *Zamindari*. Collecting detailed evidence from Purnea which had become the 'epicenter of violence and crime' due to land-caste link, the study shows how 'criminalisation' ultimately spread into everyday life. It shows how Purnea, the first place in the state to witness a caste massacre by the landlords was later pushed into the hands of gang-lords. With the state failing to fulfill its constitutional obligation, there emerged a peculiar political class that was concerned only with grabbing as much power as possible to become the "uncontested king" of the land. The nexus between politics and crime exists globally though, what is surprising is that unlike in other countries, the nexus enjoys a "cozy-comfortable-coexistence" in India. Deeply conscious of my personal limitations, this is simply an attempt to provoke a discussion, particularly among those like-minded intellectual companions who are open to look beyond the celebratory adulation of Indian democracy.

I would like to record my thanks to all the informants from the field who gave necessary inputs and helped me to understand this critical subject. I also owe a special gratitude to Dr. Amir Ali who not only helped me sharpen my views on the subject but also shape the analytical conceptions recorded here. Comments received by Professor Suranjan Das, Professor Manoranjan Mohanty and Professor Ujjwal Singh helped me make my arguments more persuasive. Working with Professor Sudha Pai over several years now has helped me a great deal in understanding the state politics in contemporary India. Thanks are due to my colleagues and students at Ram Lal Anand College (Evening), University of Delhi. Professor Praveen Jha, Chairperson, Centre for Informal Sector and Labour Studies, Jawaharlal Nehru University, also deserves special thanks for all his encouragement and support. I have also benefitted immensely from my discussions with Professor C.P. Bhambhri and Professor Barbara Harriss-White. For all errors and inadequacies that may remain in this work, of course, the responsibility is entirely mine.

This study would not have been possible without the support of my family. My mother, Smt Kanti, and my wife, Puja, both have been giving me strength through their own fortitude. The volume is dedicated to both of them. Finally, I would like to acknowledge Pranit Rawat and his team for the friendly handling of this book.

Avinash Kumar

1

Introduction

Criminalisation of politics is not a new phenomenon, but its urgency among scholars has been realised very recently.[1] Scholarly studies on the subject have remained very rare. The task has been left at the mercy of the journalists. However, journalists cannot and do not report everything that happens, and there is always a greater political meaning to every story that goes into print or on air. The public perception on seriousness of crime and its nexus with politics in the recent years has increased manifold.[2] This may have some effect of media hype, but all serious accounts suggest that the problem is real enough.[3] This study makes an attempt at academic understanding of the phenomenon of criminalisation of politics.

To specify, this study does not see the phenomenon merely in narrow terms of electoral politics. It rather considers the phenomenon as something that challenges the very survival of a democratic polity. It doesn't consider mere entry of criminals into politics, rather inquires deep into the eroding of edifice of our democratic institutional trinity of the executive, the legislature and the judiciary by show of money, muscle and gun power that has succeeded in destroying the constitutional mechanisms which are expected to uphold the rule of law.[4] The key objective is to understand how this phenomenon, in such a short span, has corroded the edifice culminating first into the crisis of governability and then into the illegitimacy of the state.[5]

The study, however, should not be confused either with a study on crime or that of politics *per se*.[6] It is an attempt to connect the the two; an attempt to wake up to the fact and check whether along with the transition to democracy there lies an insidious process of criminalisation engulfing politics and economics, which threatens the survival and legitimacy of democracy.[7] The nexus of crime and politics in India has been very unique. Unlike some countries where organised criminals and state power have run their parallel governments;[8] the nexus of crime and politics in India has enjoyed a cozy-comfortable-coexistence.

The host of crime-politics nexus is generally found in the practice of patron-client relationship, where kinship (either real or symbolic) is prioritised over relationships based on legality. Criminals themselves bolt onto or are bolted onto by politicians for vote and support in exchange of receiving protection from the law. And once this nexus is established, it never goes away. The pattern in India suggests that it all started with the use of criminals by the politicians for obtaining favours for their protection and enrichment in return. But this is not all. Entry of crime into the realm of politics also shows the weakness of political institutions and the decline in the legitimacy of the state. So how do we account for this? How do we explain the increasing criminalisation of politics in a virtually 'hegemonic democratic' age?[9] This study tries to find an answer by exploring the idea of the state from certain fundamental and unstated presuppositions of our irreversible democratic-political process that lies at the background.[10] It attempts to untangle the thicket under which crime and politics enjoys a cozy-comfortable-coexistence.

The first section of this chapter presents an overview with focus particularly on the changing nature of the state-society relationship. It suggests that the state although has to be seen as an aggregate power structure of the society, its relative autonomy cannot and should not be undermined. Section two, turns to discuss the evolution and nature of the Indian state and tries to trace the dilemmas inherent in the process. It is here that the study suggests to move beyond the celebratory adulation of Indian democracy and arrives at a more sober and thought provoking evaluation by investigating the paradoxes witnessed since independence. Based on this unravelling, the study then in the next section inquires whether the undermining of the rule of law (with processes such as criminalisation of politics), which is probably one of the most foundational aspects of democracy, is inherent in the logic of Indian democratisation or lies somewhere else. The last section of this chapter explains the structure of the study.

The State

The society today is under a deep impression of the idea of modern state.[11] With the emergence of *classical liberalism* and subsequently its hybrid variant *liberal-democracy*, the state has gained greater importance in the day to day lives.[12] However, over the years, the dilemma over the nature and features of modern-liberal-democratic state has been constantly growing. There is an intense debate on whether the state is to be seen as an 'autonomous and powerful leviathan' or a 'Gulliver tied down by an ever denser web of particularistic links to narrow social groupings'.[13] Opinion is divided according to ones preference for the models (liberal, populist, communist, etc.) which has more dissimilarity to point than commonality. But no matter where one stands, it is clear as common sense that state is a political-arena where actors use distinctive means to settle their social and economic conflicts.[14]

The most important drawback, however, of all these theories has been the expectations of a generalised political outcome in the post-colonial states regardless of historical, political, economic and social contexts that they had.[15] The experience proved to be contrary and soon all realised that most of the socio-economic changes in the third world were taking place not due to the non-state actors but because of the state itself. It thus, again generated great interest on state and shifted the focus away from the society-centred explanations to the 'autonomy of the political'.[16] It projected the state as a distinct entity, opposed to and set apart from a larger entity called society.[17]

It placed state above society, independent and capable of opposing antagonistically and frontally, the powerful social and economic interests of the ruling class.[18] However, by emphasising state as a discrete entity, it prioritised the state over everything else and ultimately failed to analyse that it was not an 'actual structure' but a 'structural effect', i.e., a "powerful, metaphysical effect of practices that make such structures appear to exist."[19] Especially in the context of country like India, assertion on the significance of the state not only underemphasised the other forces of change but also threw the evolution of the state in the background.[20] Thus, a new attempt was made to create a balance between state and society, termed as State-in-Society approach.[21] The state, now became both an independent variable (the impact made by varying state capacities) and a dependent variable (the determinants of varying state capacities), and it was conceived that the strengthening of state and society, stood squarely at the intersection of each other.[22]

However, the answers on how the state in India evolved and has functioned in the last six decades cannot be gleaned mere by understanding the differences between political vocabularies such as state and society, coercion and consent, autonomy and clientelism and the likes. This study, therefore, searching for an explanation, in addition to using approaches discussed above, also brings into use the discourse of Max Weber and Michael Foucault on the state. From the former it accepts that the state as an institution has claim over the monopoly of 'legitimate physical coercion'[23] and from the latter, it takes the principle of plurality of power, which locates it not in "appropriation" but in "dispositions, manoeuvres, tactics, techniques, functioning; that one should decipher in it a network of relations, constantly in tension, in activity, rather than a privilege that one might possess".[24] The state therefore has obligations to perform beyond reflecting of demands or interests of dominant social groups or classes in society. If this does not happen, 'criminalisation of politics' is inevitable. In more direct terms, it suggests that India has witnessed politicisation without adequate democratisation and hence it has contributed to the perpetuation of 'criminalisation of politics' in the country.[25] In what follows below, the study attempts, therefore, to use O'Donnell's term, disaggregate democracy itself.[26]

The Indian State: Rival Conjectures

An interesting and important historical aspect that one needs to keep in mind while discussing the Indian state is that power in this subcontinent has always been seen in highly personal terms and based on the traditional Hindu belief that some are born to rule while others to serve. Considerations such as birth, wealth, wisdom, education and even religiosity are the major concerns.[27] Prior to the advent of colonial modernity, kingdoms in this part of the world was dominated by a 'group of rulers distinct from society below them'. Their 'ability to affect society's basic structure was seriously restricted'.[28] Even during colonial rule this concept was riven with contradictions. The colonial masters, in order to ensure their safe existence, on the one hand brought in the concept of the rule of law and on the other hand displayed enormous sympathy for various indigenous norms (such as patriarchy, caste hierarchy, ruling elites) and included them into the legal claims to superiority of the state. The British preserved the existing situation to the extent they found it useful for themselves. Nevertheless, it provided legitimacy for British rule as a despotism based on law was said to be better than the arbitrary oriental variety'.[29] Thus, the state that the British left for the Indians, at the time of independence, was just a juxtaposition of their fondness for Hinduism and imported liberalism.

Most of the studies on Indian state, though limited in number, has described the term 'state' with a pan-Indian view. This is highly problematic. India had never existed as it exists today. The British did not conquer an Indian state, they rather 'conquered a series of independent kingdoms that became political India during ... their domination'.[30] Even the political awakening was dichotomous.[31] And last but not the least, several princely states which had no experience of democratic rule either joined or were forced to join the Indian territory at the time of independence. Thus, India became a 'union of states' (principally kingdoms) without any intellectual and theoretical debate and resulted in what Kaviraj calls 'a hybrid between an empire state of the older type and a sovereign state in the European pattern'.[32] The architectural design of the country (i.e., the Constitution) crafted by the Indian elites after three years of deliberations also reflect these rival conjectures.[33]

But the question is which of these rival conjectures have shaped and impacted upon the evolution of Indian state in the post-colonial era. This study advances a dialectical argument to prove that the trajectory of the Indian state in India has simultaneously traversed through both the conjectures. The character of the union as a whole, i.e., the state at the central level and that at the provincial level has been at variance with each other at several fronts. While the centre may have grown like a 'powerful leviathan', the states in the provinces under all apolitical variables have increasingly resembled more and more as a 'Guliver tied with an ever denser web'. The argument of 'relative autonomy' of the state though may be felt relevant at the central level,[34] at the level of provinces, it looks more problematic.[35] Coercion, as Nandy argues, may be found central to the Indian state at the centre, but the state at provincial level have seemed to be true to Philip Oldenburg's observation of a thing to be avoided or kept at bay, or a cow to be milked.[36] Though the political elites at the central level may use modernist language and depend upon Weberian 'rationality', those at the province want and have remained 'vernacular netas'. As a result, the common sense of the society at large has remained far from principles of rationality.[37]

The purpose here is not to develop a master concept of the Indian state; it is rather an attempt to move beyond the celebratory adulation and arrive at a more restrained and serious evaluation of Indian state by investigating the paradoxes inherent in the process. This unraveling is important because it will lead us to understand whether the undermining of the rule of law in the form of criminalisation of politics – which is probably one of the most foundational aspects of democracy – is inherent in the logic of Indian democratisation as it unfolds at this stage of the nation's political history or whether it lies somewhere else. What factors bring crime and politics into contact? What effect, if any, does their coming together have on democratic government? Is the relationship parasitic or symbiotic? Is it transitory or permanent?

The study comes closer to the idea that the Indian state in laying out its agenda for socio-economic change has remained universal, confident and highly interventionist but local, reactive and powerless at the same time. Construction and maintenance of state's legitimacy is a dialectic process in which the power elite have not only to create institutions but also to resist undermining them. Consequently, democratisation and political participation has come along with anomalies such as criminalisation, subversion of the rule of law, erosion of democratic institutions and naturalised simultaneously. Institutions like Election Commission, Media, etc., might have grown stronger; but the nature and functions of the executive, the legislatives and the judiciary (especially at the lower levels) have thoroughly been compromised. The state while may seem stable and strong, is actually undergoing a real crisis and decline, both as a sovereign power and as an instrument of liberation and transformation. Power lies today not in the positions or institutions but in persons of high positions. Gluttonous individuals capture institutions, change the meaning of democratic principles according to their own purpose by either cooption or elimination of those opposed to their views, and lead to the erosion of both authority and legitimacy of the state. Significant proportions of people, therefore, have lost faith in the modern Indian state, and doubt its commitment to the principles enshrined in the Constitution of India. In such a situation, criminalisation of politics slowly gains, though rancorously, a grudging social nod and become legitimate and inevitable means for democratic success.

Structure of the Book

The book is divided into six chapters. It begins with this introductory chapter, followed by an examination of the power relation, literally with the question of 'how power is exercised and what causes the changes in its pattern' in Chapter 2. The chapter shows how power and politics in India has been constantly dominated by the up-to-date knowledgeable people of the upper-caste urban elite who live with the perception that if they are not allowed to have direct access to power, democracy in India cannot be sustained.[38] When power travelled down the hierarchy with people characterised as rural and rustic, they started using it as a means to express their superiority over the former. It is this struggle that has ultimately led to the undermining of the democratic values of the institutions of the country. Interestingly, democratisation which is considered to be a good thing in itself, the chapter shows, is implicated in the phenomenon of 'criminalisation of politics'.

The chapter starting from the structural-functional analytical perspective of Rajni Kothari in his *Politics in India* to an entirely different framework of normative and empirical accounts in the later decades, comes closer to the idea 'crisis of governability' and the 'crisis of legitimacy' of the state, raised by Kohli, Vanaik in the contemporary times.[39] However, it extends itself beyond that period and analyses the situation of continued 'illegitimacy of the state' in the decades of 1990s and 2000s.[40] It finds that, although the process started changing with political intervention of the state in 1970s and 1980s, in the later years, it converted into state's incapacity to intervene. The institutions of the state started declining and the political leadership started finding themselves, increasingly, under uncertainties. Thus, in order to maintain their position, they gave way to extra-normative varieties, from money to muscle to gun power at all level of politics but mostly at the grassroot. People not knowing who else to turn to for justice and safeguard, started looking for leadership in the closed set up of their caste, religion and region. The state slowly became unable to carry out the constitutional obligations and caused a substantial shift in the understanding of the crime-punishment relationship. It explains how there has been a divorce between the crime-punishment link (being mediated through politics) for a new marriage between crime and non-punishment. The judiciary, too, failed to keep the crime-punishment link intact. In such a state, it is not surprising that the struggle for control over power has become reactive, violent and deadly.

The intention of the chapter, however, is not to say that democracy in India has become altogether lifeless. It is just to bring into light the erosions that the political process has witnessed in the increased competitive democratic set up. Though a reference has been made, in this study, of the criminalisation of political process at the central level, detailed evidence has been collected from the state of Bihar and presented in the remaining part of the book. In Chapter 3 and Chapter 4, it has been shown that the phenomenon of 'criminalisation of politics' in Bihar is not new, as it started as early as the abolition of *Zamindari* Bill in 1947. Addressing the issue of the economics and politics of change in Bihar, this focuses on the land and caste and traces the factors that led to the rise and growth of crime-politics link in the state in the later years.

These chapters further show that the state in Bihar with its feudal character 'embedded in caste' has failed to evolve as a disinterested arbiter. With the social consciousness of the people remained so rigidly attached to caste, it shows that the state has failed to witness civil society mobilisation of any form and could not even develop the spirit of agrarianism, let alone understand importance of economic development. The assertion of the backward castes since 1977, although brought some hopes among the marginalised sections of the society; the leadership's invention of a notional scheme of social justice through caste empowerment sans economic development could reach little beyond the question of 'dignity' for them. On the contrary, the opposition between the caste blocs, viz., upper and backward, transformed the state into a land of caste tensions, and in some parts even caste riots. This led to a rapid induction of socially injurious and parasitic elements into the political system, and Bihar from being a non-performer state simply became non-existent. It failed to satisfy the rising expectations of the marginalised social groups and became a state without hope. Thus, in an attempt to find the answers to the unrestricted influence of crime in politics in the state, this part digs deeper into the political economy of change in Bihar.

Chapter 5 brings the study at a level where the state meets the everyday life. Taking cases from Purnea, a district in the eastern part of northern Bihar, which has attracted news headlines over several decades now – initially celebrating the honour of being the land of the most powerful (upper caste) landlords of the country and later for being the land of the most powerful ganglords – this chapter shows how the State has remained a strong party to this conspiracy in all these years. The chapter explains how there emerged a peculiar political class that is concerned only with grabbing power to become the uncontested king of the land. With the passage of time this process accelerated from politicisation of criminals to criminalisation of politics and ultimately, the venom spread to every walk of life.

Chapter 6 makes an attempt to understand the changes witnessed in the state of Bihar after the election (2005) of Nitish Kumar as the chief minister that has attracted a world wide attention around the idea of 'replacement of caste-politics by development'. The chapter shows that caste is deeply embedded into the political-economy of Bihar and it is therefore not right to accept these presumptions without analysing critically at this early juncture. In addition to that, the victory of Nitish Kumar though may have many reasons to rejoice for; it cannot be understood in vacuum. Nitish Kumar is the culmination of the three successive terms of 'Lalu-raj'. This chapter makes an attempt to critically analyse the implication of politics under Nitish Kumar-led political formation in Bihar.

Notes

1. The first ever academic debate on the phenomenon of criminalisation of politics was organised by the Institute of Peach Research and Action with the support provided by the Ministry of Home Affairs, Government of India, on August 2–3, 1990. It brought together leading social scientists and several other eminent writers, journalists and activists to share their concern. The scholars had reached at a consensus that no analysis can be made without further research on the issue. See Susheela Bhan, (ed.) (1995). *Criminalization of Politics,* New Delhi, Shipra. More than two decades have passed, however, the term still has not found place in any Social Science – particularly in Political Science – compendia in India. The ICSSR Survey Reports in Sociology and Social Anthropology documents the studies on crime under criminological studies. The first trend report was part of 'Social Work Research' (Ranade, 1974) undertaken in the first ICSSR Survey in Sociology and Social Anthropology. The second effort was a trend report on 'Sociology of Deviant Behaviour' (1985) by K.S. Shukla. And the third effort was a report on 'Crime, Delinquency and Correctional Methods' undertaken as part of the third survey in Sociology and Social Anthropology by D.R. Singh (2000).
2. A recent study done by the Centre for the Study of Developing Societies, New Delhi on the status of democracy in India (as a part of the project on State of Democracy in South Asia) has found that a good number of people in the country have expressed concern for the declining conditions of law and order and fear from the personal and physical security than that rising from state boundaries, inter-state conflict, terrorism and insurgency. See Centre for the Study of Developing Societies, (2008). *State of Democracy in South Asia: A Report*, New Delhi, Oxford University Press.
3. See Sumanta Banerjee, (2011). 'Breeding Black Sheep', *Economic and Political Weekly,* January 8, Vol. XLVI No. 2, pp. 10–13.
4. 'Rule of law' as used in this study refers to a set of stable rules established by the law of the land, applied impartially to all its citizens, without discrimination, prejudice and biases. A necessary condition for the realization of democracy is that both the state and its citizens in general, and its political officials in particular, agree to define, accept and respect the self-enforcing limits of democratic behaviour. Not certainly as easy goal to achieve though, (as positions and interests of citizens may differ), there is a need to realise that compromise of ideal limits of self-enforcement be done by all equally. If one group of citizens' form a coalition with the state or vice-versa against another, a pattern which is most commonly witnessed and which seems workable; it is principally in violation of the rule of law.

Learning to oppose violations even if they are potential beneficiaries of that violation is necessary.

5. This invokes a suspicion of adding up to the contest between the upper castes/class and the backward/lower caste/class of the Indian society, a common thing witnessed in the recent years across India and particularly in Bihar during this study. The two groups have completely divergent conjectures, determined primarily by the side of the caste/class divide. They are rigid with their own perspective and are at loggerheads. While the former (upper caste/class) blame the lower caste/class for the change in the quality of political leadership, those from the latter argue that the political leadership in India is more representative and thus India has become more democratic. But this study has no such intention. On the contrary, it seeks to answer and explicate how individuals under the false impression of representing and settling scores of caste and faction have tried to settle their personal scores at the expense of the larger democratic system. In other words, it partially distances itself from the theories of identity politics advanced in the recent decades and aims to locate the phenomenon in the political economy of the society.
6. The study on crime in India has rarely attracted serious scholars. However, two important names that deserve mention are – Ranjit Guha and Sumanta Banerjee. Guha in his study on peasant insurgency in Bengal presented crime and rebellion as contrasting "codes" for defining the same phenomenon. He showed how the dacoit Lodhas, who kidnapped and stole from greedy moneylenders, officials, and landlords were mythic champions of justice for the peasants of the western Bengal. Conversely, persons with property and power, described the dacoits as terrifying threats to public order. Sumanta Banerjee too studies the crime and punishment in colonial Calcutta with similar approach. Analysing the criminal acts and penal measures in colonial Calcutta as "innovative responses within a symbiotic relationship in a new socio-economic environment", Banerjee provides a fascinating account of the evolution of "the criminal elite" and the "institutionalisation of crimes like extortions, bribery, and even murders, by the East India Company's men in the city". This historical element of collusion between the administration and its agents, Banerjee opines, becomes intrinsic to the city's culture and remains evident even in contemporary times between the "inhabitants of the upper tier and the underworld". However, both these studies remain strictly limited within the discipline of History and provide very little insights for a socio-political analysis. All other sources of studies on crime have been based mostly on statistical data by the government in *Crime in India* that is concerned only with the documentation of rise or fall of crime each year, rather than with causes and consequences of crime in either absolute or relative terms.

See Ranajit Guha, (1983). *Elementary Aspects of Peasant Insurgency in Colonial India*. Delhi: Oxford University Press; Sumanta Banerjee (2009). *The Wicked City – Crime and Punishment in Colonial Calcutta,* Hyderabad, Orient Blackswan; Sumanta Banerjee, (2006), 'The Underside of a City Divided', *Seminar,* 559.

7. Generally, the literature on the subjects- crime and politics- never connects the two. But recently some scholars have woken up to this fact. See Stephen Handelman, (1995). *Comrade Criminal: Russia's New Mafia*, London, Yale University Press; Bohdan Harasymiw, (2003). 'Putting Organized Crime in its Place ... Within Political Science', Paper presented at the *Annual Meetings of the Canadian Political Science Association,* Dalhousie University, Halifax, Nova Scotia, 1 June. URL: www.cpsa-acsp.ca/paper-2003/harasymiw.pdf; Accessed: 1st August 2009.
8. John Bailey and Roy Godson, (2000). "Introduction" in their edited book *Organized Crime and Democratic Governability: Mexico and the US-Mexican Borderlands*, Pittsburgh, University of Pittsburgh Press; Bohdan Harasymiw, (2003). 'Putting Organized Crime in its Place ...', op. cit. Jenkins and Potter in their case study of Philadelphia city also showed the existence of what they called "the triple alliance" of politicians, police and criminals and asserted that the initiative in this relationship came from politicians; i.e., a situation where crime did not intrude into politics, but politicians reached out and co-opted the criminals and their activities. See Philip Jenkins and Gary Potter. (1987). "The Politics and Mythology of Organized Crime: A Philadelphia Case-Study", *Journal of Criminal Justice,* 15, pp. 473–84. British historian Michael Woodwiss, in his work *Organized Crime and American Power,* demonstrated the persistence of a close link between crime and politics in the United States ever since pre-independent days to the present time; but he observed that crime in America was always seen as a social phenomenon and never a threat to the established or evolving economic and political power structures; it rather complemented them. Michael Woodiwiss, (2001). *Organized Crime and American Power: A History,* Toronto, University of Toronto Press. In other parts of the world also the criminal-politician nexus is a living, evolving one.
9. The notion of democracy, ever since the dawn of modernity, seems to have become the only essential tool for the survival of the people in this world. It has become inevitable and any argument against democracy has become futile. This is despite the fact that fulfillment of even its basic aim 'to lower the powerful and raise the low' through its pedestal principles – i.e., rights, justice and the rule of law – have been full of setbacks. A mechanism, which was essentially developed as a method to restructure the power relations within a state, by its

very nature has gone beyond the state. With the democratisation of economic, social and political relations, it has become a process, unstoppable, irreversible and rather contagiously 'hegemonic'. A google search of the term 'hegemonic democracy' although seems to have been used by Joe Lockard (see Hegemonic Democracy in the Middle East. *Tikkun 20*(3):26 (2005); accessed at http://www.tikkun.org/article.php?story=Lockard-hegemonic-democracy); he refers primarily to the imposition of the US neo-conservative vision of democracy in the context of the Middle East. However, the term here is being used to describe the nature of the democracy in India, which without any external interference has adopted a hegemonic characteristic. Principles of democracy which forms its base is used to undermine it – e.g., 'rights' is being reinterpreted here as the freedom of gluttonous individuals to fulfill their interest by hook or by crook in the midst of the vast swathes of poverty and social discrimination; yet, the idea of democracy survives beyond suspicion. As Alexis de Tocqueville had observed, democracy is not to be stopped, it is to be made the best of it when it comes by educating masses its true long-term interests. The study shows that efforts in this direction have been very rare in India and consequently it has ended up as, to use Banerjee's (2011) explanation, "the most dangerous example of how a democratic society can be insidiously turned into a totalitarian society ... where a minority of like-thinking individuals wielding power and influence ooze concurrence on every side in favour of their gluttony."

10. Important to mention is that the question of state for the purpose of this study will be concerned less about the philosophical debate and more about the prudential issues of policy and government.
11. The idea of tracing the existence of a 'modern state' for the purpose of this study is not chronological, but based on its features which are still recognisable in contemporary societies. The state has not emerged in countries all across the world, or for that matter, even in Europe, at one particular point of time. While it came into existence in Britain in eighteenth century, Germany saw its existence only in the late nineteenth century. For an interesting discussion on the uneven rise of state, see Stuart Hall, (1993). 'The State in Question' in Gregor McLenan, David Held and Stuart Hall. (eds.) *The Idea of a Modern State*, Philadelphia, Open University Press, pp. 1–28.
12. Classical liberalism, that celebrated the right of individuals to 'life, liberty and property' in its initial years remained far from democracy and was confined in the men of the new middle class or bourgeoisie. It was its variant, viz., *liberal-democracy* which celebrated upon the concept of political equality. Ibid. Also see, Chapter 2 of the same book: 'Central Perspectives on the Modern State' by David Held, pp. 29–79.

13. Kurt Weyland, (1998). 'From Leviathan to Gulliver? The Decline of the Developmental State in Brazil', *Governance,* Volume 11, Issue 1, pp. 51–75, January.
14. The difference of opinion lies only over which means – hegemonic legitimate authority or fundamentally coercive domination – the actors embody. Based on such means, the state for liberal school is an aspect of either utilitarian or value consensus, which despite having a standing force cannot be fundamentally coercive. On the contrary, Marxists and political conflict theorists see it as an organised coercion. For them the state is not dependent for its effectiveness upon value consensus or popular contentment. They suggest complete overlap between the power of the state and that of the dominant groups. For more on this debate, see Theda Skocpol, (1979) *State and Social Revolutions,* Cambridge University Press, Cambridge. While some neo-Marxist scholars, namely, Ralph Miliband, Nicos Poulantzas, Perry Anderson, Goran Therborn, and Claus Offe stated that "state should be regarded neither as a specific institution nor as an instrument but as a relation – a material concentration of class relations of a given society"; some such as Elen Kay Trimberger and Fred Block suggested state as potentially autonomous.
15. The society-centred approach had refused to consider state as an independent actor. State virtually disappeared from their political analysis for a long period only to make space for government, interest groups, voting and legislative behaviour; i.e., almost everything but 'the state'. The chief proponents of this school of thought were Gabriel Almond, James Coleman, G. Bingham Powell and David. N. Truman. Few exceptional political scientists who continued to write about the state were Samuel Huntington, Morris Janowitz, S.M. Lipset and Reinhard Bendix.
16. Peter Evans, Dietrich Rueschemeyer, and Theda Skocpol, (1985) *Bringing the State Back In,* Cambridge University Press, London.
17. Relying anew on the Weber-Hintze perspective, Skocpol stated that "state properly conceived is no mere arena in which socio-economic struggles are fought out. It is rather a set of administrative policy and military organisation headed and more or less coordinated by executive authorities. Any state first and fundamentally extracts resources from society and deploys these to create and support coercive and administrative organisation … When they exist, these fundamental state organisation are at least partially autonomous from direct dominant class control." Theda Skocpol, (1979) *State and Social Revolutions,* op. cit.
18. For a detailed critique on Statist approach, see Timothy Mitchell, (1991). 'The Limits of the State: Beyond Statist Approaches and Their Critics', *The American Political Science Review,* Vol. 85, No. 1,

March, pp. 77–96. Mitchell also points out that Skocpol (1979) eventually had acknowledged the impossibility of distinguishing state and society by bringing the two terms together in a single phrase *'statist societies'* (p. 88).

19. Ibid. Substantiating it with an example, Mitchell takes the case of the new military methods of the late eighteenth century that produced the disciplined individual soldier and, simultaneously, the novel effect of an armed unit as an artificial machine. This military apparatus appeared somehow greater than the sum of its parts, as though it were a structure with an existence independent of the men who composed it.
20. Atul Kohli, (1992). *Democracy and Discontent: India's Growing Crisis of Governability,* Cambridge, Cambridge University Press, p. 10.
21. Joel Migdal, Atul Kohli and Vivienne Shue, (1994) (Eds.) *State Power and Social Forces: Domination and Transformation in the Third World,* Cambridge: Cambridge University Press. Also see Joel Migdal, (2001). *State in Society: Studying How States and Societies Transform and Constitute One Another,* Cambridge: Cambridge University Press.
22. For more substantiated argument, see Joel Migdal, (1989). *Strong Societies and Weak States,* Princeton, N.J., Princeton University Press; Atul Kohli (1992), *Democracy and Discontent,* op. cit.
23. According to Weber, 'force is not the normal or the only means of the state ... but force is a means specific to the state'. By legitimate coercion what Weber wanted to say was not what the state could do and get away with, with its power; but what was considered right and proper in a society for the state to do. The key issue in the use of power by the state is not simply the state's violence or force, but the question of *legitimacy.* For a detailed analysis on Weber's idea of state's power, see Stuart Hall, (1993). op. cit. pp. 1–28.
24. Michael Foucault, (1977). *Discipline and Punish: The Birth of the Prison,* (translated in English by Alan Sheridan), London, Penguin Press, p. 26.
25. Democratisation, although is a commonly used concept in academic circles in India, studying its impact on the state still awaits serious examination. Due to dearth of scholarly attention on the impact of democratisation on state, the arguments cluster around two divergent conjectures. One set of ideas say that democratisation gives state a higher level of institutionalisation, makes it more cohesive and gives it more autonomy from powerful social classes and groups. With greater importance of civil society the public is in a better position to hold the state accountable, transparent and refrain from clientelism. By contrast the second view tells that democratisation corrodes the state's cohesion and autonomy by allowing

interest organisations and clientelist politicians to enhance their influence and capture public agency. The more the democratisation, the more privileged social groups take advantage of the opportunity to increase their influence in and on the state. See Kari Palonen, Tuija Pulkkinen, and José María Rosales, (2008) (eds.) *The Ashgate Research Companion to the Politics of Democratization in Europe: Concepts and Histories*, Ashgate, London. However, what is agreed universally is that the process of democratisation differs substantially from region to region and the idea of making the Western democracy a normative reference point have failed to explain it. There is a need to accommodate the variations of all the political struggles that have led to the present-day situation in different parts of the world. The experience of India though seems to be closer to the second view; this study advances a dialectical argument that combines the two opposing viewpoints. It opines that democratization though may seem to have strengthened the state; not adequate has been done to democratize before politicizing the masses.

26. Guillermo O'Donnell, (1993). 'On the State, Democratization and Some Conceptual Problems: A Latin American View with Glances at Some Postcommunist Countries', *World Development,* 21, no. 8, pp. 1355–69.
27. The idea though seems similar to Plato's argument that the origin of the state lies in the natural inequality of humanity in terms of rulers (intellect), soldiers (will) and people (desire) and that rulers were a special class of citizens with wisdom; it is actually very different from the concept of political elitehood as understood in the Hindu philosophy. State for Plato was an organic body where the pain of one member of the state was felt by the whole. He also maintained that membership in the guardian class was based solely upon the possession of appropriate skills, not on birth. He did not even allow his two highest classes, the right to their own bodies, as marriage was nothing more than mere means to procreate the state.
28. Sudipta Kaviraj, (2005), 'On the Enchantment of the State', *European Journal of Sociology,* Vol. 46, pp. 263–96. Kaviraj argues that the theory of kinship in Hindu philosophy is "simply the translation into the human scale of 'the law', the logic of a divinely given natural and social order."
29. See 'Introduction' in Michael R. Anderson and Sumit Guha, (eds.) (1998) *Changing Concepts of Rights and Justice in South Asia*, New Delhi, Oxford University Press.
30. Sudipta Kaviraj, (2005), 'On the Enchantment of the State', op. cit. p. 51.
31. G. Aloysius, (1997). *Nationalism without Nation in India,* New Delhi, Oxford University Press. Aloysius observes that there was hardly any

commonality of interest between the traditionally dominant communities of Brahmins and their allied upper castes on the one hand and the lower castes, Tribals and the Muslims on the other. While the former with the fear of withdrawal of their exclusive patronage by the British raised the slogans of nationalism to safeguard their economic and political interests, the latter effectively utilised the growing disaffection between the native and the foreign elite to their own advantage and pushed their way ahead in the new political structure against the traditional forms of caste and religious slavery. The imperialists with a view to perpetuate their rule, when doled out some fringe favours to the latter, it was projected as a commonality of interests between masses and the imperialists by the former. Thus such a situation could hardly be describes as commonality of interest or a common perception of British as the enemy between the two. The only commonality between the two was that both were interested in power – one by maintaining its monopoly over it and the other by claiming their part of share. (pp. 215–217). *Subaltern Studies* have also provided an interesting account of this dichotomy.

32. Sudipta Kaviraj, (2005), 'On the Enchantment of the State', op. cit. p. 54
33. Equating three years of deliberations of Constituent assembly with that of the intellectual and theoretical interventions experienced in Europe would be immature. In fact, interventions, if any (for instance by Gandhi, Tagore and Bhudev) were granted only hollow reverence in the Constitution; the reason primarily being that these interventions were not in conformity with modernity. Ibid. also see G. Aloysius, (1997). *Nationalism without Nation in India,* op. cit.
34. See Partha Chatterjee, (1997). 'Development Planning and the Indian State' in his edited book *State* and Politics in India, New Delhi, Oxford University Press, pp. 271–97; Sudipta Kaviraj, (1988). 'A Critique of the Passive Revolution', *Economic and Political Weekly*, 23, 45–47, pp 2429–44; Francine Frankel, (1978). *India's Political Economy 1947–1978,* Princeton, Princeton University Press; A.H. Hanson, (1966). *The Process of Planning: A Study of India's Five-Year Plans, 1950–1964.*London, Oxford University Press.
35. See Pranab Bardhan, (1990). *The Political Economy of Development in India,* Oxford University Press, New Delhi; Lloyd, I. Rudolph and Susanne H. Rudolph, (1987). *In Pursuit of Lakshmi: The Political Economy of the Indian State,* University of Chicago Press, Chicago; Achin Vanaik, (1990). *The Painful Transition: Bourgeois Democracy in India,* Verso, London; Ashutosh Varshney, (1995). *Democracy, Development and the Countryside: Urban-Rural Struggles in India,* Cambridge University Press, Cambridge.

36. See Ashis Nandy, (2007). 'The State: Fate of a Concept', in his book *Romance of the State,* New Delhi, Oxford University Press, pp. 1–14; Philip Oldenberg (2006), 'Face to Face with the Indian State', in Llyod Rudolph and J.K. Jacobson (eds.), *Experiencing the State,* New Delhi, Oxford University Press, pp. 184–211.
37. Several Indian Marxists such as Sen (1976), Kaviraj (1984, 1988) and Chatterjee (1986) have found this to be a classic political feature of India's Gramscian style of "passive revolution". See Ashok Sen, (1976). "Bureaucracy an Social Hegemony", in *Essays presented to Professor S.C. Sarkar,* New Delhi, Peoples Publishing House; Sudipta Kaviraj, (1984). 'On the Crisis of Political Institutions in India', *Contributions to Indian Sociology,* No. 2; Sudipta Kaviraj, (1988). 'A Critique of the Passive Revolution', op. cit.; Partha Chatterjee, (1986). *Nationalist Thought and the Colonial World: A Derivative Discourse?* Zed Books, London. Evidence can also be found in the arguments of a coalitional model – of the capitalists, the rich farmers and the bureaucracy – explanation of India state, in which the three although competed and aligned with one another for political space, rich farmers or agrarian capitalists within the dominant coalition won over the political clout between 1970–1990. It was only after the mid 1990s that the relative power of the corporate capitalist class as compared to the landed elites have ascended. See Pranab Bardhan (1984) *The Political Economy of Development in India,* op. cit.; Achin Vanaik, (1990). *The Painful Transition, op. cit.*; Ashutosh Varshney, (1995). *Democracy, Development and the Countryside,* op. cit.; Lloyd, I. Rudolph and Susanne H. Rudolph, (1987). *In Pursuit of Lakshmi,* op. cit.; Partha Chatterjee, (2008). 'Democracy and Economic Transformation in India', *Economic and Political Weekly,* April 19, pp. 53–62.
38. Ashis Nandy has been repeatedly arguing on this line. Kothari too has found this argument substantial. For further details see, Rajni Kothari, (1988). *State against Democracy: In Search of Humane Governance,* New Delhi, Ajanta Publication, pp. 7–9; also see Ashis Nandy, (1989). 'The Political Culture of the Indian State', *Daedaulus,* Vol. 118, No. 4, pp. 1–26.
39. See Atul Kohli, (1992). op. cit. and Achin Vanaik, (1990). op. cit. pp. 67–112.
40. Avinash Kumar, (2009). 'Illegitimacy of the State in Bihar', *Economic and Political Weekly,* Vol. XLIV, No. 44, October 31–November 6, pp. 8–11.

2

Crime, [Politics], and Non-Punishment

An understanding of the phenomenon of the criminalisation of politics in India should begin with a critical inquiry into the direct relationship between crime and punishment that has been distorted, changed and twisted over the years. This chapter makes an attempt in that direction by analysing events in the country from a variety of sources. Not definitive though, the chapter suggests that punishment in India has remained dependent on the structure of the dominant-subordinate relationship within populations, rather than the nature of the crime.

Among all post-colonial societies, India has exceptionally resisted the temptations towards non-democratic rule. Despite being a traditional society based on feudal decree of hierarchical principles, it has maintained a relatively stable and uninterrupted (except a brief disruption for two odd years) democracy. It has also seen a democratic upsurge from below, not only in terms of right to vote and representation, but also as expressing dissent, voicing their concerns and mobilisation for its fulfilment. However, this making of a 'silent revolution'[1] was not an easy process. The traditional political elite in order to maintain their status quo[2] started adopting extra-constitutional ways and means to politicize all social changes that were otherwise rather natural.

Subsequently, leaders who emerged from the silent revolution were left with little option to act exceptionally, and were forced to continue operating outside the institutional space with violent characteristics. Criminalisation of politics is a direct outcome of this contradictory process. With the growing contention and competitiveness in the electoral framework, criminality, from being an underside of politics, started being accepted openly as complementary to it. This gradually resulted in the uncoupling of the crime-punishment link, thereby making the functioning of democracy more difficult and beyond the 'rule of law'.[3]

This chapter makes an attempt to examine the uncoupling of the crime-punishment link by moving beyond the celebratory adulation of Indian democracy and analysing the significant moments of erosion in the post independence India.[4] The chapter proposes two fundamental premises. First, the country over the years has witnessed a traversal towards a divorce between crime and punishment for a new marriage between crime and non-punishment. Politics has played both as a spoiler and a mediator between the two. The use of the term politics here, does not limit itself to electoral alone. It includes affairs of all three wings of the polity – Legislature, Executive and Judiciary. Inclusion of Judiciary, which is supposedly an apolitical body, may surprise many, but the way it has been functioning in the Indian setup (as discussed in this chapter ahead), all critical understanding would accept that it has not remained apolitical, at least on most of the occasions. It is equally responsible for the uncoupling of the crime-punishment link.

Second, to maintain the link of crime with the certainty of punishment in any liberal – democracy, there is a need for a disinterested arbiter, equivalent to the state.[5] However, this has been completely lacking in the Indian case. Irrespective of the new contexts in which criminalisation of politics is generally located, the study opines that the basic reason lies in the very process of democratisation, both during the colonial and the post-independent era. The British rule although conquered and changed our political map, the society, at large, had remained unconquered and unchanged.[6] When one says that during the last phase of the colonialism, enough was achieved for the democratic transformation of the nation, it seems there is an under-estimation of the concept of democracy itself.[7] As Ambedkar has opined, "democratic temper was not an easy task to achieve, far difficult naturally" in a divided society like ours, which is structured parochially and hierarchically on the basis of region, religion, language and caste. It was "only a top dressing on a soil, which was essentially undemocratic" and thus, "it had to be cultivated".[8] In what follows, the chapter examines the changing relationship between crime and punishment through a critical evaluation of Indian politics divided into five phases.

In the Name of Politics

In the initial years after independence, power in India remained monopolised, both in the states and at the centre by the 'Congress System'.[9] Although this served well as the foundation for a consociational grand coalition, the leadership remained in the hands of a very small and homogenous (upper caste/class) elite, trained in the British style. Nehru represented this entire group of political elites.[10] Observers feel that together they attempted to bring national integration, economic development, social equality and political democracy out of the hands of the small traditional authority, based on socio-economic status and hierarchy.[11] They broadly understood the importance of a shared political culture; and despite differences of opinion – both within the party and outside – on several issues, no one ever allowed their whims to overrun the Parliamentary path.[12] Oppositions within the party were given due importance and those from outside also were able to influence the government policies because they were given considerable space by the ruling groups in the Congress (especially by Nehru), thus preventing frustration and bitterness from taking undesirable forms.[13]

Nehru gave a lot of emphasis on inner-party democracy and the rule of law, which he assumed necessary for the survival and sustenance of democracy in general and the political training of the party members in particular. During this period, the state "etched itself into the imagination of the nation in a way that no previous political agency had ever done".[14]

However, Nehru and his contemporaries failed to understand that leadership alone seldom could build effective institutions, structures and instruments that were required to transform the rhetoric of socialism into action. Lessons of democratisation to the fellow country men could not be taught through, what Seth expressed as 'political miniaturisation of the Hindu social system'.[15] Democratisation required a will to share and delegate power to those subjugated; an idea which very few leaders gave importance to. Thus, the action of some, even if they remained sincerely committed, could not contribute much.[16] Despite the dominance of progressive elements at the centre under Nehru, the power at the peripheries still stayed with the traditional rulers who were neither virtuous nor principled and tolerant.[17] The ideology of the 'Congress socialism' at the lower levels merely meant 'access to state resources'.[18] Their sole concern was to pile wealth and status as much as possible before they lost control. There was a need to shrewdly recognise the fact that political powers, added to the existing social and economic status of these traditionally powerful groups, unless checked at every step, was making them more dangerous. The possibility of realising a change in the ruler-ruled relationship for the majority of the citizens, especially the Dalits and the backward castes, under these conditions remained very low. Despite the intellectual logic to bring about a democratic and socialistic transformation in the country, it remained unfulfilled. Thus, it would not be inappropriate to invoke Jaffrelot's remark that the Congress System, contrary to the socialist programme advocated by its leaders (primarily Nehru), 'turned out to be conservative in its socioeconomic orientation'.[19]

In administrative terms too, Nehru, despite being fully aware of the inadequacy of the existing bureaucracy, could not bring in necessary changes. The attitude of the bureaucracy, especially the police, towards the people could hardly become better than the colonial times and they continued to remain increasingly unhelpful.[20] Evidences of a corrupt and dangerous nexus between multiple segments of society – the bureaucracy, the police, the political parties and the governmental agencies – were enough; yet Nehru was never enamoured with inquiries into charges of corruption and criminality and remained chary of carrying out a campaign against corruption lest it would create a general atmosphere of suspicion and accusations.[21]

Although the judiciary in this era was not entirely political; judges' rulings on land laws cannot be understood as free of conservative influences.[22] Nehru's idea to keep some subjects outside the purview of judicial review was not to challenge either the judicial independence or its power to review the legislations for constitutional validity. With a recalcitrant judiciary, he simply had no option other than pursuing the path of constitutional amendment for clarifying that 'courts should not impede executive branch programmes of social and economic engineering'.[23] This attitude of Judiciary in the initial periods of democracy became a major setback for the cultivation of the democratic culture in the country and thus its role in the process cannot be ignored.

With such attitude of the courts, the practice of cornering resources and privileges by the traditional elites and keeping the options closed for those excluded continued with high vim and vigour. The leadership failed to enlarge the scope and ambit of power and opportunities of democratising the political process, and continued to use the model of distancing the rulers from the ruled. Subordinate classes, specially the landless labourers, tenants, and the scheduled castes and tribal were never mobilised by the Congress on their own terms as an independent political force with interests and strategies of their own.[24]

In clear terms, the ability of the 'Congress System' to enable a uniform, rational and legal enforcement of public authority remained limited; and could only produce, to use O'Donnell phrase, 'a low-intensity form of citizenship'.[25] Congress effort to mobilise a wide range of interests was done primarily through an elaborate network of local notables, mostly dominant landed castes, who controlled and delivered votes in exchange for state patronage. The state remained simply too thin and too uneven to rise up as a disinterested arbiter. The authority and legality, that are supposed to be state's sole realm of domination, were left to be contested and weakened by the existing traditional feudal forces of social domination. On occasions, although Nehru condemned the acts of hooliganism carried out "in the name of the political" and appealed to the people to practice a 'politics of discipline';[26] he fell short in many ways. In a way the subtle beginning of the uncoupling of the crime-punishment link began with Nehru himself.

Nothing above Politics

Nehru's strategy to preserve the democratic legitimacy of the country in its nascent age, resisting temptations of reversing the process of democratisation, and displaying, instead, a democratic temper was remarkable.[27] It was the inability of the larger traditional elite to share power and inculcate this culture among the lower levels of the Congress and outside that made the democratisation of country more and more difficult. Democratic habits soon gave way to undemocratic forces.[28]

The most relevant evidence of this was found during the 1967 elections. D.N. Dhanagare, in an important study on the Fourth General Elections, showed how there was a steep rise in the cases of violence with the intensification of the elections.[29] As a matter of common sense, although Dhanagare had expected the rivals of the Congress to take recourse to violence in their desperate attempts to remove it, his analysis proved contrary. Congress emerged as the most frequent aggressor as well as the most frequent victim (see Table 2.1 below).[30]

Table 2.1

Aggressor-Victim Relationships during 1967 Parliamentary Election

Aggressor (↓) *Victim party (→)*	*Congress*	*Jan Sangh*	*SSP*	*PSP*	*Swatantra*	*Republicans*	*Communists**	*Independents*	*Others*	*Students*	*Agitators*	*N.I.*	*Total*
Congress	2	2	1	1	5	0	7	2	6	1	0	3	31
Jan Sangh	4	0	0	0	0	0	0	0	0	0	0	0	4
SSP	2	0	0	0	0	0	0	0	0	0	0	0	2
PSP	1	0	0	0	0	0	0	0	0	0	0	0	1
Swatantra	4	0	0	0	0	0	0	0	0	0	0	0	4
Republicans	1	0	0	0	0	0	0	0	0	0	0	0	1
Communists*	3	0	1	0	0	0	3	0	0	0	0	0	7
Independents	1	0	0	0	0	0	0	1	0	0	0	0	2
Others	13	0	1	0	1	0	0	2	2	0	0	0	19
Students	20	1	0	0	0	0	0	0	1	0	0	0	22
Agitators	18	0	0	0	0	0	0	0	0	0	0	0	18
N.I.	75	7	1	1	2	1	4	6	12	0	0	0	109
Total	144	10	4	3	8	1	14	11	21	1	0	5	222

Source: Dhanagare (1968: 155). * (both wings); Others include the Akali Dal, DMK, D.K., Jan Congress, Jan Kranti Dal, National Conference, Plebiscite Front of Jammu & Kashmir, Sampoorna Maharashtra Samiti, MGJP (Gujarat) and APHLC (Assam). Abbr. PSP: Praja Socialist Party; SSP: Samyukta Socialist Party; N.I.: Not Identified.

This was a rude shock to the political culture of the country. Congress Although saved its face at the centre with a 23 seat majority, it was voted out in eight states in favour of the coalitions of non-Congress parties. However, this was only short-lived. Leaders frequently changed their loyalties and partners and facilitated the toppling of several state governments in association with whosoever lured them with money or offered them with ministerial offices.[31] Gaya Lal, an MLA from Hassanpur changed his party thrice in a fortnight and became instrumental in establishing a new coinage "*Aya Ram, Gaya Ram*" in the Indian politics. Between 1967 and 1970, nearly 800 MLAs crossed the floor, and nearly 155 of them were rewarded with ministerial berths.[32]

Along with the wreckage of the 'Congress System', the country also witnessed a sudden elevation of Mrs Gandhi at the helm of Congress affairs. Observers believe that this was more on account of a negative decision taken by the senior Congress leaders, collectively known as Syndicate, who wanted to exploit Mrs Gandhi's inexperience and lacking substantial roots in the party.[33] But she proved them wrong and soon rose to become the most powerful personality with a capacity to alter the whole course of democratic politics of the country. Faced with dramatic and declining fortunes of the Congress witnessed in the 1967 elections on the one hand and the attempts of the managerial bosses of the Congress Syndicates to circumscribe her power and threaten her survival in the office, she started reacting like a 'dynamo and hitched her personal stakes to a new and unprecedented style and substance of conducting public affairs'.[34] She ignored the organisational set up to give rise to a more centralised power in her hands and less to the state apparatus. To secure her power and position, she started using state policies as active instruments for mustering political support.[35]

This proved detrimental and paved way for the destruction of the institutional and political preconditions of the effective pursuance of the Nehruvian strategy.[36] Making politicisation of the masses her catalytic doctrine, Mrs Gandhi although increased the party's seat more than that of the Nehru era;[37] she put India on the path of such rapid and dangerous de-institutionalisation that its capability to administer the country started growing less effective day by day.[38] The relation between electoral majority and power to administer effectively became reciprocal to each other in the days ahead.[39]

There isn't any doubt that many of our achievements today owe to her left-of-centre initiated agenda;[40] but the concern here is to trace the factors that led to the uncoupling of crime-punishment link. In what follows below, the chapter presents how a majority of these factors got shaped in the 1970s. She not only shifted the institutional base of politics, as Kothari opines, 'from the party system to the State apparatus, and within the state apparatus from a federal structure to the centre, and indeed within the centre from a dispersed ministerial set-up to prime minister's secretariat',[41] but also from the prime minister's secretariat to the Prime Minister herself and allowed criminalisation make a heady brew in the politics of the land.

Politics of Criminalisation

Criminalisation started making a heady brew in the politics of the land when Mrs Gandhi in order to diffuse the constant threat of the seasoned politicians of the Congress Syndicates, started relying on a network of the Youth Congress run by her younger son Sanjay. This soon changed the meaning of the democracy altogether as Sanjay, a distinctly inexperienced young politician, started inviting people from 'quite unusual social backgrounds, often trailing criminal connections' to the Parliament.[42] Observers opine that Sanjay understood democracy simply as a struggle for votes and winning elections.[43]

When these steps towards deinstitutionalisation were resisted by the people of the country in ways of strikes, student protests and popular demonstrations, Mrs Gandhi responded to this rising dissent very undemocratically. She suspended democratic rights and judicial procedures and imposed Emergency on June 26, 1975, only to facilitate the further concentration of power in the hands of Sanjay.[44] By April 1976, Sanjay had emerged as a parallel authority, interfering in the working of the government and administration at will.[45]

This was a clear indication of the fact that Mrs Gandhi's leadership had grown more authoritative and ignorant and the opposition, both in the party and in the Parliament, was marginalised. This deprived the political process of any channel of legitimate articulation and made politics more violent.[46] State governments too started growing ineffective, inefficient and showed no respect for the rule of law. A detailed evidence of the illegitimacy of the state by such violent politics in Bihar is presented in the following chapters, but the situation in other Congress ruled states, such as Uttar Pradesh, West Bengal, Haryana, Andhra Pradesh and Gujarat was no better.[47]

It would perhaps be unreasonable to blame the Congress, Mrs Gandhi and Sanjay alone for allowing the lumpen criminals to play as powerful arbiters in the political process. Congress regimes both at the centre as well as in the states did of course deepen the crisis; but when other political parties got an opportunity to rule, they, instead of providing an alternative, mastered the same technique. Although Jayaprakash Narayan's call for '*Sampurna Kranti*' (total revolution) was not simply for a change in the regime within the existing political system but the political system itself; JP's young lieutenants' commitment to eradicate crime and corruption could not sustain for long and ultimately dragged the nation towards a more difficult situation. Introducing a note on this tragedy, Rudolphs remarked:

> A historic opportunity to create a competitive party system, reduce over-centralisation of bureaucratic power, challenge the 'tarnished and decaying' development strategy pursued by Nehru, was lost not because of a 'policy failure', since the Janata politicians said all of these things, but because of their abysmal 'political performance' .... The demeaning political drama scenes, sometimes played separately, sometimes together, featured personal, political and institutional themes. The way family members, particularly, the sons of the politicians, were used to discredit or embarrass rivals, it could be rightfully called the age of politicians' sons.[48]

Instead of building the institutional capacity of the nation and reviving faith in democracy, it spoilt this precious opportunity through intra-party fighting and over-ambitious hate campaign against Indira Gandhi.[49]

In addition to that the Janata regime was also marked with severe egoism through a series of 'violence of the rich' on the labourers in the rural and industrial sectors throughout the country. Events in the villages of Haryana, Bihar, Uttar Pradesh and Maharashtra and those in Cotton Mills of Kanpur, Rajahara mines in Madhya Pradesh, Dhanbad ISCO factory and Bokaro in Bihar, Mukund in Bombay and Sahibabad and Lucknow in Uttar Pradesh only conformed to the same old political obstacles erected by the entrenched interests of the ruling elites to sustain power in their hands.[50] Charan Singh, the Deputy Prime Minister and Union Home Minister while speaking in the Lok Sabha on this issue said, "I, on behalf of the government, declare clearly and openly that government will not tolerate any gherao, no matter howsoever just be the intentions of the persons doing the gherao".[51]

What makes JP movement an important consideration in this analysis of the uncoupling of the crime-punishment link is that it neither paid any attention to constitutional morality nor to the principles of legality. This led to further de-institutionalisation of the party structure and politicians openly started turning to local criminals for money and muscle power. Hoodlums and gang fighting became an integral part of politics across all political parties. Sometimes, even the factions within the political parties used it for gaining superior position by eliminating the others by resorting to violence, including murder. The society at the beginning of the 1970s had started moving towards, what Nandy calls, *matsyanyaya* (the state of nature in the Indian classical tradition, in which big fishes eat the little ones and each other), and therefore, to nobody's surprise, the nation once again re-elected the biggest shark of all to overawe the others in 1980.[52]

The politics in states such as West Bengal (which had come under the rule of the Left Front government in 1977) and Tamil Nadu (under the control of regional political parties, namely Dravida Munnetra Kazhagam (DMK) and All India Anna Dravida Munnetra Kazhagam (AIADMK) since 1967), also provide an interesting example for the politics of criminalisation practised by the non-Congress governments in the states during this period. Kohli's analysis of the 'breakdown (1967–1977) to order (post 1977)' in West Bengal, therefore, seems unconvincing.[53] No doubt, in the early days after coming to power, the armed squads of CPI (M) could hardly match the Congress gangsters of 1970–77, who backed by the police had hounded out CPI (M) members and sympathisers from their strongholds in Calcutta and other parts of West Bengal; in the days ahead West Bengal became one of the most violent states in India with the beginning of the trial of strength among the CPI (M), the Youth Congress and the Naxalites.

The CPI (M) establishment wanted to leave no opportunity to prevent all threats that could dislodge it from power in the future. Though the same could have been achieved, according to a close observer of the West Bengal politics, by a process of winning over people through 'patient political campaign accompanied by measures to provide civic amenities' and wipe out corruption and criminality; the CPI (M) chose to opt for a 'short-cut of finishing off its political rival at one go'.[54]

> Local gangs of musclemen who were on the payroll of the Congress ... were either evicted from their areas of control by rival gangs hired by the CPI (M) or were won over by promises of protection by the new ruling party ... . Muscle power increasingly came to replace political campaign and ideological debates in the CPI (M)'s relentless pursuit of monopoly of power ... underworld goons enjoying protection from the ruling party became decisive factors.[55]

Musclemen, popularly called as *mastaans,* replaced political campaigns and ideological debates and were given a free hand to control the electoral machinery. In the words of a party member during that time, "often the number of the 'auxiliary groups' trained in the use of arms was more than the real party members."[56] The CPI (M) showed no signs of better state administration either. Barring 'Operation Barga', they continued with the same 'apathetic inefficiency' as demonstrated by the earlier regimes of the Congress. The CPI (M) government allowed the officials to indulge in graft and other corrupt means merely on the ground of their membership of the party. Instead of curbing the police's high-handedness, the administration 'pandered to some of the most infamous senior police officers against whom criminal charges were levelled in the past'. In such a situation the 'policemen at the lower levels' indulged freely in 'crimes ranging from extortion of hush money from offenders, to raping of women, to the killing of people in police lock-ups' and roamed freely without any fear. They went about facilitating the domination of criminal gangs backed by the CPI (M) politicians.[57]

Tamil Nadu under DMK although started with a note of caution on governance and a fair distribution of power among the non-Brahmin castes; by the 1970s, people at large started identifying the state administration, especially the police as 'the special armed force of the ruling party'. The professional integrity of its officer class came under suspicion, for most of them had reduced themselves to 'hanging around ministers' residences, with local DMK functionaries on tow, to get their preferred transfers and promotions', and mortgaged their professional pride.[58] The change of guard in the hands of AIADMK in 1977 brought no respite. Corruption and criminality became rampant and soon the state administration started 'being run by fiat'.[59] The level of mayhem had reached to such an extent that the AIADMK Chief Minister M.G. Ramachandran in 1987 gave an open call for members of his party to carry knives for their self-protection.[60]

In fact, the metropolitan newspapers in those days remained filled with several reports of gang fighting which had political backup. For instance, *The Indian Express* on its September 7, 1980 edition reported that Nariman Pithwala, a Congress leader from Surat, was murdered, first by a lorry ramming into his car, and later, when he tried to escape from the scene of the 'accident', he was apprehended by seven persons about 60 feet away from the car and assaulted with lathis (bamboo sticks), spades and axes. Two months later on November 4, *The Times of India* reported that Ram Seval Garg, a freedom fighter and Congress president of Panna district of MP was killed by a 'gang of dacoits' at his residence in Panna. *The Indian Express* again reported on November 11, the killing of Vir Singh Yadav, another Congress leader from UP and a former MLC, who was shot dead along with his brother, near the Jaithra police station in Etah.[61] Some of the other important cases were – attack on life of Bhagawat Jha Azad, the union minister for state in the Indira cabinet, and Moiddur Rehman, Bihar's minister of state for public health on his way to Patna from Purnea in January 1981. However, these are only some of the instances of the 'murder politics' being played as a result of inter- and intra-party rivalry in the politics of criminalisation.

Thus, critiques of Congress, who by all means politicised 'how not to be governed', failed to project an alternative style of governance. Their promise of equality and democracy seemed only a facade to deceive the public to capture the state power and continue the same old order. With the re-election of the biggest shark, i.e., the Congress, and with experiencing the 'murder politics' of the non-Congress governments at the centre and the states discussed above, the uncoupling of the crime-punishment finally reached to a point of divorce. The politics and the politicians of this period, who placed several lumpen elements at respectable places in the national and state political pyramid and replaced the normal administrative process by a new structure controlled by musclemen and mafias, bears a large part of the responsibility in bringing in sanctity to this phenomenon.

Politicisation of Administration, Police and Judiciary

Complaints about political interference in the law and local administration appeared though in British India[62] and continued even during Nehru;[63] evidence suggest that things became worse in the post-Nehru era. The professional ethics of administration was cast aside for a new scheme of law that was neither fair nor impartial. Mrs Gandhi's idea of 'committed bureaucracy' against the practiced philosophy of 'neutral administrative machinery' gave impetus not only to Sanjay, but even her centrally appointed chief ministers in the Congress-ruled states to interfere with day-to-day administration. Senior positions in the bureaucracy and the police were made a means of rewarding officers committed to the rulers, while those not prepared to demonstrate their commitment were sidelined. Kamalpati Tripathi, during his rule in UP between 1971 and 1973, not only transferred a large numbers of police officers and civil servants at the behest of the local businessmen and other constituents, but also completely ignored the chain of administrative command by even allowing his relatives to phone up district officials and give them direct orders.[64] The second UP Police Commission in its report submitted in 1971 complained that political interference had resulted in a 'warped enforcement of law' and a 'general decline in the police in its integrity'.[65]

This was not the case of UP alone. The National Police Commission, set up in the late 1970s, had revealed that politicisation of administration had reached alarming proportions in most of the states. The commission brought into light several cases where corrupt and committed (politically) junior officers had their more honest seniors transferred.[66] Concluding an extensive study on police in the country in the 1980s Bayley observed;

> The past decade has been a time of unprecedented stress for the Indian police … . They have become deeply involved in partisan politics. They are preoccupied with it, have been penetrated by it, and have organised collectively to participate in it. Their politicisation has produced, in my judgement, a palpable decline in the rule of law … Police officers began to feel that India was developing a dual system of justice – one through the formal channels of criminal justice system and the other through political ones.[67]

Another example of this phenomenon is found in the memoirs of a N.K. Singh CBI officer who gives an eyewitness account of the politicisation of administration, police and even the judiciary. According to Singh;

> The mid 1970s heralded an era of the 'politics of crime' at the highest level. It brought into sharp focus the involvement of high political functionaries in the alleged commission of serious crime of an unprecedented nature. It also saw the use of official machinery to strangulate political dissension, intimidate law enforcement officers, and use of 'money power' and other allurements to win over the prosecution witness. It manifested a total disregard and contempt for the judiciary.[68]

Sharing his experience in the *Kissa Kursi Ka* case, Singh explains how criminalisation raised its ugly head at the highest levels in politics and how power and position were used as a tool to twist the arm of the law and administrative machinery.[69]

Any system based on the rule of law, which claims impartiality and efficacy, should enable every citizen to get justice regardless of the wishes of the men in power. But, unfortunately, this right of citizens was put on a complete denial. The existence of independent judiciary made no difference. The executive kept interfering in the functions of the judiciary;[70] and the courts, including the Supreme Court, kept accommodating themselves to the interests and needs of the country's undemocratic political masters. The Supreme Court, which during the Janata Party regime had upheld the law passed by Parliament to create special courts to try Mrs Gandhi, Sanjay, and others for the alleged abuse of powers, excesses, and criminal acts during the Emergency; found ways of winding them up after Mrs Gandhi's return to power in 1980. Between January and June 1980, the court dismissed all the cases pending against Mrs Gandhi and her associates on the ground that the cases were merely politically vindictive.[71]

These acts of the judiciary mentioned above, however makes no attempt to undermine the fair and independent acts of some of the judges, who brought justice closer to the oppressed and put the inhumane actions of the petty oppressive agents of the State under strict surveillance.[72] It is just to point out that instead of being a facilitator in maintaining the crime-punishment link, the judiciary allowed politics and politicians to disturb this relation and make crime a non-punishable act for those in power.[73] Justice P.N. Bhagwati, who is remembered today for giving a new direction to Indian judiciary, wrote a fulsome letter of congratulations to Mrs Gandhi on her return to power in 1980.[74] In the next four years, the judiciary stooped to such a low that a scholar aptly remarks;

> It may be a fraudulent interpretation of democracy to have a government that is above its own law, but there seems no dearth of

> zealot advocates of this concept of government among the members of the ruling party. The tragedy is that some of the judges, determined not to be hurt, are undermining the very institution that is the source of their strength.[75]

The politicisation of the police and other law enforcement agencies combined with the decline in the standards of judiciary, ultimately made democracy a distant dream and restricted the state from being a disinterested arbiter. This is not to argue against politicisation *per se*. Politicisation was necessary for a society like India where freedom after independence was realised by a small section of the dominant population who controlled the power and where majority of population was still to experience a change in the ruler-ruled relationship. Politicising techniques provided ways for competitive mobilisation for access to resources available (only) through the state; but politicisation alone without the necessary steps towards democratisation proved detrimental. As a result, the key political institutions, central to democratic governance, such as political parties, elected representatives, bureaucracy, police and the courts started loosing people's trust. In the ultimate analysis, it can be said that nothing was seen above politics.

Politics as Free Style Business

In the phase dicussed above, participation in electoral politics although climbed to a higher level, it went hand in hand with the rising level of violence (see Figures 2.1; 2.2 and 2.3). Politics simply became defined as elections and crime became the most secure formula of increasing winnability. This proved to be dangerous. Representative democracy for people in a multifaceted country like India was not simply electoral politics; it was a hope and desire for change. When they did not see it coming their way through political and institutional means, they started looking for other ways. They also realised that the net gain by accepting another means was much more than the net gain derived from rejecting it.

The assassination of Mrs Gandhi, and the subsequent killing of Sikhs in which some members of the Youth Congress openly instigated the crowd in 1984, gave Congress a record majority in the Parliament and Rajiv Gandhi was crowned as the Prime Minister. In his early years, Rajiv Gandhi projected himself as an advocate of institutionalisation and as an agent of administrative reforms. But his later years confirm our premise about the failure of the Indian State to be a disinterested arbiter and hence a major cause in the rise of criminalisation of the politics.

Figure 2.1

Voter Turnout in Lok Sabha Elections 1952–1984/85

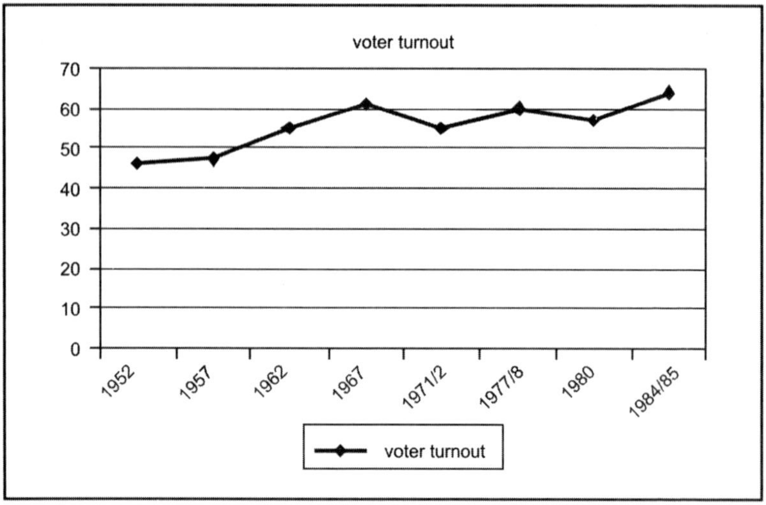

Source: www.eci.nic.in

Figure 2.2

Voter Turnout in Assembly Elections 1952–1984/85

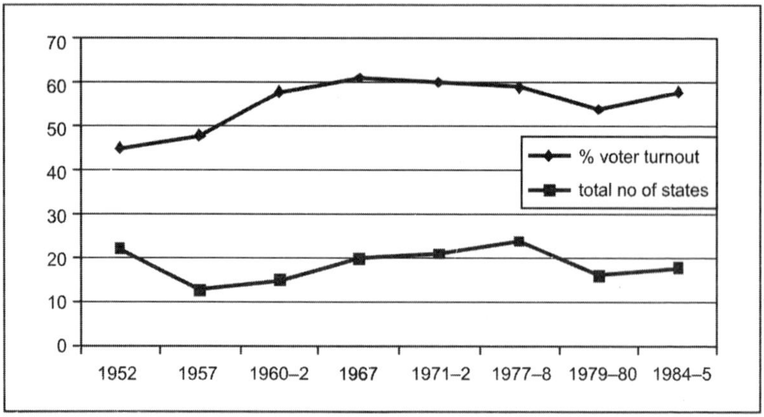

Source: Yogendra Yadav (1997: 181)[76]

Figure 2.3
Number of Riots in India 1953–1985

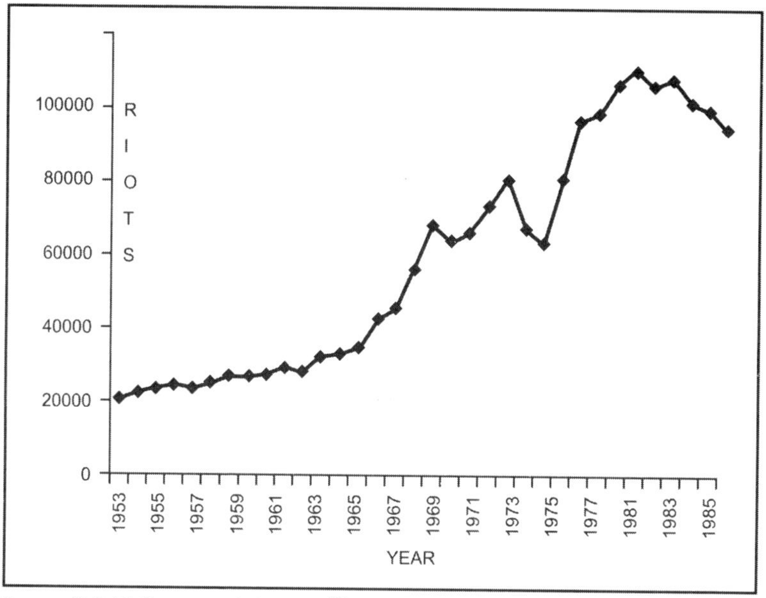

Source: K.C. Vadlamannati, (2008:7)[77]

Mr Gandhi openly showed his dissatisfaction with the working of the Congress, party and started making attempts to reform its organisational set-up.[78] During the centenary celebrations of the Congress, he delivered the most scorching critique of his own party by complaining of the Congress' 'self-aggrandised and corrupt' operations and their linkages with 'vested interests' ... 'sanctimonious posturing', and the practice where 'corruption is not only tolerated but even regarded as a hallmark of leadership.[79] Many political analysts have quoted this speech, but they have not analysed it in the crime-punishment framework. Whether the remarks of Mr Gandhi, if seriously met, would had revitalised the deinstitutionalised democratic structure and restored the uncoupled crime-punishment link may be a point of debate, but what the country has lost by not confirming to this reality is no longer hidden. The biggest contribution of Mr Gandhi's commitment to revitalise the democratic structure was the Anti-Defection Bill.[80]

However, challenges within the party from the displaced 'Indira Loyalists' grew stronger and they started blocking every single effort made by Mr Gandhi. One can understand, therefore, Rajiv Gandhi's decision to abandon his 18–month-long internal reform agenda, but what made him reverse his path completely in the later years is still unclear. His actions no longer remained committed to the idea of a 'clean government' and soon became a symbol of corruption. The practice of "*bakshish* (tip or tips) for the little guys transformed into a culture of 'bribes for the bosses' and further to 'commissions for the governing elite'."[81] Intimidation, violence, and the use of black money in election reached an all time high. Gangsterism moved from the streets to the halls and corridors of the legislative assemblies and local hoodlums, once used by the ruling party to bully and terrorise opposition party workers, were rewarded with party tickets in many states. Winning of elections increasingly turned into a fine art in which muscle power and organised terror played the most important part.

A survey in 1988 revealed that quite a large chunk of Congress legislators in the then Bihar Assembly either had past criminal records or had criminal cases pending against them. The situation in other states was also no better. The behaviour of the legislators there suggested that they were coming from a background where there was no respect for parliamentary practices.[82] The idea of a democratic party was totally abandoned by one and all.

Soon there came to light the Bofors scandal, in which Rajiv Gandhi and several others were accused of receiving kickbacks from the Swedish arms supplier Bofors AB for winning a bid to supply 155 mm field howitzer.[83] This brought the Congress to a humiliating low position in the by-elections in Parliamentary constituencies in several states. (See Appendix 1).[84]

Bureaucracy was left to be politicised and victimised (in states as well as at the Centre) at a much faster rate than ever in the past.[85] The professionalism got totally snuffed out by increasing penetration of politicians in the day-to-day affairs of administration and soon a permanent arrangement controlled by a nexus between the police, the politicians and the criminals was established.[86] The judiciary too saw a series of major controversies in the 1980s and its credibility was put to a further decline.[87]

To sum up, despite his promise and zeal for a clean state, Rajiv Gandhi failed to cleanse his own party and finally gave in before the mafia and chauvinist elements. The Indian state became a mixture of corruption and criminality. In collusion with big business (in addition to the domination of large landowners)[88] and criminals, it was no wonder that the politics of persuasion had to give place to the politics of manipulation, coercion and intimidation.

Law Breakers as Law Makers

The free style politics of Rajiv Gandhi pushed the complexities and fragility of the governments, particularly at the state level and below, where most of the actual governing happens, to its worst crisis. Even the opposition parties could not make the situation any better. Naipaul may be right in saying that violence and criminalisation in the country must be seen as a promising social revolution and not miss-governance;[89] but the changes witnessed in the Gangetic plane (discussed in detail in Chapter 3 and 4) proved much beyond his imaginative expectations. In the days ahead, street gangs were appropriated and adorned with the hallowed symbols of parliamentary democracy; their gang fights became political battles, and the gang leaders became legislators.

With the beginning of the last decade of the twentieth century, the country witnessed extreme political haphazardness with two Prime Ministers, V.P. Singh and Chandra Shekhar, in just 18 months.[90] Confirming to his commitment to the idea of social justice, Mr Singh shook the dominance of the 'upper-caste' elites by handing over the chariot of change in the hands of the scheduled/backward castes.[91] This was a great moment for people at the margins to unite beyond religious boundaries,[92] but the Bhartiya Janata Party (BJP, formerly Jan Sangha), found it hard to accept this and started using religion as a major electoral plank to bring the divide back.[93] The BJP president, Lal Krishna Advani, started a tour of the Northern states on a *rath* (a mythical chariot) to drum up support for building a Ram temple at a disputed site in Ayodhya (the birth place of Ram, one of the Gods in Hindu mythology) in the Faizabad district of Uttar Pradesh, where there had been a mosque (popularly known as Babri Masjid) since the 16th century AD. The party gave a call to present swords, spears, and maces to Mr Advani on his way.[94] This incited communal feelings against the Muslims and subsequently on the day when Mr Advani was arrested in Bihar (October 23, 1990) on charges of fomenting communal tension,[95] the party orchestrated large scale violence throughout the country. 116 riots occurred between September 1 and November 20 that year and 564 people died. UP alone witnessed 24 riots, in which 224 people got killed.[96]

After the arrest of Mr Advani, BJP withdrew its support to the National Front government and Mr Singh failed to sail through the confidence motion in Parliament on November 10, 1990. Mr Singh's decision to value the secular credentials of the country over state power was a landmark achievement. However, what happened later opened up yet another bizarre chapter. Chandra Shekhar, a member of the Janata Dal, with defected 60 JD MPs launched a new political party, Samajwadi Janata Party, to form the government with the support of the Congress (from outside). Chandra Shekhar's term as the premier depended solely on Rajiv Gandhi's whim and to nobody's surprise, it collapsed in its seventh month.[97] This was probably Mr Gandhi's last political decision as he was assassinated by a human bomb during an election campaign in Tamil Nadu in May 1991.

Mr Gandhi's assassination brought Congress back to power at the centre, a minority government though, and P.V. Narasimha Rao became the Prime Minister. Being the first Congress PM outside the Nehru-Gandhi family, expectations of a fresh whiff of clean air was very high, but Rao's political desire eventually proved to be more dangerous and assertive than his predecessors. Eliminating the Congress Parliamentary Board, he concentrated power in his own hands and allowed his ministers to use the state apparatus to their whims.[98]

During Mr Rao's regime, the country faced worst political shocks. On December 6, 1992 the BJP-led Hindu activists demolished the mosque in Ayodhya;[99] and on July 28, 1993 the Congress party bribed the MPs to save its government at the centre. Both these actions confirm our premise of the failure of the state to grow as a disinterested arbiter and finally of a new marriage between crime and non-punishment. Speaking on the demolition of Babri mosque in the Parliament, Atal Bihari Vajpayee of the BJP, who rose to become the PM of the country in 1998, constantly tried to absolve the party and its top leaders, Mr Advani in particular, of being law breakers. On the one hand, Mr Vajpayee's arguments to deny that they had done nothing to undermine the law, and on the other, Mr Advani's refusal to seek bail after being arrested from the site of demolition, clearly showed that the party believed and claimed to be above the rule of law.[100]

The country got another shock in June 1993, when Harshad Mehta, a stock broker turned semester claimed that 'he had delivered suitcases stuffed with $371,000 in cash to the Prime Minister's Office (PMO) in exchange for reining in a criminal investigation into the broker's activities'.[101] In response to this, when the CPI moved a no-confidence motion against the Congress government; it bribed 11 MPs (four of the Jharkhand Mukti Morcha and seven of the breakaway Janata Dal (Ajit) group).[102] During the investigations it was revealed that several Congress members both at the national and local levels were aware of this activity and were also a part of this conspiracy,[103] but they happily chose power over Parliamentary traditions, values, political conduct and morality.

The worst part once again was the way this case was treated by the premier investigation agency (CBI) and also the Apex Court. The affair was exposed by *Jandhama Paksh*, a Hindi weekly from Kota in Rajasthan on February 28, 1994, but the CBI moved on the matter only when it was directed by the Delhi High Court two years later on May17, 1996.[104] When the trial court framed charges against Mr Rao and 19 others,[105] the convicts moved to the Delhi High Court contending that the MPs were not public servants and had immunity from prosecution for anything said or done in Parliament by virtue of Article 105(2) of the Constitution. However, the court rejected both these contentions. The accused thereafter, moved the Supreme Court, and the Apex Court's ruling on April 17, 1998 astonished all. Though it upheld that MPs are "public servants" and therefore liable to prosecution under the Prevention of Corruption Act of 1988, it declared that only bribe givers were liable to prosecution, not bribe takers.[106] Subsequently, the alleged bribe-takers were acquitted on June 4, 1999 by the special CBI judge. Later on October 12, 2000, the Supreme Court acquitted all the accused, except Mr Rao and Mr Buta Singh, on the ground that the agency had clinching evidence against the duo but lacked 'sufficient evidence' on record against the other accused.[107] However, in March 2002 the Delhi high court, citing contradictions in Mahato's statements and the CBI's inability to prove independent evidence acquitted both Mr Rao and Mr Singh.[108]

Thus, the court judgments in the JMM case legalised the new marriage between crime and non-punishment at the highest level. Immunity for anything spoken, or voted for is necessary for free speech, but this was never intended to shield a member who takes bribes for his speech or vote. Not in any part of the world. Lord Salmon, who was the chairman of the Royal Commission on Standards of Conduct in Public Life, while submitting his report on corruption in the British Parliament in 1978 stated;

> To my mind, equality before the law is one of the pillars of freedom. To say that immunity from criminal proceedings against anyone who tries to bribe a Member of Parliament and any Member of Parliament who accepts the bribe stems from the Bill of Rights is a serious mistake ... it is ... for freedom of speech in the House; it is not ... of corruption.[109]

The democratic experience in the US too has subscribed to this view. Chief Justice Warren Burger of the US Supreme Court in the United States v. Brewster, 408 US 501 (1972) had pronounced that the Speech or Debate clause of the US Constitution does not preclude an inquiry into the alleged conduct of a Congressman or Senator and charged Senator Daniel Brewer with the solicitation and acceptance of bribes in violation of US law.[110] Pronouncing the judgement, Burger observed;

> Taking a bribe is, obviously, no part of the legislative process of function; it is not a legislative act. It is not, by any conceivable interpretation, an act performed as a part of or even incidental to the role of a legislator. It is not an act resulting from the nature, and in the execution, of the office. Nor is it a thing said or done by him, as a representative, in the exercise of the functions of that office, ...[111]

Several courts in the world have acknowledged this view. However, India's Supreme Court holding a contrary view, slammed the doors of judicial remedy and our political system decided to remain silent on the issue of law breakers going unpunished.

But this was not the end. There was a complaint of "abduction-cum-murder" at the Parliament street police station against the four JMM MPs by Amar Nath Jha, brother of SN Jha, who was working as a private secretary to Shibu Soren and had gone missing since June 2, 1994. However, the CBI registered the charge sheet only after four years on November 10 when SN Jha's dead body was found in Ranchi on August 15, 1998.[112]

While Mr Soren and four others were convicted initially with life imprisonment by the lower court (nearly after a decade on November 28, 2006); they were finally set free by the Delhi High Court on the ground of 'non-establishment of criminal conspiracy.[113]

While all this was on, nothing could deter or stop Mr Soren from getting re-elected as an MP in 1996. Later in 2002, he was elected to the Rajya Sabha with the help of the BJP during the National Democratic Alliance (NDA) regime. In 2004, Mr Soren again joined hands with the Congress and was included into the Union Cabinet as the coal minister in the Congress-led coalition, United Progressive Alliance (UPA).[114]

The JMM case might have got a special mention in this study, but instances of such skewed justice had rather become a norm. The famous murder cases of Ajit Chandra Sarkar (discussed in detail in Chapter 5), Jessica Lal, Priyadarshini Mattoo, Nitish Katara and many more which went unreported only confirms to our premise about the role of politics as a spoiler in the crime-punishment link for a new marriage between crime and non-punishment. With the institutional vacuum created by the political parties, democracy became a puppet in the hands of the armed might of ganglords, which had grown into modern mafias, viz., coal mafia, timber mafia, sandalwood mafia, lottery mafia, tender mafia and so on in all parts of the country. The working of several state administration, seems to have given in to these mafias and surviving only on their dictat.[115] This transformation of political domination in Bihar 'from landlords to ganglords' is discussed in detail in Chapter 5.

Even when a non-Congress alliance formed a government at the centre once again, under a BJP-led coalition (NDA) between 1998 and 2004; it instead of learning from its past, rather obliged the country with two other shameful experiences of corruption and criminality in the form of the Tehelka scam in 2001 and the Gujarat massacres in 2002. The investigative journalism of a web portal, Tehelka, caught the Indian government officials, army officers, the president of the BJP – Bangaru Laxman, and the general secretary of the Samata Party – Jaya Jaitely (who was a close colleague of the Union Defence Minister George Fernandes of the same party) accepting bribe from journalists, posing as defence dealers.[116] A Special CBI Court convicted Bangaru Laxman of the charge of accepting bribe in April 2012 and also framed charges against Jaya Jaitely and three others for the offence of hatching criminal conspiracy under section 120 B of the IPC and various other sections of the PCA dealing with "taking gratification for exercise of personal influence with public servant". The trial is still on.

Under the same NDA regime in 2002, Gujarat (under the rule of BJP) more than 2,000 Muslims were killed brutally under the active support of the state administration. Chief minister Narendra Modi (since October 2001) justified the killings by describing them as a reaction to what had happened in Godhra on February 27 the same year.[117] The report of a nine-member Concerned Citizens Tribunal headed by former Supreme Court judge justice V.R. Krishna Iyer, comprising former judges and other eminent citizens, quoted a minister (name withheld in the original report) of the Modi cabinet saying;

> At a meeting called by Modi, that was attended by the DGP, the Commissioner of Police, Ahmedabad, the Chief Secretary, the Home Secretary, Secretary to the Home Department (a serving police officer of IG rank on deputation), DGP (IB), and several officers from the CM's office on the day of the Godhra carnage, Modi instructed senior police officials to allow *"people to vent their frustration"* over the torching of two coaches of the Sabarmati Express during the VHP *bandh* the following day. In addition to that, Modi also ordered the police not to come in the way of *"the Hindu backlash"*. The officers who vehemently protested were harshly told by the chief minister to simply shut up and obey.[118]

The report concluded that all the violence and rioting happened with the complicity of the state police and the bureaucracy. Honest officers who sought to stop the violence in their areas were immediately transferred by the state government. Some of the ministers of the state government actively led the mob. Many mosques and mausoleums were demolished. Some accounts put the number of such religious structures destroyed or severely damaged at 700. Property worth more than ₹ 10,000 crore was looted or burnt and loss of business due to closures and migration of labour was several times that figure. The carnage continued for more than five months and more than 1.5 lakh Muslims were totally uprooted, and were forced to live in refugee camps.[119] But, all this was again justified by the BJP in the name of nationalism. Even the coalition partners of the BJP did not come out with any serious criticism.

A censure motion in the Lok Sabha on the government's handling of the Gujarat carnage was defeated (276 votes to 182).[120] Although Modi returned to power in the state assembly election that followed the carnage, people rejected the divisive politics of the BJP in the next general elections held in April-May 2004. Maya Kodnani, the then minister of women and child welfare has been convicted and trial against several others is still on.

The politics of the day owes considerable credit for creating this disequilibrium. But it would not be an exaggeration to say that even the judiciary's efficacy owes a lot of responsibility for the misplacement of the public trust and the undermining of the rule of law equally. More the people have looked upon the judiciary as the last straw of legal redress and restitution, more it has failed to be a reliable and efficient arbitrator. Not only inordinate delays in issuing effective orders, but reducing itself as a helpless spectator in cases involving prominent politicians is a matter of grave concern.

In addition to that, even when these criminal-politicians were sent to prison under court orders, they enjoyed all the privileges of a special suite in a bungalow (or similar arrangements made inside the prisons), with free access to all his cronies and special medical treatment. The equality before law simply means that either they be sent to the common jail where the ordinary prisoners live and suffer, or prisoners in the common jail be given the same facilities that politicians accused of corruption and criminal acts enjoy today even after arrest. Upendra Baxi, a close observer of the working of Indian judiciary commenting on the system in the early 1980s said:

> The idea that legal rules are binding upon all sections of society has been rejected in practice by the governing elite. Modern India seems

> to have at least two parallel legal systems: one for the rich and the resourceful and those who wield political power and influence, and the other for the small men without resources and capabilities to obtain justice or fight injustice. Normatively, the law is the same for all citizens. In practice, the incidence of enforcement of right and liabilities varies depending on the location of persons involved in the socioeconomic structure.[121]

Thus, during the 1990s, people with political fortune managed to make politics the escape route of punishment. In other words, the divorce of the crime-punishment link successfully completed a new marriage between crime and non-punishment. One can accept, as most of these criminal-politicians claim, 'cases are falsely implicated and exaggerated', but does it really satisfy the working of the parliamentary democracy? Is it not an evidence of statelessness and partisanship, where a man with a strong criminal background gets into positions such as that of a Union Minister? The only impression that goes around is that repressiveness in the surveillance nail only innocents, and criminals who have strong political connections are allowed to become the law unto themselves. Is it not sufficient to show that the criminal justice system, or for that matter the state itself has grown illegitimate? Heinous criminals charged of several murders and riots openly take the politico-judicial route to emerge as winners. While poor, petty and simple criminals, once sentenced by the lower courts, can seldom afford to appeal, and thus languish in jail to serve the sentence; those with the political fortunes, flushed with money and power obtain bails even at midnight and enjoy their punishment-free-crime.

The Tyranny of Democracy

Aristotle observed that the duty of a legislator is to make citizens good by habituation. Those who do not carry it out, fail to achieve their objective.[122] The situation today has reached at such a low that 'if corruption and criminality, shrouded in the garb of hypocrisy, need a higher centre of learning and excellence, the place to choose is India.'[123] The sensational revelation that the law makers were once again bribed to cross-vote to save the UPA-I in the trust motion moved by it in 2008 have not reached to any conclusion.[124] The undesirable situation of law breakers becoming law makers and moving around under police protection is still in place. One wonders therefore, what led several political commentators and analysts to conclude the outcome of the Parliamentary election of 2009 as the start of a new beginning; an opportunity to correct mistakes done in the past.[125] A brief analysis of the legislators based on the available data (discussed later) explains how our popular hope sounds euphoric and the conclusions of the political commentators disillusioning. Things have changed, for sure, but only for worse.

Though the phenomenon of 'criminalisation of politics', as traced in the discussions above, has roots in the politics since 1950s, the only effort till date to understand this issue was made in the early years of 1990s through a Committee constituted under Justice N.N. Vohra. However, the committee's report, instead of addressing widespread criminal-politician-bureaucrat axis which has become a menace to the common citizen in the villages or cities, rather chose to highlight only the threat to national security, posed mainly by the smugglers of Mumbai, who enjoy the protection of local political leaders and who allegedly were used by Pakistan's ISI to plot the Bombay blasts.[126] As pointed by an observer, the report did not consider the other dimensions of the axis, as manifested in the daily suffering of the landless Dalits terrorised by criminal musclemen in the party of the local landlord-politician, protected by the district administration; or the middle class citizens being bullied for extortion by the local mafia patronised by MLAs and MPs, again protected by the police. By ignoring these everyday manifestations of the criminal-politician-bureaucrat nexus at the ground level, the report, with its full intention, reduced the entire issue of criminalisation of the Indian political system to a non-serious act.[127]

Nevertheless, the report did ignite some discussion on the ground. The PUCL-Tamil Nadu and Pondicherry, led a major campaign called 'Citizens' Campaign for Clean Elections' during the state assembly elections in 1996 to vote for the right candidate in their respective constituency.[128] The same year in its judgement to a PIL regarding election expenses incurred by political parties by an organisation named Common Cause, the Supreme Court held that purity of election is fundamental to democracy.

> The political parties in their quest for power spend more than one thousand crore of rupees on the General Election (Parliament alone), yet nobody accounts for the bulk of the money so spent and there is no accountability anywhere. Nobody discloses the source of the money. There are no proper accounts and no audit. From where does the money come, nobody knows. In a democracy where rule of law prevails this type of naked display of black money, by violating the mandatory provisions of law, cannot be permitted.[129]

In response to this, the Election Commission in August 1997 showing concern towards this issue disclosed that in the 1996 general elections, it seized a large number of illegal arms and that out of the total 13,952 candidates, who contested the election, nearly 1,500 had criminal records. It further added that the number of MPs and MLAs who have cases pending against them (in 1997) was 40 and 700 respectively.[130] It was then that the Supreme Court ordered a directive to the government to explain 'what it had done by way of follow-up action on the Vohra Committee report'.[131] The same year, the Election Commission came with an order to prevent participation in elections of all those who had been convicted for non-cognisable offences under various sub-sections of the Section 8 of the Representation of People's Act, irrespective of whether the convicted person is released on bail or not during the tendency of appeal (subject, of course, to the exception in the case of sitting members of Parliament and State Legislatures under sub-section (4) of the said section 8 of the Representation of the People Act, 1951).[132] This has been mentioned by several Ethics Committees started since 1998; but, it has never been able to issue directives and proposals that could stop the rapid declining of legitimacy of the state due to the growing influence of the criminality in the political process. On the contrary, the self-styled criminal-politicians have established their own hegemony and control over the management of their custody and bail, even if implicated in offences such as murder. This is largely due to the generosity of the courts and to the police who invariably in league with these criminals, make the prosecution cases deliberately weak.

It was due to this sense of helplessness that in the year 1999 a Public Interest Litigation (PIL) was filed asking for a mandatory disclosure of criminal, financial and educational backgrounds of candidates contesting elections to the Parliament and State Legislatures, prior to the polls.[133] After a long wait of three years, the Supreme Court on May 2, 2002 (later revised in 2003) finally directed the Election Commission to call for information on affidavit from each candidate seeking election to Parliament or a State Legislature as a necessary part of his nomination paper, furnishing therein, information on the aspects in relation to his/her candidature of: (1) All past convictions, (2) Current cases in which charges have been framed (under trial), (3) Assets of candidate, spouse and dependent children, (4) Liabilities – including debts to Government (rent, telephone bills, etc.) and Banks, etc., and (5) Educational Qualifications essential for the candidates to contest any election.[134]

Although this landmark judgement of the Supreme Court has empowered the voters with the right to know about the candidates contesting in the country, it, could not however, strengthen the existing laws to make convictions of the accused fairly possible. On the contrary, politicians accused of crimes easily escaped conviction by a variety of means ranging from intimidating witnesses and destroying evidence to delaying indefinitely the final disposal of their cases. Just to think of depending on conviction to debar criminals from entering the electoral fray seems illusionary, given the low rate of conviction for even serious crimes like murder or rape, not to mention corruption.

Proposing an amendment to this practice, the Election Commission in its report submitted to the Government of India on Electoral Reforms in July 2004, suggested that 'any person who is accused of an offence punishable by imprisonment for five years or more should be disqualified from contesting election even when the trial is pending, provided that the charges have been framed against him by the competent court'. The Commission reiterated that the counter view to this proposal based on the doctrine that 'a person is presumed to be innocent until he is proved guilty' should be ignored for greater public interests. However, as a precaution against motivated cases by the ruling party, the Commission opined that only those cases would be considered merit for disqualification 'which were filed prior to six months before an election'. It is also suggested that 'persons found guilty by a Commission of Enquiry should also stand disqualified from contesting elections'.[135] In the meantime, the Patna High Court in a petition filed by an organisation People's Watch, passed an order that 'persons behind bars cannot contest elections'. But unfortunately, the Election Commission, on the ground that the Court passed the order during the course of the election process in 2004, obtained a stay order from the Supreme Court. The issue is still pending before the Supreme Court for final disposal;[136] and the Government of India has hardly bothered to consider this issue seriously.

A closer look at the disclosure of criminal background of candidates contesting/winning assembly and parliamentary elections held across country since 2003 clearly exposes both the interest of the politicians and their growing nexus with the judiciary (see Table 2.2).

Out of a total of 44,183 candidates contesting various state assemblies and parliamentary elections between 2003 and 2008, nearly 4,790 (10.9%) had pending criminal charges against them. Among those who won in these elections (4,653), 1,168 (25.10%) had pending criminal cases against them. The numbers, if taken separately, say that there were 38,748 candidates who fought various assembly elections between 2003 and 2008 and 5435 fought in the parliamentary elections in the year 2004. Out of the 543 members of the Lok Sabha elected in the year 2004, 120 (22.09%) were with pending criminal cases against them; and out of 4,114 assembly seats, 1,048 (25.5%) were occupied by those who had pending criminal cases against them. In each of these elections, the proportion of candidates with criminal charges among the winners is higher than that of the contesting. Some cases, this ratio has even multiplied nearly three times (see Uttarakhand Assembly Election 2007, row no. 15 of the Table 2.2).

The age old practice of political parties to go by the yardstick of winnability of the candidate calculated on the basis of caste and religion is now complemented by that of 'money, muscle and gun power'. This is nothing but a tyranny of democracy. This can be substantiated more by the fact that out of 478 candidates who had pending criminal cases against them in the Lok Sabha election 2004, 120 (25.10%) had won, and among the 4,312 candidates who had criminal backgrounds in the assembly elections, 1,048 (24.30%) won. This means every fourth candidate with a criminal record won both in the Lok Sabha and the State Assemblies.

In the last nine years, the situation has got even worse. According to the recently released reports of ADR & NEW, out of the total 8,790 MPs/MLAs analysed since 2004, almost 30 per cent have criminal charges (self-declared) and half of these have serious criminal charges (self-declared) against them. All political parties in India, without exception, reaffirm their commitment to rooting out criminalisation and restoring law and order, whenever asked to speak on the issue; but when asked to perform, always prefers the factor of 'winnability' of candidates and favour the criminal antecedents. As a matter of fact, over the years the chances of winning an election with serious criminal record has grown much higher than the chance of winning election with a clean record.[137]

The Practical Syllogism

The purpose of this chapter is not to hold a brief of history-sheeters in politics. These have been discussed only to highlight the point that people with criminal records managing to become law makers and ministers is a matter of serious concern, and therefore needs necessary consideration. A detailed analysis by disaggregating democracy (in addition to what approached here at the macro-institutional level of the Parliament, and the Elections) at the intermediate and the local level institutions where both state and society meet and where 'everyday' forms of democracy takes shape is attempted in part II and III.

However, what becomes clear from the discussions made earlier is that the newly-born political structure in the country which includes the state, the political parties, the executive bodies and the judiciary is

Table 2.2

Details of Candidates with Pending Criminal Cases in the state legislative assemblies since 2003

S.No.	A	B	C	D	E	F	G	H	I
1.	MP	Nov 03 Assembly	2,171	753	NA	NA	230	36	15.65
2.	Maharashtra	Oct 2004, Assembly	2,678	1,625	366	22.5	288	86	29.86
3.	Karnataka	Dec 04, Assembly	1,715	1,715	211	12.3	224	56	25.00
4.	Orissa	May, 2004, Assembly	802	802	135	16.83	147	41	27.89
5.	Bihar	Feb, 2005, Assembly	1,279	1,199	418	34.86	243	102	41.97
6.	Harayana	Feb, 2005, Assembly	983	529	60	11.34	90	23	25.56
7.	Jharkhand	Feb, 2005, Assembly	1390	518	151	29.15	81	25	30.86
8.	Bihar	Nov, 2005, Assembly	2,135	1,613	451	28	243	119	49
9.	West Bengal	May, 2006, Assembly	1654	1129	217	19.22	294	45	15.31
10.	Assam	May, 2006, Assembly	997	698	35	5.041	126	7	5.56
11.	Tamil Nadu	May, 2006, Assembly	2,586	1,366	201	14.71	234	77	32.91
12.	Pondicherry	May, 2006, Assembly	218	145	12	8.28	30	4	13.33
13.	Manipur	Assembly 2007	308	308	4	1.3	60	1	1.66
14.	Punjab	Assembly 2007	1,043	612	74	12.09	117	20	17.09
15.	Uttarakhand	Assembly 2007	806	806	59	7.32	70	13	18.57
16.	UP	Assembly 2007	6,086	5,940	881	14.83	403	160	38.3
17.	HP	Assembly 2007	336	336	50	14.88	68	21	30.88
18.	Meghalaya	Assembly 2008	None of the candidates contesting the assembly elections had any criminal cases pending against them.						
19.	Nagaland	Assembly 2008	218	218	2	0.92	60	0	0.00
20.	Tripura	Assembly 2008	313	313	6	1.92	60	1	1.67

Cont'd...

...Cont'd

21.	Gujarat	Assembly 2008	1,268	1,268	233	18.38	182	45	24.73
22.	Karnataka	Assembly 2008	2,242	2,242	142	6.33	234	42	17.95
23.	MP	Assembly 2008	3,179	1,168	208	17.81	230	54	29.00
24.	Chhattisgarh	Assembly 2008	1,066	904	76	8.41	90	11	12.22
25.	Rajasthan	Assembly 2008	2,194	2,194	225	10.26	200	30	15.00
26.	Delhi	Assembly 2008	875	645	92	14.26	70	27	38.57
27.	Mizoram	Assembly 2008	206	206	3	1.46	40	2	5.00
28.	Lok Sabha	May, 2004	5,435	3,182	478	15.02	539	120	22.26

Source: http://www.adrindia.org/downloads/Analysis_Since_2003.pdf. A: State; B: Election; C:Total Candidates Contested; D: Total Candidates Considered; E: Candidates with pending criminal Cases; F: percentage of Candidates with pending cases w.r.t. candidates considered; G: Total Winners; H: Total Winners with Pending cases; I: percentage of winners with pending cases w.r.t. total winners.

on a ethical decline. The governance of the Indian State has nearly failed to be socially meaningful for the majority of citizens. Survival of the fittest, a prime characteristic of our democratic history, has increased sharply in the 1970s and in the later decades became the life saving *mantra*. Temptations to use the power to settle scores without adhering to the democratic ethos and to be in positions of power, even by the worst undemocratic means (including murder politics) have became the order of the day. Even the new participants, emerged through the process of 'silent revolution', has failed to show any sign of rebuilding the country's ruined institutional structure. Looking beyond the leadership of one's own group of caste/community/religion/region and working as individuals have become unimaginable. In other words, it further narrowed down the meaning of politics to imply simply as symbolic actions that inspired triumphalism only among their social base.

This rise of politics on the basis of caste/community/religion/region is a direct product of the politics practiced by the traditional elites and therefore, 'it is wrong to see them as atavistic forms that repudiate or attack the ideas of the State and democracy'. On the contrary, 'they exemplify the triumphant success of these ideas'.[138] However, this success has been paradoxical. The country has fallen not only into the trap of Weber's, 'political capitalism'[139], but also 'criminal capitalism', i.e., criminals gaining social legitimacy by winning ballots by the power of bullets. A close look at elections ever since the Independence shows that election years have been closely associated with increase in the intensity of riots over the years (see Table 2.3).

Table 2.3

Election Years and Increase of Riots (1958–2004)

States	*No. of Elections/scheduled elections*	*No. of times Rate of Riot growth was positive*
Andhra Pradesh	9	7
Assam	8	4
Bihar	8	2
Gujarat	8	7
Haryana	8	4
Jammu & Kashmir	8	4
Karnataka	9	8
Kerala	9	6
Madhya Pradesh	8	4
Maharashtra	9	7
Orissa	9	6
Punjab	8	5
Rajasthan	8	6
Tamil Nadu	8	6
Uttar Pradesh	8	4
West Bengal	8	4
National	133	87

Source: K.C. Vadlamannati, (2008). op. cit.

Transition from feudalism to democracy not only require adult franchise, but a strong political will to democratize the power structure. Attempts made in the initial years after Independence couldn't achieve any substantial success. In the later days, the experience, however, remained only dramatic. The relationship between crime and punishment was disturbed, and the criminals were granted the privilege of law-making.

This further assured the criminals of their non-conviction. All remained reluctant to prosecute their rivals with a fear that the same may happen to them when they are out of power. This has led them to make use of all means to retain their hold on power. Adding to this are the delays in investigations. Our judicial system, with its shortfall in judges but excess of corrupt lawyers, has a huge backlog of 29.2 million cases pending across hundreds of subordinate courts, 21 high courts and the Supreme Court. According to figures released by the Supreme Court in 2008, out of this mind-boggling number, over 25.4 million cases are pending in subordinate courts, 3.7 million cases in various high courts, while the Supreme Court is sitting over 45,887 cases.[140] More importantly, according to the global anti-corruption group Transparency International, as many as 77 per cent of Indians in 2008 believed the country's judiciary was corrupt; and 36 per cent acknowledged coughing up bribes to the judiciary in 2007:

> An estimated [$600 billion] was the amount Indians shelled out as bribes to the judiciary, higher than the bribes paid out in any other sector in the country ... . The average amount of money [roughly $90] paid in bribes by a household in India in 12 months was maximum in the judiciary compared to other sectors.[141]

Even the data on prosecutions of cases by the CBI was no different. In April 2000, the CBI had more than 6,000 cases pending for trial, 220 of them over 20 years old, in various courts while another 1,600 cases were still under investigation. More important, as several observers comment, even the quality of investigation has declined, leading to more acquittals. In 1999, only 58 per cent of the cases ended in conviction against 67 per cent in 1997.[142] Though our democracy has withstood the test of time (except during the two odd years of Emergency), the meaning of citizenship throughout the vast regions has remained limited by the persistence of traditional feudal system that is based on the concept that someone is born to rule and someone to be ruled.

Thus, criminalisation of politics is a much larger threat to democracy than the mere presence of men with criminal records in politics. It concerns growth of all such forces that instead of upholding the rule of law, pulls it apart. There isn't any risk in saying that this process started in the 1970s and in the years that followed, the system could never get restored. Politicians have misused public opinion (in the form of votes gained through fair or foul means) as a tool to save themselves from all odds on the premise that "*hume to janata ne chuna hai*" (we have been elected by the people). As a result, it has led to an increase in criminalisation of the political system and the strengthening of the bond between crime and non-punishment.

Notes

1. Borrowed from Christophe Jaffrelot's work *India's Silent Revolution: The Rise of Lower Castes in North India,* London, Hurst and Co (2003).

2. The 'status quo', as used for the purpose of this study, is a situation in which upper-caste elites hold the (public) monopoly of politics and policymaking uncontested.
3. Paul Brass in his recent work on politics in the north Indian states has expressed his dissatisfaction with using glorifying terms such as democracy, freedom and rule of law while describing the working of the Indian system of government and expressed it simply as a 'corrupt bureaucratic state' (see Paul Brass, (2011). *An Indian Political Life: Charan Singh and Congress Politics, 1937–1961,* Sage Publications, New Delhi, p. 158). This study, on the contrary, believes that since the task here is less about fixing terms to describe the working of the Indian government and politics and more of finding the roots and causes of its increasing criminality and illegitimacy; avoiding these glorifying terms is actually impossible.
4. This is not to suggest that criminality traversed into politics only after India's independence. It was endemic to the system even before independence, in all its local conflicts from village to town to district and state; but this study confines itself to the phenomenon of criminalisation of politics in independent India. To know more on the criminality in politics in the colonial period, see (Ibid.).
5. A disinterested arbiter in the form of the state has remained one of the most contested concepts in the past and even today. The idea of the state as a disinterested arbiter has increasingly been the position of the Western liberal societies; but it was first challenged by Marx and later by the other neo-Marxist scholars. However, as a matter of fact, all agree that, to be politically effective, the state must be able to differentiate itself from the ruling class factions and not be a party to it (see Gregor McLennan, David Held and Stuart Hall (eds.) (1993). *The Idea of the Modern State,* Philadelphia, Open University Press, pp. 1–79). This study understands state as a disinterested arbiter for its commitment to uphold the rule of law, which is very necessary for the sustenance of democracy with a liberal format. Rule of law can be simply understood as protection of the rights of common people from arbitrary and abusive use of people in power. It is adherence to the Constitution that confers the rights of 'equality before law' and 'equal protection of law' for every citizen of the country. One cannot deny that a regime cannot be autonomous of society, pursuing its own agenda of interests, but at the same time, it should not be directed by the concentration of private economic or social power of one caste/class, almost free from accountability. It cannot allow criminals, who defy the law to administer over others. For more on rule of law. See Chapter 1, Footnote 4.
6. For details see chapter 1.
7. Ashutosh Varshney, (1998). 'India Defies the Odds; Why Democracy Survives', *Journal of Democracy,* Vol. 9, No. 3, July, pp. 36–50; Myron

Weiner, (1989). 'Institution Building in India', *The Indian Paradox: Essays in Indian Politics,* New Delhi, Sage Publication, pp. 77–98. With the establishment of Indian National Congress (henceforth INC), democratic norms certainly had begun to penetrate down to the political imagination of a few Indians, who in return tried their best to build a democratic stage for the generations to follow; but a lot more was needed to democratize a country as vast as India.

8. Excerpts from Ambedkar's speech on the floor of the Constituent Assembly on November 4, 1948; see *Constituent Assembly Debates,* Vol. VII, November 4, 1948, p. 38.
9. Rajni Kothari, (1964). 'The Congress System in India' *Asian Survey,* 4 (12), December, pp. 1161–73. This expression by Kothari refers to the identification of the capacity of the Congress party, i.e., the 'party of consensus' to remain in power by adjusting to and co-opting the social movements within the party, which he described as the 'parties of pressure'. The only exceptions were states of Jammu & Kashmir, Kerala and Nagaland. In J&K the ruling party was the National Conference and in Kerala there was a CPI-led government for a brief period during 1957–59. Nagaland became a state in 1963 and had a Naga National Organisation government. The Congress in this era won around 45 per cent of the votes and 75 per cent of the seats in Parliament against 10 per cent of votes and 5 per cent of the seats by the successive opposition parties – the Socialist Party in 1951, the Praja Socialist Party in 1957 and the Communist Party of India in 1962. Congress enjoyed uninterrupted power at the centre until 1977. See Partha Chatterjee, (2004). 'Introduction: A Political History of Independent India', in Partha Chatterjee (ed.) *State and Politics in India,* New Delhi, Oxford University Press, pp. 1–39. Also see Bipan Chandra, et al. (1999). *India After Independence,* New Delhi, Penguin Books, p. 136.
10. Some of the important names other than Nehru were N. Sanjeeva Reddy (Andhra Pradesh), B.P. Chaliha (Assam), Sri Krishna Sinha (Bihar), Y.S. Parmar (Himachal Pradesh), S. Nijalingapa (Mysore), Y.B. Chavan (Maharashtra), H.K. Mahtab (Orissa), Pratap Singh Kairon (Punjab), Mohan Lal Sukhadia (Rajasthan), K. Kamraj (Madras), Sampoornanand and C.B. Gupta (Uttar Pradesh) and B.C. Roy (West Bengal). Although B.R. Ambedkar was an exception representing the 'lower castes', he too was educated at London and Columbia. The credit to bring in political equality and pull democracy out of the hands of the small traditional authority based on caste hierarchy, goes primarily to Ambedkar, who was never a member of the Congress.
11. Though there are variations in the degree of acceptance of this theory, all seem to be in consent that Congress during the Nehru era

had a high regard for democratic norms. See Rajni Kothari, (1988a). op. cit. p. 24; Ashutosh Varshney, (1998). op. cit.; Achin Vanaik, (1990). *The Painful Transition: Bourgeois Democracy in India,* London, Verso, pp. 67–112; Granville Austin, (2005). 'The Expected and the Unintended in Working a Democratic Constitution' in Zoya Hasan, E. Sridharan and R. Sudarshan, (eds.) *India's Living Constitution: Ideas, Practices and Controversies,* London, Anthem Press, pp. 318–342.

12. W.H. Morris-Jones, (1975). 'The Achievement of Parliament' in his book *Parliament in India,* Philadelphia, University of Pennsylvania Press, pp. 316–33.
13. Rajni Kothari, (1988a). op. cit. p. 26. In fact, most of the members in opposition had a Congress background. But even those who didn't, such as CPI (3.3% of MPs in the 1950s belonged to this party), had accepted to adhere to the Parliamentary path. See B.L. Sankar and Valerian Rodrigues, (2010). *The Indian Parliament: A Democracy at Work,* New Delhi, Oxford University Press, pp. 27–69.
14. See Sunil Khilnani, (2004). op. cit. p. 41.
15. D.L. Seth, (2004). 'The Crisis of Political Authority', in Rajendra Vora and Suhas Palshikar (eds.) *Indian Democracy: Meanings and Practices,* New Delhi, Sage, pp. 65–66.
16. See W.H. Morris-Jones, (1975). op. cit. p. 324.
17. The rulers as understood here include the kingdoms, the big and small landlords and the middlemen. For further details see Christophe Jaffrelot, (2003). 'The Congress; Party of the Intelligentsia, or of the Notables?' in his book *India's Silent Revolution: The Rise of Lower Castes in North India,* London, Hurst and Co. pp. 48–88.
18. See Achin Vanaik, (1990). op. cit. p. 82.
19. See Christophe Jaffrelot, (2003). 'Congress in Power or India as a Conservative Democracy', in his book *India's Silent Revolution: The Rise of Lower Castes in North India,* London, Hurst and Co. pp. 11–253. Other scholars too have argued that one of the major problems of Congress in the Nehru era was intra-party rivalry. There was a clear divide between the right wing of the Party (Purushottamdas Tandon) and Nehru. On several occasions the deadlock between the two leaders had reached to such level that on August 6, 1951 Nehru finally resigned from the Congress Working Committee asking Congressmen to choose between the two. However, Tandon instead of accepting Nehru's resignation, decided to resign himself. In the later days, this division – between Nehru's commitment to socialism and the right-wing led to a rot in the party. This is not to suggest that the democratic habit within the party was on decline. When Tandon was replaced by Nehru as Congress President graciously asked Tandon to join his Working Committee

and the offer was immediately accepted. Nehru also asked dissidents to rejoin the party, and several of them followed. See Bipan Chandra, et al.1999. op. cit. pp. 185–198.

20. See Bipan Chandra, et al. (1999). op. cit., p. 140.
21. Paul Brass, (2011), op. cit.; Prakash Singh, (2001). "Crime, Politics and Governance', *Seminar,* 502; also see Bipan Chandra, et al.1999. op. cit., p. 141. Some of the popular scandals of this period were jeep scandal, the LIC-Mundhra deal, etc. It was only the H.G. Mudgal affair (a Congress legislator from Bombay who had received bribe in connection with his dealings with the Bullion Merchants Association) in which Nehru, rising above the party lines, moved the resolution for his removal.
22. Political scientists have only made referential comments about the executive-judiciary relations of this era. For a detailed analysis on the conditions for creation of the Ninth Schedule during the First Amendment to the Constitution in 1951, see Granville Austin, (1999). *Working A Democratic Constitution: A History of the Indian Experience,* New Delhi, Oxford University Press.
23. Ibid. p. 325; also see Pratap Bhanu Mehta, (2006). 'The Promise of Uncertainty', in Pran Chopra (ed.) *The Supreme Court Versus the Constitution: a Challenge to Federalism,* New Delhi, Sage Publication, pp. 155–77.
24. For a seminal analysis, see Francine Frankel, (1978). *India's Political Economy, 1947–1977.* Princeton, Princeton University Press.
25. For a helpful introductory account, see Guillermo O'Donnell, (1993). 'On the State, Democratization And Some Conceptual Problems: A Latin American View with Glances at some Post communist Countries', *World Development* 21, no. 8, pp. 1355–69. I draw this argument from Patrick Heller who says that the most important precondition for the effective exercise of civic and political rights requires a state capable of securing the even, uniform, and rational-legal enforcement of public authority. In much of the developing world, the states have failed to do so and produced only 'a low-intensity from of citizenship'. See Patrick Heller, (2000). 'Degrees of Democracy: Some Comparative Lessions from India', *World Politics,* 52, pp. 484–519.
26. Deepesh Chakrabarty, (2005). "In the Name of Politics: Sovereignty, Democracy and Multitude in India", *Economic and Political Weekly,* July 23, pp. 3293–3301.
27. See Ashutosh Varshney, (1998). op. cit.
28. See Sunil Khilnani, (2004). op. cit. p. 41. For a seminal analysis, see Rajni Kothari, 1988a. 'Decline of Parties and Rise of Grassroots Movements, in *State Against Democracy,* op. cit. pp. 37–54. A large

number of Congressmen were no longer satisfied with party work and hungered for official positions, influence and patronage. Nehru's last effort to infuse new life into the party and restore the balance between the party and the government in August 1963, popularly known as the Kamraj Plan, though received enthusiastically (with 300 resignations from ministerial posts), was too late to cure the damage. The plan on the whole failed to cleanse the party of the dross. The morale of the party continued to sink, and the Congressmen's obsession for power and patronage increased even more. See Bipan Chandra, et al. (1999). op. cit. p. 197.

29. Dhanagare noted that highest number of cases of violence occurred in Bihar, alone accounting for 21 per cent of the total. On the contrary the arrests made in Bihar were relatively very few. Dhanagare credited the political leadership for this situation. For a seminal analysis see, D.N. Dhanagare, (1968). 'Violence in the Fourth General Elections: A Study in Political Conflict', *Economic and Political Weekly,* Annual Number, January, pp. 151–156.
30. Ibid. He, however, suggested that violence during election can be understood as an indication of healthy democratic system.
31. During this period Bihar saw seven governments, Uttar Pradesh four, Haryana, MP, Punjab and West Bengal three each, and Kerala two. In addition to that these states also underwent a total of eight spells of Central rule.
32. See Bipan Chandra, et al. (1999). op. cit. p. 228.
33. Bipan Chandra, et al. (1999). op. cit. Also see Rajni Kothari, (1988a) and (1998b). op. cit.
34. For a detailed analysis, see Rajni Kothari, (1988b). op. cit. Also see Bipan Chandra, et al. (1999). op. cit. pp. 232–45
35. See Sunil Khilnani, (2004). op. cit. p. 90.
36. Sudipta Kaviraj, (1986). 'Indira Gandhi and Indian Politics', *Economic and Political Weekly,* Vol. XXI, Nos 38 and 39, September 20–27, pp. 1697–1708.
37. In the 1971 election Indira's Congress (R) swept the polls winning 352 of the 518 Lok Sabha seats.
38. For a seminal analysis, see Rajni Kothari, (1988a). op. cit. p. 107. The first step in this direction was her call during the Presidential election to vote according to one's 'conscience', following the split in the party in 1969. The second step was the *garibi hatao* (remove poverty) slogan during the 1971 election. Kothari opined that both these occasions could have been used to give a new institutional structure to the Indian State.
39. See Atul Kohli, (1994). 'Centralization and Powerlessness: India's Democracy in a Comparative Perspective' in Joe Migdal et al. (ed.)

'*State Power and Social Forces*, op. cit. pp. 89–107. Also see Atul Kohli, (1992). op. cit.; Rajni Kothari, (1988a). op. cit.; and Sunil Khilnani, 2004. op. cit.

40. In August 1970, she derecognised the Princes and stopped all their monetary and other privileges by proclaiming a presidential order. She pushed for rigorous implementation of the existing land reform and land ceiling legislations. She also doubled the investment outlay of the Five Year Plan. She kept her focus on the growth of the public sector and brought legislations for imposition of a ceiling on urban property. By the 24th and 25th Amendment to the Constitution, she tried to rectify the conservative position of the courts on issues such as agrarian reform legislation, nationalisation of industries, banks and other business enterprises and hindered measures to check concentration of wealth and economic power in private hands. India also achieved a major success in nuclear atomic science during her regime.
41. Rajni Kothari, (1988b). op. cit.
42. See Sunil Khilnani, (2004). op. cit., p. 47.
43. See Rajni Kothari, (1989a). op. cit. p. 216; also see Sunil Khilnani, (2004). op. cit. p. 48.
44. Ibid p. 253–58. Though Mrs Gandhi had announced a 20–Point programme during the Emergency; it was the only the four points of Sanjay that actually remained more important throughout the period – don't take dowry at the time of marriage; practice family planning and limit families to only two children; plant trees; and promote literacy. Moreover to achieve these, Sanjay pushed the state towards initiating several steps against the unsterilised and unbeautified poor. The civil service's and the judiciary's commitment to the government was rather made mandatory.
45. For details, see Ibid. p. 253–58; also see Sunil Khilnani, (2004). op. cit. pp. 46–7. Anyone who declined to take orders from Sanjay's gang [Bansi Lal (defense minister), Mohammad Yunus (special envoy of the PM) and R.K. Dhavan (PS to the PM)], had to go unceremoniously. Inder Kumar Gujaral was the first casualty; because his instructions to the All India Radio and Delhi Television conflicted with those that were given orally on telephone by Sanjay. See C.S. Pandit, (1977). *End of an Era: The Rise and fall of Indira Gandhi*, New Delhi, Allied Publishers, 180–196.
46. Sudipta Kaviraj, (1986). op. cit.
47. For a seminal analysis of politics of this period in some of these states, see James Manor, (2002). 'Changing State, Changing Society in India', *Journal of South Asian Studies,* South Asia, 25(2), pp. 231–256; (for Uttar Pradesh) see Paul Brass, (1997). 'National Power and Local Politics in India: A Twenty-year Perspective' in

Partha Chatterjee, (ed.) *State and Politics in India,* op. cit. pp. 303–35; Paul Brass, (1980). 'The Politicization of the Peasantry in a North Indian State', *Journal of Peasant Studies,* July, pp. 395–426 and September, pp. 3–36; (for Gujarat) see Atul Kohli, (1992). *Democracy and Discontent,* op. cit. The only exception among the Congress ruled states in the 1970s was Karnataka, under Devraj Urs. Urs not only had tactically prevented the dominant castes from misuse of state apparatus, but also successfully shared power with the backward and scheduled castes. Thus, it was less due to the character of the Congress and more of the personal charisma and leadership of Urs that had prevented the over-politicisation of the polity in the state. See Atul Kohli, (1992). *Democracy and Discontent,* op. cit. pp. 93–122.

48. See Rudolph and Rudolph, (1998) (1987). op. cit. pp. 159–177.
49. Observers feel that although the various constituents of the Janata Party formally merged to form a single organisation; they largely retained their separate identities on the ground. They had very less in common in terms of policies and programmes and failed to utilise the anti-Emergency mood of the country to build an alternative politics. See Partha Chatterjee, (ed.) (2004). *State and Politics in India,* New Delhi, Oxford University Press, pp. 1–39; also see Bipan Chandra, et al.1999. op. cit. p. 250.
50. Sumanta Banerjee, (1978). 'Violence of the Rich', *Economic and Political Weekly,* January 7, pp. 11–12. Also see several other stories published during that period (1977–1980) under the regular column 'From Our Correspondents' in *Economic and Political Weekly.*
51. As quoted in ibid.
52. Ashis Nandy, (1980). 'Indira Gandhi and the Culture of Indian Politics' in his book *At the Edge of Psychology: Essays in Politics and Culture,* Delhi, Oxford University Press, pp. 112–130. Indira won from two constituencies – Medak and Rai Bareli; while Sanjay won from Amethi in 1980 (Both of them had lost from the Rai Bareli and Amethi seats respectively in 1977). The dissatisfaction with the three-years of Janata Party rule (1977–1979) was so high that in the next two years, after coming back to power, Indira even won majority of the Parliamentary by-elections (see Appendix 1). This placed Sanjay once again at the top of the political pyramid, and the lumpen elements, which included a large number of persons with a record of either criminal or civil offences, emerged from the backstage and entered the political mainstream as MLAs, MPs and even ministers. See Rajni Kothari, (1988a). 'Democracy and Fascism in India', in *State against Democracy,* op. cit. pp. 282–298. The first setback of this unhindered power was seen in Karnataka where Devraj Urs war replaced by Gundu Rao, as the Chief Minister of the state, who pushed the

Karnataka government to a brink of collapse. See Atul Kohli, (1992). *Democracy and Discontent,* op. cit. pp. 93–122. Few years later the country witnessed another tragic episode of this unchecked power in Punjab in June 1984, where Indira Gandhi along with Sanjay scripted a heavy-handed army operation – 'Operation Blue Star' – in the Golden Temple in Amritsar, to finish off the separatist, J.S. Bhindranwale, whom they themselves had earlier encouraged for their narrow partisan gains. This led to the killing of many innocent pilgrims and later became the reason for an organised communal violence against the Sikhs in connivance with the state (in the aftermath of Indira's assassination by her Sikh bodyguard on Oct. 31, 1984) See Sunil Khilnani, (2004). op. cit. pp. 51–3.

53. Atul Kohli, (1992), 'From Breakdown to Order: West Bengal' in *Democracy and Discontent,* op. cit. pp. 267–296
54. Sumanta Banerjee, (1990). "West Bengal Today: An Anticipatory Postmortem", *Economic and Political Weekly,* August 18, pp. 1812–1816.
55. Ibid.
56. Arun Prakash Chatterjee, as quoted in ibid.
57. For a detailed analysis of the criminality of the police and the state and their nexus with the criminals, see Sumanta Banerjee, (1990). op. cit. Banerjee reports how policemen who were convicted on the charge of killing a youth in the Golabari police station in Howrah in February 1980, despite arrest warrants served upon them, moved freely and threatened those who had given evidence against them.
58. For details see "Leviathan Unbound", *Economic and Political Weekly,* December 8, (1973), pp. 2163–2165; "The Politics of Repression", *Economic and Political Weekly,* August, (1973), pp. 1392–1395.
59. See "Police of Rampage", *Economic and Political Weekly,* December, (1977), pp. 2000–2001; "Rising Crime against Scheduled Castes", *Economic and Political Weekly,* December, (1979), pp. 1941–1948;
60. See Atul Kohli, (1992). *Democracy and Discontent,* op. cit. pp. 154–183.
61. 'Murder Politics', *Economic and Political Weekly,* January 31, (1981), p. 131.
62. In UP, for example, the governor complained to Pandit Pant in 1937 that '... in some districts the activities of Congressmen in interfering with police work and in establishing a regular system of complaints against whatever the police do are producing some deterioration in the morale of the police force and are beginning to affect their authority and to be reflected in some weakening of control over crime.' Sir Harry Haig, confidential letter to Pant, November 3, 1937. *United Provinces Governors Reports 1937,* India Office Records

L/PJ/5/264, as quoted in Steven I. Wilkinson, (2001). 'Cleansing Political Institutions', *Seminar,* Oct 20; URL: http://www.india-seminar.com/2001/506/506%20steven%20i.%20wilkinson.htm. Nehru himself in conversation with Rammanohar Lohia in 1946 had shared the degrading picture of the UP Congressmen who in their internal fight were showing no respect to the penal codes and had put the working of the state administration at stake. See Rammanohar Lohia, (1960). *Guilty Men of India's Partition,* Allahabad, Kitabistan, p. 20.

63. Steven I. Wilkinson, (2001). Every independent inquiry into policing that was carried out in the 1950s and early 1960s – in Bengal (1960–61), UP (1959), Kerala (1959), Punjab (1961–62) and Delhi (1961–62) – complained that, 'the greatest obstacle to efficient police administration flows from the domination of party politics under the state administration .... The result of partisan interference is often reflected in lawless enforcement of laws, inferior service, and in general decline of police prestige followed by irresponsible criticism and consequent widening of the cleavage between the police and the public affecting the confidence of the public in the integrity and objectives of the police force.' cited in *Report of the Punjab Police Commission 1961–62*, p. 20.
64. *Times of India*, 26 June 1973, as cited in Steven I. Wilkinson, (2001). op. cit.
65. See Steven I. Wilkinson, (2000). op. cit.
66. The Inspector General of Madhya Pradesh was demoted to an insignificant post when he refused to make large numbers of politically motivated transfers. See *Ninth Report of the National Police Commission*, Government of India, (August 1979), pp. 20–35.
67. Bayley, a student of Graduate School of International Studies, University of Denver, in his paper 'The Police and Political Order in India', presented at the *Tenth Annual Conference on Southeast Asia* at Madison in 1981. As quoted in N.K. Singh. (1999). *'The Politics of Crime and Corruption: A Former CBI Officer Speaks',* New Delhi, Harper Collins, pp. 37–98.
68. N.K. Singh in personal conversation with the author in July 2009.
69. N.K. Singh. (1999). *'The Politics of Crime and Corruption* op. cit. 58–66. *Kissa Kursi Ka*, a film produced by Amrit Nahata, was a satire on the style of the functioning of Indira Gandhi, particularly her promotion of Sanjay Gandhi as power centre and her successor. But this film could not be screened and released. It was banned under the Defence of India Rules. The buried facts came into light only when the investigation was taken up during the Janata Party government of Morarji Desai. After a protracted trial, the sessions' court on February

21, 1979 convicted Sanjay and his associate V.C. Shukla for entering into a criminal conspiracy. They were sentenced to two years rigorous imprisonment with fines of Rs 25,000 and Rs 10,000 respectively. Interesting is to read the day-to-day events of the trial days where Singh shows how on the day of conviction, hoodlums, led by Arjun Das attacked and caused physical harm to the senior counsel of CBI and others (including N.K. Singh) and broke the glass panes, damaged the furniture of the courtroom, held a mock trial acquitting the accused persons. It was only later that they appealed against this judgement in the Supreme Court. Singh explaining the aftermath of the judgement in a personal interview to me added, "I was forced to proceed on leave from the CBI. My official residence at Chanakyapuri was surrounded by Haryana policemen, sent by Sanjay's friend Bhajan Lal. I was falsely implicated in a case and other CBI officers of the team who were associated with the investigation of the case were harassed and transferred to distant places". Later, when elections to the Lok Sabha were held in 1979, both were allowed to fight the election on the ground of the pending judgement in the Supreme Court and eventually, after Congress' return to power, both of them were acquitted on the grounds of 'allegations not proved'.

70. In 1973, Indira Gandhi appointed A.N. Ray as the Chief Justice of the Supreme Court, superseding three senior judges, who then resigned in protest from the court. Though the appointment was politically motivated, the Prime Minister defended her action in the name of social justice. A similar act was repeated in January 1977. For more details, see Robert L. Hardgrave and Stanley A. Kochanek, (1999). *India: Government and Politics in a Developing Nation,* 6th ed. Fort Worth, Texas, Harcourt College Publishers, pp. 107–8.

71. For further details on court's accommodating ways in the interest of the ruling politicians, see Rudolph and Rudolph, (1998 [1987]). op. cit. pp. 118–121; also see N.K. Singh. (1999). op. cit. pp. 58–66.

72. Several practices established by Justices V.R. Krishna Iyer and P.N. Bhagwati opened the doors of the Court (complaints written even in postcards were considered as writ petitions) for the oppressed and the marginalised; expanded the scope of fundamental rights; and increased attention on issues of state impropriety and lawlessness.

73. For more on the executive-judicial conflict in this period, see Bhagwan D. Dua, (1983). 'A Case in Executive Judicial Conflict: The Indian Case', *Asian Survey,* Vol 23. no. 4, April, pp. 463–83; "After the *Keshavananda* decision was delivered on April 24, 1973 ... the government announced the appointment of Justice A.N. Ray as the Chief Justice of India in preference to three senior judges who had dared to interpret *Keshavananda* boldly and in the face of open threats from the regime .... The suppression of the judges provoked

volumes of protest from across the country, but the government refused to admit that it had compromised the independence of the judiciary by its unprecedented action." (p. 466) Later during the Emergency, it was Justice Ray who agreed, voluntarily or otherwise, with the President of India to the mass transfer of the High Court judges who were allegedly out of line with the regime (p. 467). Also see, A.G. Noorani, (1980). op. cit. There were instances when people in power were even made aware of what each of the judges was going to decide quite some time before the judgments were pronounced in the courts. For further details see P. Jaganmohan Reddy, 1999. *The Judiciary I Served,* New Delhi, Orient Blackswan.

74. A.G. Noorani, (2003). 'The Betrayal of India' *Frontline,* Vol. 20, January 18–31, URL: http://www.hindu.com/fline/fl2001/stories/2003011-7001007700.htm; also see, Bhagwan D. Dua, (1983). op. cit.
75. Bhagwan D. Dua, (1983). op. cit. p. 479.
76. See Yogendra Yadav, (1997). 'Reconfiguration in Indian Politics: State Assembly Election 1993–1995' in Partha Chatterjee (ed.) *State and Politics in India*, op. cit. 177–207.
77. K.C. Vadlamannati, (2008). 'Does Time of Elections Instigate Riots? A Substantial Study of 16 Indian States, 1958–2004', *William Davidson Institute Working Paper Number 939,* University of Michigan; URL: http://www.wdi.umich.edu/files/Publications/WorkingPapers/wp939.pdf; also see Atul Kohli, 1992. op. cit. p. 7.
78. See Atul Kohli, (1992). op. cit. pp. 339–377.
79. See *India Today,* January 15, (1986), p. 53.
80. L.I. Rudolph and S. Rudolph, (1998) (1987), op. cit. p. 152. see Atul Kohli, (1992). op. cit. 337–377.
81. For more on this, see L.I. Rudolph and S. Rudolph, (2001). 'Redoing the Constitutional Design', in Atul Kohli (ed.). *The Success of India's Democracy,* Cambridge University Press, pp. 127–162.
82. For more details on the behaviour of the legislators, especially of the Congress Party, see 'Hoodlum days', *Economic and Political Weekly,* April 30, (1988), p. 868.
83. The case was revealed through investigative journalism by Chitra Subramaniam and N. Ram of the newspapers *The Indian Express* and *The Hindu* respectively. For details on Bofors scandal, see http://indiatoday.intoday.in/index.php?issueid=89&id=39264&option=com_content&task= view&sectionid=4; also see Vir Sanghvi, 1999. 'Bofors' Ghost', *http://www.rediff.com/news/1999/sep/23vir.htm*; last accessed in May 2009.
84. Out of the total 26 by-elections during Rajiv Gandhi's regime, Congress lost twelve. It lost the election in Allahabad (UP), Sirsa,

Faridabad (Haryana) and Godhra (Gujarat) and won in Udhampur (J&K), Tura (Meghalaya) and Pali (Rajasthan). The most popular defeat of Congress among these was the defeat in Allahabad in 1988, where V.P. Singh, ousted from the Congress Party defeated the Congress candidate S. Shastri (son of Lal Bahadur Shastri) fighting as an independent. The seat had fallen vacant after the resignation of the Congress MP Amitabh Bachhan who had resigned in the aftermath of Bofors scandal.

85. The most dramatic of all the incidents was the public announcement of the replacement of the then foreign secretary A.P. Venkateswaran, ('who was appointed in the post only ten months before), before a nationally telecast press conference. Venkateswaran was present at the press conference and he was left totally stunned. For details, see Hardrave and Kochanek, 1999. op. cit. p. 93, 103.
86. Atul Kohli, (1992). op. cit. pp. 203–338.
87. Ibid. p. 111. Also see, 'The Judiciary: Crisis of Credibility', *India Today*. July 15, 1990, pp. 18–23.
88. For an interesting discussion, see Pranab Bardhan, (1984). 'The Dominant Propriety Classes', in his book *Political Economy of Development in India, The Political Economy of Development in India,* New York. Basil Blackwell, pp. 40–53.
89. V.S. Naipaul, (1992). *A Million Mutinies Now,* New Delhi, Penguin Books.
90. V.P. Singh became the PM with the support of the BJP and the Left parties and stayed in this capacity for eight months (December 2nd 1989–November 10th 1990); Chandra Shekhar formed the government with the support of the Congress between 10th November 1990 and 21st June 1991.
91. V.P. Singh declared the implementation of 27 per cent reservation for the Other Backward Class (OBC), as recommended by the Backward Class Commission (popularly known as Mandal Commission) in 1980. This indirectly empowered even the Scheduled Castes (SCs).
92. The OBC movement in Maharashtra is an excellent example of the Hindu-Muslim unity. For more details, see Gurpreet Mahajan and S.S. Jodhka, (2009). "Religions, Democracy and Governance: Spaces for the Marginalised in the Contemporary India", *Religions and Development Research Programme,* Working Paper 26, University of Birmingham, UK; available at www.rad.bham.ac.uk.
93. The BJP, a right-wing party declares its objective as, "The Party aims at establishing a democratic state which guarantees to all citizens irrespective of caste, creed or sex, political, social and economic justice, equality of opportunity and liberty of faith and expression". Religion, which has been included in the Indian Constitution in the list of non-discriminatory category, does not find similar space in BJP's

ideology. See http://www.bjp.org/ index.php?option=com_content&view=article&id=128&Itemid=426

94. *The Organizer* (the mouth piece of VHP), October 14, 1990.
95. Bihar in 1990 had a Janata Dal government under the premiership of Lalu Prasad Yadav. Yadav's decision to arrest Advani was supported by the then Prime Minister V.P. Singh (for more details, see Chapter 3).
96. Amrita Basu, (2001). 'The Dialects of Hindu Nationalism' in Atul Kohli (ed.). *The Success of India's Democracy,* Cambridge University Press, pp. 163–189; also see her chapter 'When Local Riots are Not Merely Local: Bringing the State Back In, Bijnor, 1988–1992', in Partha Chatterjee, (1997), op. cit. pp. 390–435.
97. Congress alleged that Chandra Shekhar's government was spying on Rajiv Gandhi. Dipankar Sinha, (1991). 'V.P. Singh, Chandra Shekhar, and No-Where Politics of India', *Asian Survey,* Vol. 31, No. 7, July, pp. 598–612.
98. For details see, Hardgrave and Kochanek, 1999. op. cit. p. 94.
99. The failure of the BJP government, in UP and the Congress leadership in Delhi to take decisive action finally led to the escalation of communal riots in a big way and made the fate of India's largest minority, a world-wide anxiety. For a detailed analysis on the politics of Hindu nationalism, see Katherine Adeney and Lawrence Saez, 2005. *Coalition Politics and Hindu Nationalism,* London and New York, Routledge. For a detailed analysis on the situation of the demolition of Babri mosque and its aftermath, see John McGuire, Pater Reeves and Howard Brasted, (1996). *Politics of Violence,* New Delhi, Sage Publications. Also see the documentary *'I Live in Behrampada'* produced by Majlis and directed by Madhusree Dutta.
100. For an in-depth analysis of the discussion made in the Parliament on this issue, see B.L. Shankar and Valerian Rodrigues, (2011). *The Indian Parliament*, op. cit. pp. 144–147.
101. Edward A. Gargan, 1993. 'Indian Government Survives Parliament Votes', *The New York Times,* July 29.URL: http://www.nytimes.com/1993/07/29/world/indian-government-survives-parliament-vote.html, last accessed on 29th June 2008.
102. See *UNI Report*; URL: http://www. rediff.com/news/nov/04jmm.htm
103. During the investigation, the approver Shailendra Mahato said that the then Congress president Sitaram Kesri, the then Congress treasurer, was aware of the bribing of MPs. See *UNI Report,* Kesri Knew MPs were bribed: Mahto; URL: http://www.rediff.com/news/nov/04jmm.htm
104. It registered a case against Rao under Section 120(b) (criminal conspiracy) and several other Sections of the Prevention of

Corruption Act of 1988. Four cases under Section 13(2) and Section 13(1) (d) (iii) of the 1988 Act were filed against JMM MPs Suraj Mandal, Shibu Soren, Simon Marandi and Shailendra Mahato. Subsequently, in pursuance of an order by the Delhi High Court, another case was registered against Congress leaders like V.C. Shukla, Satish Sharma, R.K. Dhawan, Lalit Suri and others. After completing the investigation, the CBI submitted three charge-sheets in the special CBI court in New Delhi. A.G. Noorani, (2000). 'The Law and its Potency', *Frontline,* Volume 17 - Issue 22, Oct. 28 - Nov. 10, URL: http://www.thehindu. com/fline/fl1722/ 17220990.htm

105. Only one of the four MPs of the JMM, Shailendra Mahato, was granted pardon after he turned to become an approver.
106. However, the court opined that the bribe givers had no such immunity and could be prosecuted. The decision was held by a narrow majority of 3:2. For further details, see *P.V. Narasimha Rao Vs State (CBI)* (1998) 4 SCC 626.
107. For further discussion on the case, see A.G. Noorani, (2000). op. cit.
108. "Foul Play and Punishment", *Indian Express,* July 23, (2008); http://www.indianexpress.com/news/foul-play-and-punishment/339059/0
109. As quoted in T.R. Andhyarujina, (2006). 'Shibu Soren's Unpunished Crime of Bribery, *The Hindu,* Dec. 16. URL: http://www.thehindu.com/2006/12/16/stories/2006121605311000.htm Last accessed on 7th Aug. 2008.
110. Mark Grossman, (2003). *Political Corruption in America: an Encyclopedia of Scandals, Power, and Greed,* ABC-CLIO publishers, California, USA, p. 342.
111. Ibid.
112. 'Knowledge of JMM-Congress Deal Led to Soren Secy's Murder: CBI', The Indian Express, November 16, 1998; URL: www.indianexpress.com/ ie/daily/19981116/32050354.html, last accessed on August 7, 2008. Also see High Court Judgement of the Criminal Appeal No. 64 of 2007 and Criminal Appeal No. 158 of 2007 on August 22, 2007, URL: http://delhi courts.nic.in/Aug07/Shibu%20Soren %20Vs.%20CBI.pdf.
113. See High Court Judgement of the Criminal Appeal No. 64 of 2007 and Criminal Appeal No. 158 of 2007 on August 22, 2007, op. cit.; also see Harish V. Nair and Satya Prakash, (2007). 'Shibu Soren's Aquittal on Expected Lines', *Hindustan Times,* August 7; URL: www.hindustantimes.com/.../storypage.aspx?...Headline=Shibu+Soren's+aquittal...expected+lines; last accessed on August 7, 2008.
114. See 'Soren Back in Union Cabinet', *The Hindu,* Nov 28, 2004; URL: http://www.hindu.com/2004/11/28/stories/2004112808950100.htm, last accessed on 21 August, 2008.

115. Congress leader and former CM of Andhra Pradesh, YSR belonged to a family known in the Rayalseema region as Baryte granite illegal miners. Several cases are pending in the courts against the family members and his father Raja Reddy, who was killed in a factional feud in Kadapa district on May 23, 1998 while he was heading the Congress party. According to news reports, one of the accused, Perla Uma Maheswara Reddy, was hacked to death in retaliation on the same day and four of the other accused died during the trial. 'Rayalseema is the legendary badlands of Andhra Pradesh – notorious for its endemic culture of violence, murder and unbridled factionalism .... A report in Frontline in 2005 said an astounding 670 Congressmen and 560 TDP men had lost their lives to factional rivalries in just the previous 15 years. Even the police admit that the "only ideology" in these testosterone faction-ridden villages is violence'. YSR's empire of an estimate of 1.5 lakh crores earned in just six years was evident. YSR's son Jaganmohan Reddy, who after his father's death, has made several attempts to become the CM of the state, has been 'accused of orchestrating the murder of controversial TDP leader Paritala Ravindra in 2005. The police filed an FIR against him, but a CBI enquiry exonerated him. Still, many lesser stories abound of him of unleashing his fury on police constables or inspectors who dared to stand up against him. In one such incident, a police inspector caught several men hunting rabbits without license in Simhadripuram town. They turned out to be Jagan's acolytes. When he landed up at the police station to rescue his friends, there was such a violent melee that the inspector locked himself inside the cell, refusing to come out. See Sanjana, (2009). 'Into The Madding Crown', *Tehelka Magazine,* Vol. 6, Issue 38, September 26. The Karnataka state under the BJP regime during 2008–2013 also functioned in similar style. The mining mafia, under Reddy brothers who were Ministers in the BJP government), ran the government at their whims. It is said that between 2003 and 2010, over 30 million tonnes of iron ore has been illegally mined and exported from Karnataka causing a huge revenue loss to the state exchequer. See Soroor Ahmed, (2010): 'BJP caught between Yeddy, Reddys and sleazy business', *twocircles.net,* July 16. The former CM of Karnataka, B.S. Yeddyurappa allegedly doled out land via denotification to his family and lieutenants. The matter is sub-judice. The Reddy mafias of both the states have established a vice-like grip over both the Congress and the BJP; the signs of which they have already shown in the recent past.

116. See Madhu Trehan, (2009). *Tehelka as Metaphor,* Lotus Roli Books, New Delhi.

117. Godhra has remained known for its high communal sensitivity for long in Gujarat. On February 27, 2002 a coach of the Sabarmati Express carrying kar-sevaks coming from Ayodhya was set on fire killing many people. Official evidence of 'who and how was the coach

set on fire' has not been established by any investigating agency, but forensic report says that the fire was lit from inside the coach and required at least 60 litres of an inflammable substance like petrol. The Tribunal of Concerned Citizens comprising retired Supreme Court judges and other eminent personalities has found that nothing can be said with certainty. This happened on the morning of February 27 and all hell broke loose all over Gujarat the next day'. For more details, see Asgar Ali Engineer, (2003). 'Communal Riots in 2002: A Survey', *Economic and Political Weekly,* January 25, pp. 280–2; also watch *Final Solution,* a film documenting the changing face of right-wing politics in India through a study of the 2002 genocide of Muslims in Gujarat by Rakesh Sharma (2004); also available at http://video.google. com/videoplay?docid= 3829364588351777769#.

118. For more details on the minister's disposition before the tribunal, see Manu Joseph and S. Anand, 2002. 'A Plot from the Devil's Lair', *Outlook,* June 3. URL: http://www.outlookindia.com/article.aspx? 215889. last accessed on 27th July 2008.
119. Asgar Ali Engineer, (2003). op. cit. also see Arundhati Roy, (2002). 'Who's She when She's at Home?' *Outlook,* May 6; URL: http://www.outlookindia.com/article.aspx?215477. Last accessed on August 2012.
120. For more details on the censure motion, see Alistair McMillan, (2005). op. cit. p. 32 and f.n. 19, p. 35. 8.
121. Upendra Baxi, (1982). 'The Crisis of Legitimation of the Law' in his book *The Crisis of the Indian Legal System,* New Delhi, Vikas Publishing House Pvt. Ltd. pp. 1–40.
122. Aristotle, (1953). *Ethics,* Book II. Translated by J.A.K. Thomson, Penguin Classics, 1955, Britain, p. 93.
123. Sumanta Banerjee, (2011), 'Breeding Black Sheep', *Economic and Political Weekly,* January 8, Vol. XLVI, No. 2, pp. 10–13.
124. The trust motion was moved during the first term of the UPA when the Left parties withdrew their support (62 seats) from UPA following Congress' decision to go ahead with the India-US civil nuclear deal in 2008.
125. While for some, it signals a major shift in the political landscape that could open up a new hope for institutional politics and the opportunity for state representing a grand coalition of interests, some see it as the voter's desire to bring down the arrogance in the political representatives. See Yogendra Yadav, (2009). 'Making Sense of the Verdict', *The Hindu,* 18th May. URL: http://www. thehindu.com/ 2009/05/18/stories/2009051854961100.htm, accessed last on June 20th 2008; and Ashis Nandy, (2009). 'The Hour of the Untamed Cosmopolitan' *Tehalka Magazine,* May 30, pp. 6–9.

126. Editorial, 1995. 'Diversionary Tactics', *Economic and Political Weekly*; September 2, p. 2152.
127. Ibid.
128. The response of the voter was, "Whom do we vote for? We do not find a single good candidate among the contestants". See Sudha Ramalingam, 2002. 'Do We Really Adhere to the Rule of Law?' *PUCL Bulletin*, September.
129. See Common Cause (A registered society) v. Union of India and Others [(1996) 2 SCC 752]
130. Editorial, 1997. 'Ritual Rhetoric', *Economic and Political Weekly* August 30, p. 2176.
131. Ibid.
132. See Election Commission of India, (1997). *Election Commission of India No. 509/Disqln./97 - J.S.I.* Dated: 28th August. According to the section 8(4) of Representation of People Act, 1951, the disqualification of a sitting member of parliament or legislature of a state, even if convicted of any offence with a sentence of imprisonment for two years, does not take effect until three months have elapsed from that date or, if within that period an appeal or application for revision is brought in respect of the conviction or the sentence, until that appeal or application is disposed of by the court. For more details see Sec. 8, *Representation of People Act, 1951.*
133. This PIL was filed by the Association for Democratic Reforms (ADR), an NGO founded in 1999 by a group of Professors from the Indian Institute of Management (IIM), Ahmedabad and National Institute of Design and some alumni of IIM. For details, see http://www.adrindia.org/about/about.asp
134. Union of India Vs. Association for Democratic Reforms and Another (Civil Appeal No. 7178 of 2001 and Writ Petition (C) No. 294 of 2001), date of order 02.05.2002; The revision was done in People's Union for Civil Liberties (PUCL) and Another vs. Union of India and another writ petition civil No. 490, 509, 515 of 2002), date of order 13.3.2003, see Election Commission of India, (2006). *Landmark Judgements on Election Law: A Compilation of important Judgements of the Supreme Court of India and High Courts and Opinion tendered by the Election Commission,* Vol. 4. New Delhi.
135. Election Commission of India, (2004). *Proposed Electoral Reforms,* New Delhi, July, p. 4.
136. See SLP (No. 9204–05/2004– ECI Vs. Jan Chowkidar (Peoples Watch) and Ors.)
137. See ADR and New (National Election Watch) Press Release, July 29, 2013; accessed at www.adrindia.org on July 29, 2013. Of the criminal records analysed of 4181 repeated candidates, 1072 of them had a

criminal case the first time they contested an election and 788 had cases the second time also. That is, political parties gave tickets of 74 per cent of candidates with criminal records the second time despite having information on their criminal background from previous elections. However the total number of candidates with criminal cases still increased the second time as there were 507 other candidates (out of 4181) who showed no criminal cases in the first election but declared cases in the second round of elections. Therefore the total per cent of candidates with criminal records given tickets by political parties rose from 26 per cent to 31 per cent. Of 540 candidates with serious charges, 353 (65%) were given tickets for the second time. In addition to that, there were 289 other candidates with no criminal cases in the first election, but who had declared cases in the second found of elections. This also shows that the total per cent of candidates with serious criminal records given tickets by political parties rose from 12 per cent to 15 per cent. The break up when seen party wise is headed by Shiv Sena with 75 per cent of MPs/MLAs since 2004; RLD with 46 per cent of MPs/MLAs since 2004; JD(U) with 44 per cent of MPs/MLAs since 2004. Among the two major national parties, BJP leads the race with 31 per cent of MPs/MLAs since 2004 (out of the 1689 MPs/MLAs from BJP, 520 have declared criminal cases) followed closely by 22 per cent of MPs/MLAs from the INC (out of the 2451 MPs/MLAs from INC, 527 have declared criminal cases) since 2004.

138. Sunil Khilnani, (2004). op. cit. p. 58.

139. It means the accumulation of wealth through political power, often wielded deceitfully and coercively. For more details on 'political capitalism' see Max Weber, (2001). *The Protestant Ethics and the Spirit of Political Capitalism* (edited and translated by Stephen Kalberg), London, Taylor and Francis, pp. 13–38.

140. See Neeta Lal, (2008). 'Huge Case Backlog Clogs India's Courts', *Asia Times,* June 28. URL: http://www.atimes.com/atimes/South_Asia/JF28Df02.html. Last accessed on 13 August 2008.

141. '*Global Corruption Report 2007: Corruption in Judicial Systems*' as cited in ibid.

142. See Farzand Ahmad, (2000). 'CBI: Zzz Files', *India Today,* May 29; URL: http://www.india-today.com/itoday/20000529/nation3.html. last accessed on 13 August 2008. also see Source: N. Vittal, 'Tackling Corruption in Public Service', March 2000, URL: http://cvc.nic.in/vscvc/cvcspeeches/march2k9.html, as produced in Wilkinson, 2000, op. cit.

3

The Economics of Change

> There is no society anywhere in the world – except for marginal cases – with resources so scarce that it could not, were it reasonably and rationally organised and governed, become well-ordered [...] The crucial element in how a country fares is its political culture – its members' political and civic virtues – and not the level of its resources.
>
> —John Rawls, *The Law of Peoples*

India is an economy which is primarily rural and agrarian, yet the majority of its population do not own land. The specificity of numerous caste groups divided and placed hierarchically on the basis of ritual superiority has made the situation more complex. Caste being the only crucial factor in the exercise of power and authority at the rural level has kept land ownership primarily with castes, higher in hierarchy. We are a country where 'to own land is the highest mark of esteem, to perform manual labour, the lowest'.[1]

Agrarian class relations in Bihar have been "firmly embedded in caste, because whether a person controls land or not is conditioned by that person's caste status".[2] Caught in the paradox of paucity amidst plenty and the preference for status quo among the traditionally dominant, the society here has witnessed brutalisation in various forms. The social prelude to the present stage of criminalisation in Bihar has grown out of this background. With its deep feudal character 'firmly embedded in caste', the state in Bihar has failed to achieve any degree of relative autonomy from that of the ruling elite. Rather it has chosen to be a party to exploit the majority of poor even in the conditions of scarcity.

The social consciousness of the people in Bihar have remained so deeply attached to caste that the state has hardly witnessed mobilisation of any form, other than caste. People could not develop the spirit of agrarianism, let alone economic development. Even, the setting up of a few heavy industries in a highly antiquated agrarian base failed to alter the basic structure of the state's economy in any significant way.

The gradual assertion of the backward castes in politics, who were kept excluded from electoral competition for a lengthy period, raised some hopes among the marginalised sections of the society. But faced with the stiff opposition from the traditional political elite, this soon got transformed into caste tensions, and in some cases even caste riots. This led to the erosion of social harmony, and produced a lumpenised political culture.[3] In simpler terms, it failed to satisfy the rising expectations of the marginalised social groups. Attempting to find the answers to the unrestricted influence of crime in politics, this chapter digs deeper into the economics of change in Bihar.

The Land Question

Bihar moved the Abolition of Zamindari Bill in the State Assembly in 1947, but it was challenged by the state's biggest landlord, Kameshwar Singh of Darbhanga in the Patna High Court.[4] While the decision was pending, the Bihar Government replaced it by the Bihar Land Reform Bill, 1949, which after receiving the Governor's assent became the Bihar Abolition of Zamindari Repealing (Land Reforms) Act, 1950.[5] Unfortunately the Patna High Court struck it down and so was the decision on the state government's appeal in the Supreme Court.[6] Consequently the provisional Parliament passed the Constitution (First Amendment) Act, 1951 to insert the Ninth Schedule into the Constitution and placed the Bihar Zamindari Abolition (Land Reforms) Act, 1950 in this schedule.[7]

The aim of the Act was to abolish the interests of the *zamindars* and *bataidars* (tenure-holders) legally, and put it under the direct control of the state. But with the state machinery in the hands of the same gentry class, the process of implementation could never gather momentum. On the contrary, the degree of resistance and the number of legal obstacles that were produced in its way sufficiently decided its future course of action. Land survey records were very old (30 to 40 years), field survey was progressing at a very slow pace and, most importantly, in spite of the government orders, *zamindars* refused to give the rent-rolls and related land records to the state (essential for determining the extent of land ownership of individuals). Ultimately the state was forced to create its own record (a process known as field *Bujharat*). However, it's a hard reality that even two decades after the passing of the legislation, the state government could not create its land record.[8]

To eliminate the loopholes, the Act was amended twice; first in 1954 and then in 1959. But on both occasions nothing substantial was altered to disturb the built-in safeguards of the *zamindars*.[9] The state also introduced the Bihar Agricultural Lands (Ceiling and Management) Bill in 1955, but, the opposition from within the ruling Congress forced the Bill to be shelved. Six years later it was passed as the Bihar Land Reforms (Fixation of Ceiling Area and Acquisition of Surplus Land) Act 1961, but only after making enough space for the landlords to maintain their status quo.[10] The Act provided numerous supplementary provisions that granted land holdings in much excess of the ceiling provisions.[11] By 1976, the Act could consolidate only 3 per cent of the total cultivated land. This Act was amended twice in 1973 and 1976.[12]

Along with the ceiling measures, the state government, simultaneously, passed the Tenancy Act, popularly known as the Bataidari Act in 1955. The Act, although aimed to empower the actual tillers of the soil, received similar fate.[13] Despite the long lists of safeguards to protect the tenancy rights, a number of studies show that no benefits have really reached to the *bataidars* or under-*raiyats*. Eviction in large numbers continued for long, and probably, continues even today. A very large percentage of productive land is still in the hands of feudal powers, and not the tillers. The spread of the semi-feudal productive system is little changed even today as 20 per cent of the cultivable land is still tilled by the sharecroppers.[14]

The Land Ceiling Act implemented in April 1962 had by the end of 1980s benefited only 2,92,470 landless families, though their number, according to the 1981 Census, was at 73.40 lakh in the state.[15] The situation improved only a little in 1990, when the state government conducting merely a legitimising ritual, acquired 3.85 lakh acres and distributed 2.62 lakh acres. Of the rest, 71,542 acres were disputed, 19,948 acres were unfit, 24,288 acres were debarred by courts and only 6,749 acres were pending distribution. In the days ahead, the situation remained virtually stagnant. According to the Commissioner of Land Reforms Task Force (1992), only 1 per cent of the land in the state was distributed. On the contrary, almost 23 per cent of the land assumed to be surplus was reversed to landlords on various grounds. According to agricultural census figures (which are generally pro-landlord) the land acquired by the government was just 21.7 per cent of the actual surplus disclosed by its own records.[16] The number of beneficiaries increased only marginally to 3,52,703 with a total land accumulation of 3,85,013 acres and distribution of 2,77,491 acres by 2001.[17]

During the Bhoodan Movement, although Bihar accounted for more than 50 per cent of the land, (a total of 21,17,756 acres), gifted throughout the country; majority of it could never be distributed. More important, even among the distributed land, only 25.71 per cent was actually allotted (see Table 3.1 below).

Table 3.1

Allotment of Bhoodan Land

States/Total Land Received (acres)	*% of Land Allotted*	*Beneficiaries*					
		Number			*Area*		
		SC	*ST*	*Others*	*SC*	*ST*	*Others*
AP/(1,95,509)	47.14	35.91	8.36	55.73	28.52	14.3	57.15
Bihar/(21,17,756)	25.71	27.83	22.91	49.26	29.28	29.6	41.12
Punjab/(9,801)	100.00	84.70	—	15.30	95.30	—	4.70
Maharashtra/(88,462)	0.69	56.83	18.06	21.11	57.17	15.8	27.04
Orissa/(13,46,966)	12.39	21.77	45.63	32.60	22.56	58.0	19.44

Source: Report of the Commissioner for Scheduled Castes and Scheduled Tribes, April 1980–March 1981.

The Bhoodan committees that were set up to ensure fair allotment gradually lost their momentum, and land meant for the landless never reached them.[18]

Landholding Pattern

Although the landholding pattern changed over the years, the land ownership largely remained extremely unequal. The Figures 3.1, 3.2 and 3.3 show the pattern of landholdings during 1970–71, 1976–77 and 1980–81.

Figure 3.1

Size, Number, and Area of Operational Land Holdings in Bihar: 1970–71

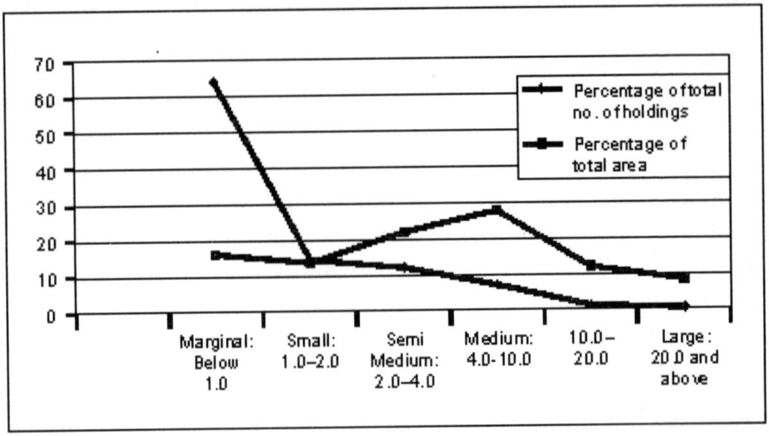

Source: Bihar Agricultural Census, 1981.

Figure 3.2

Size, Number, and Area of Operational Land Holdings in Bihar: 1976–77

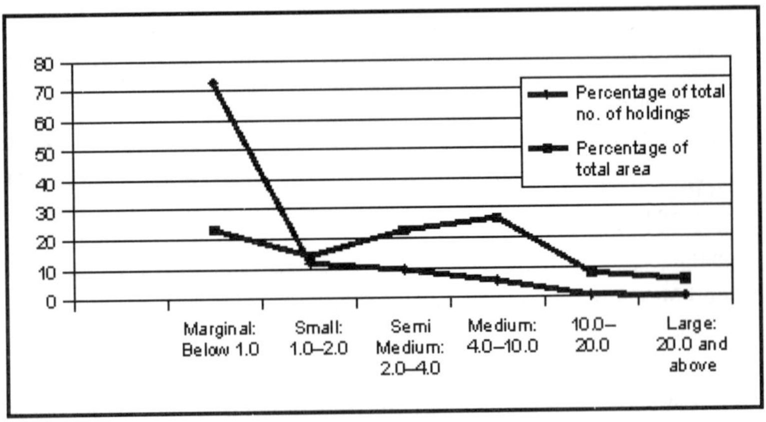

Source: Bihar Agricultural Census, 1981.

Figure 3.3

Size, Number, and Area of Operational Holdings in Bihar: 1980–81

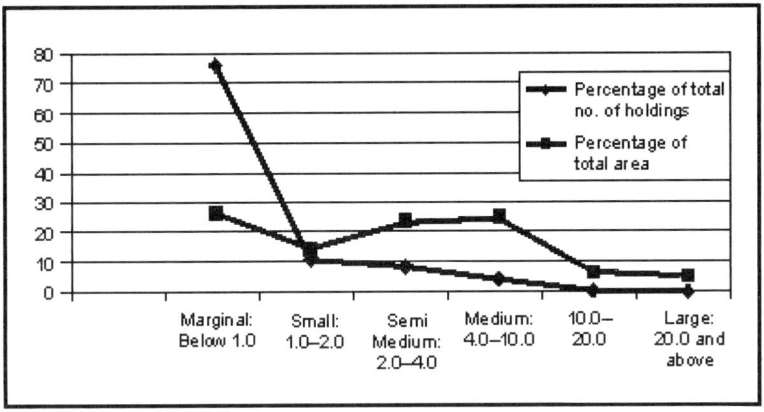

Source: Bihar Agricultural Census, 1981.

Table 3.2

Size, Number, and Area of Operational Land Holdings in Bihar: 1995–1996

Size class (Hectares)	*Total Holdings*			
	Number ('000)	*Percentage*	*Area ('000) (Hectares)*	*Percentage*
Below 0.5	8,422	59.51	1,752	16.40
0.5–1.0	2,922	20.64	2,119	19.84
Marginal	**11,344**	**80.15**	**3,871**	**36.25**
1.0–2.0	1,526	10.78	2,018	18.89
Small	**1,526**	**10.78**	**2,018**	**18.89**
2.0–3.0	640	4.52	1,534	14.36
3.0–4.0	301	2.13	1,031	9.66
Semi-Medium	**941**	**6.65**	**2,565**	**24.01**
4.0–5.0	170	1.2	750	7.01
5.0–7.5	99	0.7	597	5.99
7.5–10.0	45	0.32	402	3.75
Medium	**314**	**2.22**	**1,749**	**16.37**
10.0–20.0	24	0.17	336	3.15
20.0 and above	5	0.03	143	1.34
Large	**29**	**0.2**	**479**	**4.48**
Total	14,155	100	10,682	100

Source: Directorate of Statistics and Evaluation, Government of Bihar.

The extent of inequality remained nearly the same even in the mid-1990s, as shown in Table 3.2. The share of marginal operational holdings despite being as high as 80 per cent, accounted for only 36 per cent of the total land area. At the other end, the medium and large operational holdings of over 4 hectares comprising less than 2.5 per cent of all holdings, occupied over 20 per cent of the total operational land area.

A comparison shows that this inequality, over the decades, has continued to increase significantly (see Table 3.3 below).

Table 3.3

Number and Area of Operational Land Holdings (1970–71 to 1995–96)

Size class (Hectares)	*Number of Operational Holdings (Percentage)*				*Area of operational Holdings (percentage)*			
	1970–71	*76–77*	*80–81*	*95–96*	*1970–71*	*76–77*	*80–81*	*95–96*
Marginal	64.3	72.6	75.8	80.1	16.0	23.3	26.7	36.2
Small	14.6	12.0	10.9	10.7	13.6	14.4	14.9	18.8
Semi- medium	12.1	9.4	8.5	6.6	22.1	22.5	23.4	24.0
Medium	7.2	5.2	4.2	2.2	27.6	26.6	24.5	16.3
Large	1.8	0.8	0.6	0.2	20.7	13.2	10.5	4.4
Total	100	100	100	100	100	100	100	100

Source: Directorate of Statistics and Evaluation, and Bihar State Planning Board.

One positive note, however, is that the proportion of small and semi-medium holdings appears to have increased as far as the distribution of land is concerned. Their percentage has been steadily decreasing, while their share of the land area has been proportionately increasing. But, if semi-medium and medium landowners are taken together, 9 per cent of land owners still occupied 40 per cent of the total land area of Bihar 1995–96. In 1980–81, the percentage of medium landowners that controlled nearly 50 per cent of the total land area was 13 per cent. This shows that distribution of operational area has continued to remain more unequal in the case of medium holdings. In the case of large holdings, land concentration in some districts, particularly in Purnea, Katihar, East and West Champaran, remained very high. Official surveys in 1991–92 disclosed that in Purnea, 210 landlords had more than 200 acres each, (nine of them having over 1,000 acres each), in West Champaran, 11 landlords had over 500 acres each.[19] More importantly, the upper/dominant caste landowners continued to own a significant percentage of the agricultural land. Figures 3.4 and 3.5 illustrate land possession and land cultivation by different social categories.

Figure 3.4

Percentage of Land Possessed by Social Categories

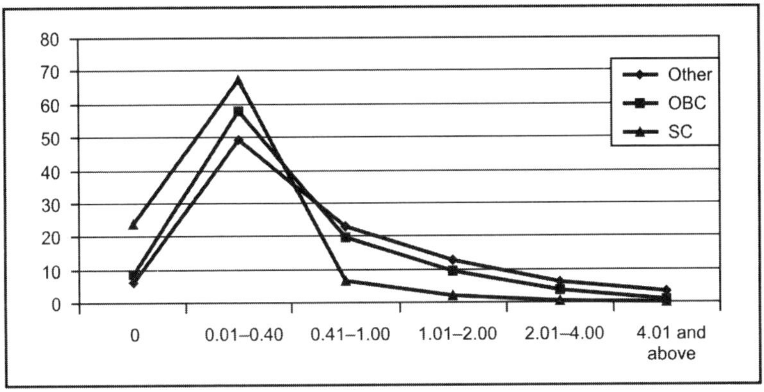

Source: Graph prepared from the data of the 55th round of NSS (1999–2000).

Figure 3.5

Percentage of Land Cultivated by Social Categories

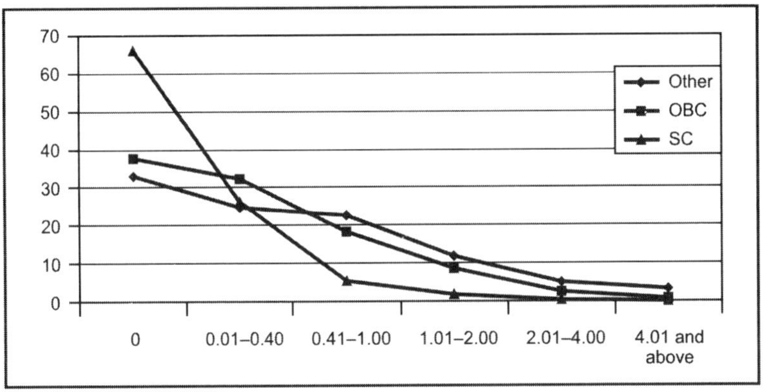

Source: Graph prepared from the data of the 55th round of NSS (1999–2000).

In both the figures, as regards the percentage of landless and the marginal landholders, the Scheduled Castes continue to be at the top, followed by the OBCs. There was a sharp decline in the case of the semi-medium holdings. Only 2.7 per cent of SC households possessed land somewhat larger than marginal holdings and an even lesser (2.2) percentage cultivated on those lands. Among the OBCs, the percentage of households possessing and cultivating semi-medium or higher landholdings was 0.7 per cent only. However, the upper castes continued with both the privilege of owning and cultivating semi-medium, medium and large holdings. The same was evident in the pattern of increase in land-leasing. While leased-in land constituted less than 5 per cent of the cultivated land in 1992, this increased to nearly 25 per cent by 1998. Figure 3.6 displays the pattern of leased-in land by social categories. It clearly shows that households with marginal and small operational holdings cultivated the largest percentage of leased-in land and the upper/dominant castes were the most that leased out land to them.

Figure 3.6

Leased-in Land by Social Categories

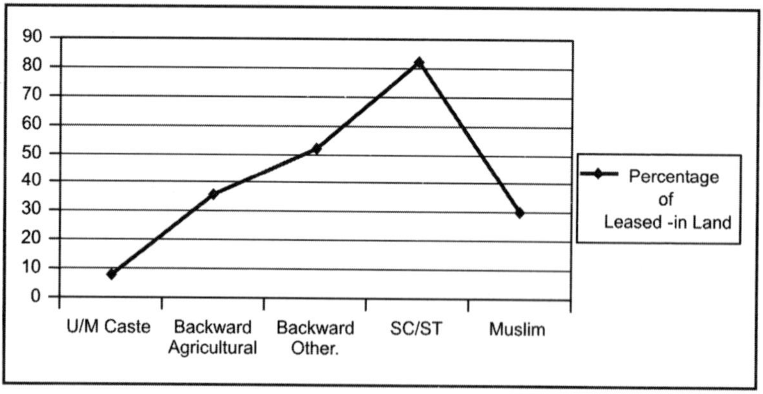

Source: Srivastava (2003) as cited in World Bank, (2005). *Bihar: Towards a Development Strategy,* Washington DC, p. 16. URL:siteresources.worldbank.org/.../Bihar_report_final_June2005.pdf, last accessed on 12 April 2009.

Absence of Agrarianism

Thus, the story of land reforms in Bihar presents a picture of total administrative and political apathy. There was a strong nexus of the landlords – the politico-administrative machinery and the judiciary, a characteristic found common in all the regimes. The *zamindari* system was highly institutionalised and the dominant groups were very strongly entrenched in the state machinery itself.

Explaining the situation an observer writes:

> Bihar's dismal performance in the field of land reforms has been largely due to the overbearing sway of large landlords over rural society and their dominant influence over the state's politics and administration. Moreover, the legal system is heavily tilted against

> the disadvantaged ... . Without a radical transformation of the objective conditions obtaining in Bihar there is *[sic]* no reason to expect any marked improvement in the implementation of land reforms.[20]

The fact that actions continued to be determined through the lens of caste restricted them from establishing a political constituency of development.[21] As a result, the basic resources such as land and rivers remained only a victim of neglect and the state failed to develop the spirit of agrarianism, let alone economic development. Despite the wide possibilities for irrigation, particularly in the northern and the eastern planes, they were not properly exploited. The negligence was so high that the river Kosi, instead of being a resource[22] has turned out to be a cause for national disaster.[23] With the annual rate of growth of agriculture between 1951 and 1987 stagnant at 1.8 per cent, Bihar became the only state to experience a decline in per capita income in the 1990s and remained trapped in a stage of backwardness.[24]

In all these years, however, what increased constantly was violence based on caste. Bihar witnessed several brutal caste massacres and it was dalits who were burnt alive, shot dead or even butchered by the private armies of the upper/dominant castes (see Appendix 3; details discussed later). With no respite from the state, the poor and the oppressed started organising themselves under the banner of Naxalism, which paid real attention to their demands and mobilised these hapless poor to struggle for their rights. However, the fact remains that throughout these decades; they still remained at the receiving end of the violence and could not gather enough strength to retaliate.

The Naxal Movement

With the support of the ruling Congress to the landlords, the landless and the poor found respite in the Naxal movement, that emerged in the neighbouring state of West Bengal. During its formative phase, the Naxal movement in Bihar remained sporadic in areas like Muzaffarpur, Bhojpur, Patna, Hazaribagh, Ranchi, Singhbhum, and Dhanbad. Although various members of the All-India Coordination Committee of Communist Revolutionaries (AICCCR) or its successor, the CPI-ML, as well as from Naxal groups outside the AICCCR fold (mainly the Maoist Communist Centre) took part in the protest; it remained ideologically disoriented, internally dissented, and far from taking a sustainable shape.[25] The movement never actually became as powerful as to challenge the state, but, the state in order to suppress the movement, started outsourcing even its raison detre function. It decided to provide arms to the upper caste landlords in order to facilitate them create their own militias. In a press note issued by the DIG (Naxals) as reported in a local newspaper on May 28, 1975:

> The Bihar government has decided to arm all able bodied persons in Bhojpur and Patna districts for self-defence to face the extreme menace, who have recently launched an armed struggle … . District magistrates of both these districts have been asked to visit the affected villages and issue licenses for firearms on the spot to those who are able to possess them … . The decision was taken following a spurt in the armed attacks on landowners by the extremists in these villages. The trouble was mostly of agrarian nature.[26]

It was during the same time that Jaya Prakash Narain had openly expressed;

> Since Independence … there has been no real change in the social, economic and political structure of our society. Zamindari is abolished, land reform laws have been passed, untouchability has been legally prohibited, and so on. But the village in most parts of India is still in the grip of the higher castes and the bigger and medium landowners. The small and marginal landowners are the landless, the backward classes and the Harijans … . Yet their position continues to be miserable. Harijans are still burnt alive.[27]
>
> It is not the so-called Naxalites who have fathered their violence but those who have persistently defied and defeated the laws for the past so many years – be they politicians, administrators, landlords, or moneylenders. When such happens to be the situation and when the institutions and process of democracy are found to be so woefully lacking, is there any wonder that discontent, frustration, anger, and what should turn the minds of some towards violence as the only possible saviour?[28]

However, this could not help landless Dalits and the poor in any way. The repression was so severe and tough that by the mid-1970s, the movement got weakened beyond recognition.[29] The upper caste militias, in connivance with the state created a record of atrocities on the Dalits (see Appendix 3). The real economic problems were ignored and the democratic institutions of the state were undermined by the politics and politicians of the day. According to an estimate, between 1985–1986, there was nearly a quarter of Bihar's available land that could not be cultivated due to agrarian conflicts,[30] and there were a number of cases in which the Dalits were killed by the men of the caste militias after *pattas* (legal right of land on paper) had been allotted to them.[31]

During the regime of Karpoori Thakur, a backward class leader who became chief minister in 1977, people hoped that things would change for better. But Thakur, surrounded by the same land-owning upper/dominant castes, could not do much on the issue of land reforms. In 1980, however, when the Congress came back to power in the state, all hopes of change faded away. Ironically, in 1982, despite its small presence, the government of Bihar in its 'Notes on Extremist Activities-affected Areas' reported that as many as 47 out of a total of 587 blocks, spread over 14 districts, were affected by the Communist extremist movements.[32] Subsequently, the Naxals were forced to start their open mass activities.[33]

Post-1990 Phase

With the change in the corridors of power in 1990s, hopes raised once again when Lalu Prasad became the chief minister. However, Lalu Prasad proved them completely wrong, as far as the issue of land was concerned. Throughout his tenure and later during his wife Rabri Devi's regime, the government took not even a single concrete step on the land reform front (details discussed in Chapter 4). During his initial days (1991) Bihar witnessed five caste massacres in which 54 Dalit agricultural labourers were killed by the upper/dominant caste landlord *senas* (for details see Appendix 3).[34] And the state, as usual, did nothing beyond being a mute spectator. A year later, however, when in a retaliatory move, the Dalits (some of whom were Maoist Communist Centre cadres) killed some 34 upper caste landlords, the state responded by invoking the Terrorist and Disruptive Activities (Prevention) Act (TADA), and gave a unique twist to Bihar's caste wars. The upper caste army has been harassing the lower castes in the state for decades, but in no case where the Dalits were killed was TADA invoked. The anti-terror law was brought into play only when those killed were from the upper castes.[35] This clearly showed that the attitude of Lalu government towards the agrarian and rural situation in Bihar was no different from that of earlier regimes. And thus, year after year, the massacre of Dalit agricultural labourers continued.

In addition, when the central government decided to build an anti-Naxalite central paramilitary force, Lalu Prasad played a leading role in getting it created. Analysing the deteriorating law and order situation in the state, a note prepared by the government said, "the crumbling of the feudal system and the emergence and assertiveness of the new economic and social forces have added a new dimension to the law and order situation resulting in socio-economic tension in the state".[36] Soon the state police started a large combing exercise in areas identified as Naxalite-affected and peasant movements were repressed. The lives of the poor, the Dalits and the tribals continued to be miserable, insecure and strife torn and the governance went on becoming more corrupt, criminalised and violent (details discussed in Chapter 4). In response to a question on land reforms in 1999, Lalu Prasad responded:

> The land is not the question .... There is no land in Bihar because the density of population is much higher as compared to the land. I've finished their (Naxalites) base. The day Lalu is gone; these Naxalites will surround the cities and butcher everybody. I say give the land to the tiller. The government is even ready to buy excess land from absentee landlords and distribute them among the landless.[37]

It is hard to believe that Lalu Prasad simply could not understand the political economy of the turmoil; but a closer examination of such ignorance probably says that the upper strata of the backward castes, (whom we call the upper backward castes or the dominant castes), to which Lalu Prasad himself belonged, had joined hands with the upper caste feudal lords as the ruling class in the state; and in the process employed equally oppressive tactics against the most under-privileged but numerically the largest class of poor peasants and agricultural labourers. That apart, an IAS officer who was appointed as the additional chief secretary of the state and was assigned to look into the issue of land reforms, rural development schemes and problems of agricultural labourers and other sections of unorganised labour, said:

> The Janata Dal rule was no different from its predecessors. One should not think that the Janata Dal was Lalu Yadav or vice-versa. It was still dominated by the same upper caste feudal lords. Despite Lalu Yadav's keen interest on the issue of land reforms, the party never allowed him to take any step.[38]

In other words, because the demands of the underprivileged, exploited and oppressed sections of society posed a threat to the interests of the alliance, on which the Lalu Prasad government was based, the demands could not find a place in the government's scheme of social justice. And hence it resolved, like its predecessors, to term them as Naxalism. The state government, as usual, not only allowed men responsible for massacring Dalit peasants and labourers to go scot-free but at times even provided them with necessary protection. From Janata Party to Janata Dal to Rashtriya Janata Dal, the state contrary to everybody's expectations continued to grow more and more illegitimate in all spheres.

Notes

1. See Gunnar Myrdal, (1968). *Asian Drama: An Inquiry into the Poverty of Nations,* New York. Vol. 2, p. 1097.
2. Anand Chakravarti, (2001), 'Caste and Agrarian Class: A View from Bihar', in Manoranjan Mohanty (ed.) *Class, Caste and Gender,* New Delhi, Sage Publication, p. 47. (47–88).
3. See A.N. Das, (1992). *Republic of Bihar,* New Delhi, Penguin Books.
4. See *Kameshwar Singh v. State of Bihar,* AIR 1951, Pat 91. The suit was instituted in the Court of the Subordinate Judge at Darbhanga. On 25–11–1949, it moved to the High Court.
5. The Bill received assent from the Governor General and became known as the Bihar Abolition of Zamindaris Act, 1948 (Bihar Act XVIII [18] of 1948). On 9–12–1949 a Bill entitled the Bihar Land Reforms Bill, 1949 was published, and was later introduced in the Bihar Legislative Assembly. Subsequently, an amendment to the Bill was added and a new Act entitled "Bihar Abolition of Zamindaris Repealing Act, 1950 (Bihar Act IX [9] of 1950) was passed by the Bihar legislature, that received the assent by the Governor of Bihar on 18–1–1950. See ibid. also see A.N. Das, (1992). op. cit. 35; also see Jose J. Nedumpara, (2004). *Political Economy and Class Contradictions: A Study,* New Delhi, Anmol Publications, p. 104.
6. The land laws of other states such as Uttar Pradesh and Madhya Pradesh was also challenged, but the High Courts of these two states had upheld them. See *Surya Pal v. U.P. Government.* AIR 1951, All 674; *Ram Dubey v. Government of the State of Madhya Pradesh,* AIR 1952, MB 57. The suit at Patna High Court was instituted with a demand to declare the Bihar Abolition of Zamindaris Act, 1948 as unconstitutional on the ground of mere technicality and the court succumbed before the landlord's tactics. Ibid.
7. Article 31 (A) and Article 31 (B) were added to nullify the effect of Article 14. Art 31 (A) created a Ninth Schedule for 'estate' laws, and Art 31 (B) declared that any law placed in the Ninth Schedule would be immune from any challenges based on violation of Fundamental Rights. See Raju Ramachandran, (2006). 'The Supreme Court and the basic Structure Doctrine', in B.N. Kripal, et al. (eds.) *Supreme but not Infallible: Essays in Honour of the Supreme Court of India,* New Delhi, Oxford University Press, pp. 107–133.
8. See F.T. Jannuzi, (1974). *Agrarian Crisis in India: The Case of Bihar,* Austin, Texas University Press, p. 25.
9. *Report from the Flaming Fields of Bihar,* CPI (ML) Document, Kolkata, (1986), no 23, p 30; also see Jannuzi, (1974). op. cit. 32; D. Thorner, (1980). *The Shaping of Modern India.* New Delhi, Allied Publishers, p. 30–35; G. Ojha, (1977) *Land Problems and Land Reforms,* New Delhi,

Sultan Chand, p. 142. The changes that these amendments made were as following: while the original Act had provisions of individual notification for 'proprietors' or 'tenure-holders' that their estates have been vested in the state, the 1954 amendment provided the option for a general notification of all the intermediaries. In other words, the state was now given a power to proclaim within a specified period, all intermediary interests located in any region of the state, or even all such interests in the state as a whole. This was in no way a substantial change, as the *zamindars* continued to challenge the notifications in the court and keep the possession in their hands for a time. In fact, in the amendments in Sections 5, 6 and 7, it included in the '*khas* possession', lands cultivated not only by them in person, but also by their employed servants, hired labour or stock. This allowed the landlords to claim all the land under their control, until the state of the intermediaries produced some contradictory proofs. However, this possibility was very rare and the privileges of the landlords to hold all their land were left intact.

10. See G. Ojha, (1977). op. cit. p. 116. For the purpose of ceiling, the Act classified the land into five categories. Class I (the Finest) land were those irrigated by flow irrigation works; Class II lands were those irrigated by 'lift' irrigation works or tube wells; Class III lands were those used for orchards or horticultural purpose; Class IV lands were *diara* (near the river) lands and Class V were those considered as hilly, sandy, or incapable of production of any kind of crops. The Act provided for an individual possession of 20 acres of Class I, 30 acres of Class II, 40 acres of Class III, 50 acres of Class IV and 60 acres of Class V.
11. *Bihar Land Reforms (Fixation of Ceiling Area and Acquisition of Surplus Land) Act,* 1961, Clause 5, Provision to sub-clause 3, as cited in Jose J. Nedumpara, 2004. op. cit. p. 106. For example, 'a landowner could retain in addition to his ceiling area: (a) land forming part of his homestead not exceeding 10 acres in area. (b) He could transfer within one year following the commencement of the Act, any land held by him as a *raiyat* to any person or persons who might have inherited the land or have been entitled to a share it at his death. (c) He could also retain any land in consolidated blocks not exceeding 15 acres in area used for growing fodder. Exemptions were also granted to the landowners for several categories of lands including a) land previously donated to the Bhoodan movement, (b) land held by educational institutions and public religious institutions, (c) plantations and (d) lac-wood farms, sugarcane farms, etc.'.
12. Kalpana Wilson, (1999). 'Patterns of Accumulation and Struggles of Rural Labour: Some Aspects of Agrarian Change in Central Bihar', *Journal of Peasant Studies*, 26 (2–3), pp. 316–54. The power to take

cognizance was transferred from the judiciary to the executive from April 1, 1973. Amending Act of 1973 also created a sixth category providing 45 acres as ceiling and also provided that specified landlords cannot hold orchards and homestead in excess of the ceiling. The amendment in 1976 provided for "voluntary surrender" which resulted in landlords surrendering the land not in their actual possession, thereby bringing a big gap between 'acquired' and distributed land. Another amendment in the same year increased the executive's power of intervention and created an appellate jurisdiction of Board of Revenue. The amendment of 1976 took away the right of parties other than landowners (i.e., landless and poor peasants) to file objections thereby debarring their involvement in these disputes. Also see, Jose J. Nedumpara, (2004). op. cit. p. 106.

13. Ibid. The usual practice was that a landlord can at any time and due to any or no reason, eject an under-*raiyat* (*bataidar*) from his land. The ejected *bataidars* could take the course of the civil suit but they were not economically sound to meet the expenses of the litigation. Therefore, they had no option but to depend on the whims of the land owning groups. The Tenancy Act not only attempted to provide them a legal support, but also fixed the maximum amount of rent (nearly one third of the produce) to be drawn from the land. The Act was further amended in 1970.
14. A study done by the Institute of Social Studies, Patna and the International Labour Organisation (1983). Accessed at URL: http://www.cscsarchive.org/MediaArchive/liberty.nsf/(docid)/65 DD3DD4 5C07BB77E5256AD30013065E
15. A report of the revenue and land reforms department in the late 1980s. Patna, UNI, August 7, 1990.
16. http://www.cpimlnd.org/on-new-democratic-revolution-and-land-problem/peoples-democratic-revolution-in-india-and-land-problem.html, last accessed at October 25, 2008.
17. T.K. Rajlakshmi, (2001). Land Rights and Wrongs in Bihar, *Frontline*, Volume 18 - Issue 22, October 27–November. 09.
18. Today the committees are defunct and are unable to settle disputes or coordinate with the state government. See T.K. Rajlakshmi, (2001). op. cit.
19. CPI (M-L) Approach Paper – New Democracy, (2007). People's democratic Revolution in India and Land Problem. URL: http://www.cpimlnd.org/on-new-democratic-revolution-and-land-problem/peoples-democratic-revolution-in-india-and-land-proble m.html

20. As quoted in Anand Chakravarty, (1986). 'The Unfinished Struggle of Santhal *Bataidars* in Purnea District', *Economic and Political Weekly,* XXI, 42. October 18, p. 1857.
21. See P.S. Appu, (1993). 'A Modest Programme for the Nineties' in B.N. Yugandhar and Gopal Iyer (eds.), *Land Reforms in India*, Vol. I, Sage Publications, New Delhi, pp. 50–55. P.S. Appu served as an IAS officer in the state since the early days after independence and later became the chairman of the committee on land reforms (and also state chief secretary).
22. Though a detailed study of this negligence is not available, Wolf Ladejinsky in a comparative study of Bihar and Punjab in 1969, the period of Green Revolution, explained how Punjabi farmers were doubling and tripling their yields with the new miracle seeds but Bihar remained stagnant. Wolf Ladejinsky, (1969). 'The Green Revolution in Bihar: The Kosi Area: A Field Trip', *Economic and Political Weekly* Vol. 4 (39), 27 September; and 'The Green Revolution in Punjab: A Field Trip', *Economic and Political Weekly,* Vol. 4 (26), 28 June.
23. See Dinesh Kumar Mishra, (2008). 'Bihar Flood: The Inevitable has Happened', *Economic and Political Weekly,* Sep. 6, pp. 8–12. Mishra observes that though the extent of the flood, certainly was the largest in 2008, its character had remained same over the years. Writing a note on the situation Mishra argues, "... this is the eighth incident of its kind ... the first breach in the embankment had occurred in 1963 near Dalwa in Nepal, much before the Kosi project was completed. Binodanand Jha of the Congress was the chief minister then and the responsibility of the breach was at that time placed on the rats and foxes that had dug holes in the body of the embankments through which water had seeped in! The second incident took place in 1968 near Jamalpur in Darbhanga when five breaches occurred in October. Engineer P.N. Kumra of CWC had conducted an inquiry and had once again identified the rats and foxes as the culprits. The state was then under the Presidential rule. The third incident occurred at Bhatania in 1971 when the approach bundh collapsed between the 10th and 19th km below Bhimnagar, and many villages were washed away but the eastern embankment did not breach. Since only eight villages were affected, the incident did not get wide publicity. The next incident occurred in 1980 near Bahuarawa in Salkhua block of Saharsa district near the 121 km mark below Bhimnagar. The river eroded the embankment but just after the breach, it receded very quickly and the water did not spill on to the countryside. The state was at the time ruled by Jagannath Mishra of the Congress. In 1984, a tragedy as terrible as Jamalpur struck the eastern embankment near Hempur village in the Navhatta block of Saharsa district, 75 km

below the Bhimnagar barrage. The floods uprooted half a million people and engulfed 96 villages in Saharsa and Supaul districts. People could go back to their villages only after Holi in 1985 when the breach was plugged. Bindeshwari Dubey of the Congress was the chief minister then. In 1991, there was a breach in the western embankment near Joginia in Nepal that led to a political crisis in Bihar and the minister of water resources had to resign. But his resignation was never accepted by Lalu Yadav who was the chief minister at the time. This was a repeat of the Bahuarawa breach where the river had receded after eroding the embankment. The Kusaha breach took place during the regime of Nitish Kumar ... . Thus, virtually no ruling party including the administration under President's rule can claim that it was not involved in such an accident."

24. See Pradhan H. Prasad, (n.d.) 'Neglect of Land Resources: Misfortune of Bihar', available in the archives of Loksahi Hakk Sangathan, URL: http://www.cscsarchive.org:8081/MediaArchive/liberty.nsf/(docid)/65DD3DD45C07BB77E5256AD30013065E. Also see, Gaurav Datt and Martin Ravallion, 1998. "Why Have Some Indian States Done Better Than Others in Reducing Rural Poverty?" *Economica*, London School of Economics and Political Science, vol. 65(257), February, pp. 17–38; and S.D. Naik (2001) "Census 2001: Disturbing Inter-State Disparities," *Business Line Internet Edition*, April 3, at www.blonnet.com/businessline/2001/04/03/stories/01032001.htm
25. Bela Bhatia, (2005a). 'Naxalite Movement in Central Bihar', *Economic and Political Weekly,* April 9, pp. 1536–1549.
26. Reported in *Indian Nation,* as cited in Mukherjee and Yadav, 'For Reasons of State: Oppression and Resistance, a Study of Bhojpur Peasantry', in A.N. Das (ed.) (1992). op. cit. pp. 119–147.
27. Ajit Bhattacharya, (1975). (Selected and Introduced), "Notes on Bihar Movement", Transforming the Polity – Centenary Readings from Jayaprakash Narayan, New Delhi, Rupa. Accessed online URL: http://www.mkgandhi-sarvodaya.org/jpnarayan/total_revo.htm.
28. K.C. Vadlamannati, (2008). 'Socioeconomic, Institutional and Political Determinants of Human Rights Abuses: A Substantial Study of India 1993–2002', *William Davidson Institute Working paper No 926,* July. URL: papers.ssrn.com/sol3/Delivery.../SSRN_ID1253482_code599.pdf.
29. But this does not mean that the movement had collapsed. In the words of Das, "indeed, the grim agrarian situation and overall deterioration of the political scenario in the state created a new and more vital left ... . The largest surviving faction was known as the CPI-ML-*Liberation* group, so called on account of its party organ, Liberation. Over a period of time, this group reorganised and has today grown into a formidable force. Another faction which had a small presence

in the area in the 1970s but which has grown subsequently goes by the name of the Central Organising Committee of the CPI-ML- *Party Unity*. These two have minor ideological differences with each other but retain their separate identities. They also have separate mass organisation .... Many of these organisations combined in the 1980s into a large umberella organisation known as the Indian Peoples' Front (IPF)". For a seminal analysis, see A.N. Das, (1992). op. cit. pp. 111–3.

30. Pradhan H. Prasad, (1987), 'Agrarian Violence in Bihar', *Economic and Political Weekly,* May 30, 22 (22), pp. 847–52.
31. For details see B.B. Mohanty, (2001). 'Land Distribution among Scheduled Castes and Scheduled Tribes', *Economic and Political Weekly,* October 6, pp. 3857–68.
32. The note showed that 10.28 per cent of the village, 8.23 of the population, 7.24 of the area, 9.46 of the net sown area and 11.98 of the gross sown area had been affected by Communist extremist movement by May 1982.
33. A.N. Das, (1992). op. cit. pp. 111–3.
34. Prakash Louis, (2002). *People Power: The Naxalite Movement in Central Bihar,* New Delhi: Word-Smiths, pp 242–46.
35. K. George Varghese, (2004). 'Massacres in Bihar Never Invited TADA Until Bara: Killers in This Case Were Dalits', *Indian Express*, 2 December. URL: http://www.indianexpress.com/oldStory/60023/.
36. Krishna Chaitanya, (1991). 'Social Justice, Bihar Style', Economic and Political Weekly, 16, November, p 2612.
37. Rajesh Joshi in interview with Lalu Prasad. "If Laloo Goes, Naxal will Surround the cities", *Outlook,* 22 March, 1999.
38. Avinash Kumar, (2009). 'Illegitimacy of the State in Bihar', *Economic and Political Weekly,* Vol. XLIV, No. 44, October 31– November 6, pp. 8–11.

4

The Politics of Change

Ambedkar on the floor of the Constituent Assembly on November 25, 1949 had expressed that although independent India granted equality to its citizens politically, inequality in social and economic life remained as wide as ever before. 'We must remove this contradiction at the earliest moment, or else those who suffer from inequality will blow up the structure of political democracy'.[1] Six decades have passed, but equality beyond "one-man-one-vote" continues to remain a distant dream even today. In the last chapter we discussed how socioeconomic inequalities in Bihar has continued to exist without any substantial change, and the state therefore, has witnessed many political fires and mutinies. The current chapter attempts to show how even in the name of political democracy, the state has witnessed nothing more than a massive charade in which a large number of voters, particularly the landless poor from the Scheduled Castes/Tribes and women, were left disenfranchised for decades. The condition in Bihar today indicates that things have gone terribly wrong in this politics of change. Along with experiencing criminalisation of politics for a long period, the state in the last few decades has reached a point where people have been left to face the tyranny of democracy.

Politics of Caste and Criminalisation: 1947–1966

Politics of caste and criminalisation, as suggested in Chapter 2, is not a recent invention. Politics in Bihar, particularly, has a longstanding reputation of being violent dut to caste restrictions. Caste and land has set the condition of Bihar's politics since the very beginning, and so is the history of criminalisation of politics in the state. Presenting the anecdote, Das writes;

> *K.B. Sahay (the anti-zamindari revenue minister) was run over by a truck, allegedly hired by the Raja of Ramgarh,* who was ideologically opposed to *zamindari* abolition … . The finance minister, A.N. Sinha, himself a *zamindar,* was reluctant to do so and even the premier (chief minister) Sri Krishna Sinha who represented both petty *zamindari* and Bhumihar *junker-kulak* interests, was not very enthusiastic in spite of having been one of the founders of the Kisan Sabha. The assembly met in Ranchi which was Bihar's summer capital in those days … *Even as ministers rose to deputise for their injured colleague, K.B. Sahay, swathed in blood-stained bandages, made a dramatic entry.*
>
> *The immense wealth and guns and muscle power at the command of such landlords made them invaluable allies of the politicians.* Thus, while the Bihar Assembly was debating the Land Reforms Bill after independence, its finance minister A.N. Sinha … was attending a banquet given by his caste brother, the Raja of Kursela, one of the largest of the *nouveaux-rentiers.*[2] *(Emphasis added)*

The state remained under the premiership of Krishna Singh until his death in 1961 and nothing much could change in politics during his regime. But, as soon as Mr Singh died, the other upper caste leaders of the Congress instead of addressing the problems of the state preferred to engage in a 'race for successorship' and ultimately into a 'process of parochialisation of politics and sectionalisation of political leadership'.[3] Within two years, one faction (under the leadership of K.B. Sahay, a Kayastha) forced the ouster of the second chief minister Binodanand Jha (a Brahmin). But when K.B. Sahay, who was known as an espouser of the farmers and the landless (during *Zamindari* abolition), became the chief minister, he ended up being only a political manipulator. Sahay went on to become Bihar's first chief minister indicted by a commission of inquiry for corruption.[4] In 1967, the Justice T.L. Venkataraman Aiyar Commission (set up by Mahamaya Prasad Sinha, a Bhumihar chief minister, who was heading the first non-Congress government) indicted K.B. Sahay and over half-a-dozen ministers of his government for financial irregularities.[5] Thus, when there was lot to be done to establish a healthy political culture in the state, the leadership remained busy experimenting a rapid change of caste coalitions, primarily among the four upper castes.

The Period of Political Confusion: 1967–1980

The 1970s, saw the rise of a competitive politics, when the backward castes started realising the effect of this profound and systematic violation of the basic principles of electoral democracy by traditional political elites.[6] Soon the forward castes lost control over backward-caste votes and the course of politics in the state changed very rapidly. Unfortunately, this change could not make the situation any better. It rather, aggravated the existing political confusion.[7] Between 1967 and 1972, the government changed nine times (see Table 4.1).

Table 4.1

Coalition Governments in Bihar (1967–72)

S.No.	Chief Minister	Parties in coalition	From	Number of days
1.	Mahamaya P. Sinha	SSP, PSP, JS, CPI, JKD	5.3.67	327
2.	Satish Prasad Singh	Minority ministry backed by Congress	28.1.68	4
3.	B.P. Mandal	Soshit Dal backed by Congress	1.2.68	47
4.	Bhola Paswan Shastri	LTC, CPI, Janata, JS	23.2.68	96
	President Rule		29.5.68	247
	Mid-Term Polls 1969			
5.	Harihar Singh	Congress, Janata, Soshit Dal	26.2.69	115
6.	Bhola Paswan Shastri	LCD, Soshit, BKD, Jharkhand, backed by SSP, JS, CPI	21.6.69	11
	President Rule		2.7.69	229
7.	Daroga Rai	Cong (R), Jharkhand, Soshit Dal backed by CPI, PSP	16.2.70	306
8.	Karpoori Thakur	SSP, Cong (O), JS, SWT, Janata, BKD, Soshit Dal, a section of PSP	22.12.70	163
9.	Bhola Paswan Shastri	Congress (R), CPI, PSP, Soshit, Jharkhand (Horo)	2.6.69	209
	President Rule		28.12.71	81
10.	Kedar Pandey	Cong (R)	19.3.72	470

Among the ten chief ministers between 1967 and 1972, only one could hold the chair beyond one year. In the meantime, the political scene in New Delhi had started being deinstitutionalised during Mrs Gandhi's 'nothing above politics' regime (discussed in Chapter 2). The involvement of Sanjay Gandhi had a great impact on the polics of states throughout the country, particularly in Bihar. Sanjay appointed his man, Jagannath Mishra, as the state chief minister in 1975 and the politics in the state adopted a new top-down characteristic. According to Kohli:

> Mishra's period … turned out to be "a dark period in the state administration [when] corruption, favouritism and nepotism reached [their] zenith". Prior to the Emergency rampant factionalism, governmental instability, politically motivated rioting, and escalating criminalization of politics were the major characteristics of political decay. The trend toward criminalization intensified under Mishra. Moreover, two new developments contributed to the government's growing ineffectiveness: the continuing decline of the police and civil bureaucracies as professional institutions, and the arming of private groups to cope with the agrarian violence.[8]

Throughout the Emergency period, it manifested a reign of terror by constantly providing licenced arms to the private armies of the landlords. Legions of examples can be presented to unveil the attitude of the Mishra regime towards the landowners.

> Dinesh Singh, the Raja of Kursela state and leader of the Congress legislature party in the state's upper house, was expelled from the party for obstructing land reforms, but within months he was unconditionally welcomed back into the party, of course with his vast land-holding entirely intact. Madhuri Singh, the daughter of Maul Babu of Purnea, who is said to have as much landed property as the Darbhanga raj, was given a Congress ticket with the Mishra regime taking the help of Maul Babu and vice versa. Most Congress politicians from the days of L.N. Mishra have been courtiers of the Darbhanga raj. According to Rajmangal Pandey, MLA, who left Congress to join CFD with Jagjivan Ram, the chief minister had given protection to the members of his family who own more than 1,000 acres of land.[9]

Abandoning even its minimum task of maintaining a monopoly over the use of coercion necessary for the protection of the citizens, the state openly displayed its virtual breakdown at all levels. The growing tendency to bypass institutions, particularly by those in power, finally culminated in a 'feeling that there is no point in complaining to those in authority', for it can only bring in more trouble.[10] However, the leadership, both in Delhi and Patna, had no idea that this increasing distance from the masses would culminate into people's urge for counter-violence. It continued with its usual style of politics. According to Navin Chandra Mishra, the superintendent of police (SP) in Purnea, a district in the north-eastern part of the state, during the 1977 State Assembly and Parliamentary elections:

> The chief minister, the agriculture minister and a deputy inspector-general of police sought to pressurise him to release about 100 goondas, including some requisitioned by a former union minister

from different parts of Bengal, whom he had detained a few days earlier.[11]

The SP specifically stated that, 'Goondas were brought to Purnea to capture polling booths on behalf of the Congress candidate'. When he refused to oblige the CM, he was transferred immediately. But he got an interim injunction from the court which then also issued 'a show cause notice to the chief minister, the agriculture minister and the DIG (Kosi range)'.[12] However, this could not protect the Congress and it was thrown out of power, both at the centre as well as in Bihar. Karpoori Thakur (a backward caste leader of the Janata Party) became the chief minister (see Appendix 2).

Thakur, by this time (his second term) had realised that land reforms in Bihar was not an easy task and therefore he successfully ignored it.[13] However, attempting to build his political constituency, Thakur invented two new agendas – to reserve seats (establishing quotas) in government jobs and in educational institutions for members of the backward castes and to remove English as a compulsory subject at the higher secondary level.[14] The policy of reservation was promulgated in 1978 by declaring 26 per cent reservation for the Other Backward Classes (OBCs).[15] Both these actions of Thakur, as expected, attracted strong reaction from the forward castes. They viewed this institutional change as a conspiracy to diminish their access to power and they took to streets, pushing political riots in Bihar to a new peak. Soon Thakur fell to a vote of no-confidence in the Assembly in 1979 against an alliance formed between the forward castes and the Scheduled Castes in the Assembly. This new alliance placed Ram Sunder Das, a Scheduled Caste leader of the Janata Party, as the chief minister and re-established the dominance of the forward castes both in the ministry as well as in the Assembly (sees Table 4.2 below).

Although Ram Sunder Das promised to implement the reservation policy as promulgated by Thakur, he actually became a puppet in the hands of the upper castes, who once again had captured all important positions in his government (see Table 4.2). They amended Thakur's reservation policy in such a way that recruitment of SCs/STs, OBCs and MBCs, including those on merit would never go beyond the prescribed quotas.[16] Das neither could act full-heartedly for strengthening the voice of the Scheduled Castes nor could continue with the policy initiated by Thakur for the backward castes.[17] His ministry fell a year later in 1980 only to bring the Congress back in the state once again. However, the 1970s was a decade of great change in Bihar and the underlying trends in the state in the following decades show that it successfully started a tilt in favour of the backward castes.

It brought in a noticeable decline in the forward castes' representation from the non-reserved seats from 54.8 to 48.6%.

Thus, what does the politics of change in the 1970s actually show? According to Blair, the decline in the strength of the forwards and increase in the strength of the backwards was actually the loss and victory of just one caste group, i.e., the Brahmins and the Yadavs respectively.[18]

> That entire decline was borne by the Brahmins, whose strength dropped from 18.3 per cent of the general seats in 1975 to only 7.6 per cent in 1977, or in numerical terms from 36 to 19 MLAs. The other three castes among the forwards even gained a bit; in fact, their collective share (for the Bhumihars plus the Rajputs plus the Kayasthas) went up from 36.5 to 40–9 per cent .... For the other upper backwards, their representation has been essentially stationary over the period (the Banias and the Koiris) or even declining, as with the Kurmis, who thrived under the Congress patronage back in the days of Binodanand Jha's chief ministership in the early 1960s, but who have faced leaner times since then. The category of other backward castes like the Shudras has consisted of a different mix each time, with never more than two entering the fray from these caste groups. ... primarily

Table 4.2

Caste Composition (in %age) of the Ministries in Bihar 1962–1979

Year	*CM*[19]	*Upper Castes*	*Upper Backward castes*	*Lower Backward Castes*	*Muslim/ Bengalis*	*SCs/ STs*	*Others*
1962	B.N. Jha	58	8	0	8	25	0
1963	K.B. Sahay	40	20	0	20	20	0
1967	M.P. Sinha	67	20	7	7	1	0
1968	B.P. Mandal	19	33	9	13	28	0
1968	B.P. Shastri	52	16	—	8	16	8
1968	H. Singh	45	26	—	9	24	—
1969	D.P. Rai	33	20	0	13	33	0
1970	K. Thakur	42	26	6	8	16	2
1971	B.P. Shastri	44	20	0	3	30	3
1972	K. Pandey	38	23	0	15	23	0
1973	A. Gafoor	38	23	5	10	24	0
1975	J. Mishra	40	20	0	13	27	0
1977	K. Thakur	**29**	**38**	**4**	**13**	**17**	**0**
1979	R.S. Das	**50**	**20**	**0**	**15**	**15**	**0**

Source: Harry W Blair (1980: 69); also see Jose J. Nedumpara, (2004). op. cit. p. 66.

the Annexure I Backwards, such as the Dhanuks, the Hajjams, the Kahars, the Kewats, the Mallahs and the Noniyas. Among the backwards, the upper backwards have been consistently over-represented. Even back in 1962, the four upper backward castes had 28.8 per cent of the general seats, as against only 24.3 per cent for the non-Scheduled population. By 1977, their percentage had grown to 34.9. The lower backward castes, on the other hand, were 40 per cent of non-Scheduled population, but never had more than 3.6 per cent of the general seats. The backwards' participation in state politics, then, has been a very uneven business, confined for all practical purposes to the upper backward community.[20]

At the administrative level too, the Janata government did not bring any significant change. It witnessed the brutal massacre of dalit landless labourers in Belchi on May 27, 1977, by the rising backward castes (the perpetrators were kurmi landlords led by Inderdeo Chaudhary and Mahavir Mahto). With no check on their rising criminality, the landlords soon transformed their musclemen into a private militia, popularly known as Bhoomi Sena. The other massacre a year later in Kaila (Jehanabad, 1978) only further exposes the failure of the state under the Janata regime. In addition to that, elections to the 11,740 gram panchayats held in 1978 state resulted in the further consolidation of the feudal elements, strengthening them against the rapidly advancing mobilisation of the rural proletariat.[21] The month-long elections turned out to be the bloodiest in Bihar. In fact, barring the 1971 parliamentary elections in West Bengal, it proved to be the bloodiest in the country. According to some observations, more than 700 people were reported killed during the elections.[22] According to a report published in *Economic and Political Weekly*;

> Well before the polling began the landlords used all kinds of influence to get votes in their favour. They found out who were to officiate as presiding and polling officers in their constituencies and so manipulated that only their favourites would come. *They manoeuvred to get the nomination papers of stronger rivals rejected; they kidnapped their opponents; they bought votes. In all these manoeuvrings they were helped by their relatives in the government posts* ... the most clever device of landlords was to have the polling booths at their doorsteps where none else but their supporters could gather and vote. The booths required brick buildings in the village; and these were invariably either the property of the landlords or local schools. *Nowhere were booths set up in the Harijan ghettoes* ... the landlords of village Bathnaha in Saharsa block got the polling booth shifted to their village from the Harijan *busti* of Agma. *Here the*

> *Mukhiya candidate was a big landlord who had recently used these guns on the share-croppers. Where the Harijans protested, they were attacked.* Ten days before the poll, in Siarna panchayat in Jagdishpur block of Bhojpur district, two Harijans were wounded and their houses burnt by the gang of a Mukhiya candidate ... *the Mukhiya of Akodhi-Ladai panchayat of Rohtas district is none else but Jamuni Rai, the main accused in the Bishrampur carnage in which four landless and poor peasants were massacred and their houses burnt last March. Rai filed his nominations from jail; came out on bail a couple of days before the poll and won by a large majority.* The violence was one-sided. In many cases, one section of the ruling class fought with the other but largely the violence was directed at the landless peasants and lower classes of peasantry. *This was sought to be given the description of 'inter-group clash', while the fact was that in several cases the poor were shot dead from close range or just lynched.* The role of the police was either indifferent or collaborationist. When the police were indifferent, they shut their eyes to booth-capturing and bogus voting; in this lay the secret of 'peaceful polling'. But there were also some 100 police firings reported in the month of polling. These firings, which killed more than two dozen people, were mostly ordered when some candidate violently opposed bogus voting by his rival. *The police nowhere fired on the landlords who were scaring the poor people away from the polling booths. The involvement of ... representatives in the violence in panchayat elections was in many cases direct.* A Janata party MP, according to a police case, was alleged to have shot dead an opponent in a panchayat in Gaya district. The gun of another Janata Party MP was found in the possession of a mercenary in Nalanda district.[23] (*Emphasis added*)

The much hyped talk to decentralise power proved only to be an eyewash. Nevertheless, the Janata Party failed to achieve what it had hoped for, as the majority of the elected Mukhiyas were either from the Congress or their supporters.

> Topping it all ... *more than 90 per cent of the Mukhiyas were reportedly wealthy people with big or substantial interests in land, contracts or trade and more than 40 per cent of them and sarpanchs had a criminal background.* Whatever little developmental funds trickled down to panchayats were cornered by those vested interests. Panchayats [had] failed to meet expectations and the panchayati system virtually died out. (emphasis added)[24]

The Politics of Intrigue: 1980–1990

With a strong lumpenised base at the grassroot, Congress did not had to work very hard to return to power in 1980. Thereafter, throughout the decade, even the re-election of the backward castes could not re-build the political capital that could promote their interests in the state. Social conflicts in villages continued to smoulder, more often resulting in flaming houses and lives of the poor, landless and Dalits (for details see Appendix 3). With Jagannath Mishra at the top of Congress leadership in the state, the governmental ineffectiveness touched an all-time high. Neither Mishra in his initial three years (June 1980–August 1983) nor his successor Chandra Shekhar Singh (August 1983–March 1985) made any effort to curb the political violence. On the contrary, a parade of horrors marched through a long darkness to create a parasitic nexus of politicians, criminals and contractors who brutally silenced whatsoever little protest was shown by the society. According to some observers;

> Crime was rampant ... Every twelfth person in the state owned an unlicensed firearm. Hundreds of clandestine gun factories had sprung up in the rural districts around Patna, Nalanda, Gaya, Jehanabad, Begusarai, Bhojpur ... Politicians used hired criminals ... Just before the 1980 elections, Kamdeo Singh, a wanted upper caste gandster-smuggler from Begusarai in central Bihar, was killed in an encounter. Politicians formed queues to pay homage to him. Jagannath Mishra led a delegation of Congressmen to his village to console his family and apologise for the encounter and seek their support in ensuing polls .... In November 1980, soon after Jagannath Mishra took over reins of the state, the Bihar Assembly was stunned when some opposition members entered the house with a stretcher carrying an injured MLA from the chief minister's own party. Ramdeo Singh had been shot at near Patna allegedly at the instance of Jagannath Mishra's minister of state for finance, Prabhunath Singh. Mishra's way of punishing him was to change his portfolio ... . Corruption had been institutionalised ... Transfers in government jobs cost ₹ 20,000; postings ₹ 25, 000 and promotions ₹ 50,000. Every contract had a cut; every job needed to be done carried a price tag.[25]

> Both the Lok Sabha elections in 1984 and the Legislative Assembly elections in early 1985 were considerably more violent than those in 1977. For example, violent incidents (including assaults, bomb explosions, booth capturing, civilian shootings, and police shootings) increased from some 260 in 1977 to 617 in 1984. Moreover, nearly 100 people were killed in the 1985 election, compared with 34 in 1977, including four candidates running for office.[26]

> The setting up of the *Matdata Suraksha Samitis* (voters' protection committees) by the Indian People's Front (mass organisations of the

> Naxals that participated in the election for the first time) was primarily to counter the process of booth capturing and actualising democracy at the grassroots … . Defying severe police repression and attacks by the landlords' armed gangs, the peasants casted their first ever vote in their life. While all the champions of parliamentary democracy – the Congress, the Lok Dal and the CPI like – were busy capturing booths, the fighting peasants of Bihar, through their conduct in the elections, proved that they are the real representatives of democracy.[27]

To say it simply, 'law and order was taken out of the purview of the state government and was effectively privatised'.[28] To hide its inability, however, the state government started presenting Naxalism as the only reason for the worsening condition of law and order situation. Although it's true that the Naxals, after losing on all fronts, had vowed to wage an open war with the landlords; discussions in Chapter 3 have clearly demonstrated that at no point in time did they become as strong as the armed caste militias that were working in connivance with the state machinery. But because the political will to confront the real problems in the state had completely withered away, nobody cared for how democratic institutions of the state were being undermined by politics and politicians of all hues, especially the ruling party. The dividing line between local government and police on one side and local society of landowning families on the other was being erased cleverly. The state supported the local elite by arming them to put down all discontents against them. Throughout the 1980s 'much of the attention of the political leadership was focused on political intrigue'.[29]

After the 1985 Assembly election, Congress placed four upper caste CMs, viz., Bindeswari Dubey, Bhagwat Jha Azad, S.N. Sinha and Jagannath Mishra in the next five years. Mr Dubey's government, busy in scripting a medical scandal, hardly paid any attention to the series of massacres of Dalits and agricultural labourers taking place across the state (for details see Appendix 3). The brutal act of marauder at Arwal (Jehanabad), clearly exposed state connivance with upper caste landlords during Congress regimes.[30] However, the chief minister's position had no threat on this ground. What caused Mr Dubey's replacement after three years by a Brahmin leader, Bhagwat Jha Azad, was his increasing feud with Jagannath Mishra. Azad after coming to power in 1988, promised to hold panchayat elections, but soon backtracked.[31] The officially stated reason for this was that the matter was sub-judice;[32] but in reality, the decision was much more political in nature. An annual confidential report of the district magistrates regarding the political affiliation of the *Mukhiyas* of *gram panchayats* in April 1988 showed that 60 per cent of the Mukhiyas in the gram panchayats were either Congressmen or ardent supporters of the Congress.[33] Disturbing that could have jeopardised their prospects of manipulating the general elections due in 1989.

However, an important achievement of Mr Azad's government was its campaign against the Mafiosi who had defrauded the co-operatives of vast sum of public funds. Though their nefarious games were well known, no chief minister before Mr Azad had dared to take any action against them. He dismissed the dons heading the apex bodies of co-operatives, including some Congress MPs and MLAs and also dropped the tainted minister's of the previous cabinet.[34]

The retaliation of these mafias was swift and suave. Using their clout over the Congress MLAs, the dismissed co-operative bosses launched a sustained campaign for Mr Azad's ouster. There were reports of sudden increase in the bank balances of the close relatives of some Congress MLAs.[35]

One can understand the venomous role being played by the removed mafias but why did the Central government decide to remove Mr Azad.[36] Probably, the steps initiated by Azad were against the wishes the high command and he was replaced by a Rajput leader S.N. Sinha (son of A.N. Sinha, popularly known as the Chhote Sahab).[37] The Sinha government not only dropped the campaign initiated by his predecessor, but also facilitated the process of the rehabilitation of the co-operative mafia. Tapeshwar Singh, the man removed by Mr Azad was invited to the swearing-in-ceremony, and just after taking oath, the CM declared "there is no mafia in the state". A few weeks later he further specified that "all the co-operative bosses are my friends and colleagues". Later events revealed that they had managed their 'men' even in the judiciary.[38] The chief minister continued to show his commitment towards rehabilitation of the mafia dons by appearing in the public and shared the dais along with them. Describing the situation, an observer writes:

> The government's attitude towards them was so soft that they were not only given the lead in organising Prime Minister Rajiv Gandhi's public meeting at Gandhi Maidan in Patna on June 16, 1989 but also presenting their strength both at the airport to receive the Prime Minister and at his public meeting. Ironically, the very day Rajiv Gandhi was in Patna, local newspapers carried damaging reports of an FIR lodged by the state government against Tapeshwar Singh, Rajo Singh and Narendra Singh, four other Congress MLAs, two former Congress legislators and three others, in which they had been

> charged with embezzlement of the cooperative bodies' funds by submitting bogus travelling bills to the tune of lakhs of rupees. The FIR had mentioned as many as 112 such instances in barely two financial years. But no follow-up action was taken. The lodging of the FIR was mainly a propaganda exercise by the government to show to the people on the eve of the Prime Minister's visit that it was getting tough with the co-operative mafia. However, these reports could not gather any attention of the PM.[39]

These reports were speaking loud about the mood of the public of Bihar, but the Congress had chosen a different path. They had forgot that citizens can make appropriate use of their public autonomy, as guaranteed by the constitution, at appropriate time. In the 1989 hustings, the Congress was forced to bite the dust in all but four of the 54 Parliamentary constituencies in the state. The fortress that the Congress had built in Bihar crumbled like a pack of cards. The Janata Dal emerged as the winner with 31 seats followed by the Bhartiya Janata Party with nine seats.[40] The Left parties also secured seven seats, showing a remarkable rise in the awareness of the peasants.[41] Muslims voted against the Congress en-mass in the wake of a chain of manslaughter at Sasaram, Munger and Bhagalpur due to the rising tide of *Ram Shila Pujan*. According to an observer;

> Even the blatant use of the state machinery in the constituencies where from CM's close kin were fighting could not prevent their defeat. Sinha had to suffer the defeat of his daughter-in-law at Aurangabad, the 'Chittorgarh' of Bihar, and of his wife, Kishori Sinha, the sitting MP, at Vaishali. The case of the Brahmin leader Jagannath Mishra, supposed to be the representative of the aspirations of the Brahmins of Mithilanchal, also was not very different. The Brahmin voters not only rejected his brother-in-law Gauri Shankar Rajhans, but also supported Shakeelur Rehman, the ousted vice-chancellor of the Mithila University against a well known Brahmin leader Nagendra Jha. For Rehman this victory came as sweet revenge as it was Jha who had dismissed him as vice-chancellor during the Azad regime.[42]

Dalits overwhelmingly backed the Indian People's Front (IPF) in the 11 constituencies where it contested.[43] Remarkably, Tapeshwar Singh, Kali Pandey, and several other criminals also lost their seats.[44]

However, this was only a trailer of the real political drama due in 1990 Assembly election. Congress, in its last attempt to rebuild its ruined fort, brought back the old guard Jagannath Mishra;[45] but all proved futile. Mishra in his third stint as the chief minister, started distributing largesse to his old friends – industrialists, landlords and bureaucrats.[46] He also realised that one of the most important reasons of Congress debacle in the Lok Sabha election was dissatisfaction among the Backward Castes and the Dalits. He therefore announced that his government would acquire surplus land from big landlords and distribute it to the landless. The state cabinet also waived off farm loans up to ₹ 15,000. Irrigation tax was abolished for farmers of all categories and all the arrears of irrigation tax and power tariffs were waived off. He also made provisions of free electricity for irrigation to farmers with up to 10 acres of cultivable land.[47]

Panchayats elections, for the reasons explained above, remained out of question. Assured with the confidential report about Mukhiyas affiliation and preference for Congressmen, Mishra on the contrary, kept addressing meetings of Mukhias throughout the state and promised to extend the facilities of pension, railway concessions and liberal travelling allowances for them.[48] It is worth mentioning that these decisions of the state government, according to some estimates, brought 'an additional burden of ₹ 1,500 crore on the state exchequer'.[49] More importantly, the government started these additional expenditures even before the legislative sanction was sought.[50]

However, the matter would not have gone worse in the days ahead, had other political parties preferred to play a politics based on ideology and relevant issues. All political parties in the 1990 Assembly elections fielded several criminals and started aggravating caste rivalry openly. Those criminals who could not get party tickets decided to fight the polls independently. There were around 60 such candidates in the fray who were convicted for murder, rape, *dacoity* and so on.[51] The Janata Dal alone had given tickets to more than 50 hardened criminals, including the chief convict in the Belchi massacre. It also chose to provide a safe harbour to retired bureaucrats who were involved in scandals and against whom cases were still pending. Twenty such retired bureaucrats were given party tickets.[52]

In such a complex scenario, violence became inevitable. Fought largely on the personal influence of candidates' caste and communal loyalties, it was the bullet and not the ballot, which decided the outcome. More than 125 people were killed and nearly double the number was injured. Re-polling had to be conducted at a record number of over 1,200 booths spread over 175 constituencies. People were so terrified that in many areas where criminals were in the fray, they did not come out to vote. As a result, as many as 40 hardened criminals, with cases of murder, dacoity and rape, managed to enter the Assembly.[53]

Janata Dal emerged as the single largest party (122 out of 324 seats) in a hung assembly.[54] To facilitate the selection of the chief minister of Bihar, prime minister VP Singh sent a group of observers (including George Fernandes and Ajit Singh) to Patna. The selection of leader of the Janata Dal in Patna proved to be a proxy war between the top party leaders both in the state and at the national levels. PM's personal choice was Ram Sunder Das, but the other senior leader, Chandra Shekhar, backed Raghunath Jha. Devi Lal (the then Deputy Prime Minister), however, had a different game plan. He wanted to show that he was no less than V.P. Singh, and therefore supported Lalu Prasad Yadav.[55] Some other names that were floated for the post of CM were Nitish Kumar (a Kurmi) and Raghuvansh Prasad Singh (a Rajput). All these were the lieutenants of JP who had pledged to fight for socialism together, but the political chaos in Bihar was telling a different story altogether. Failing to reach at a consensus on the leadership they finally opted for an intra-party election.

Lalu Prasad Yadav, a man well known for his satirical oratorial skills, emerged as a lucky winner in this chaotic political game. He secured 58 votes as compared to Ram Sunder Das' 50 and Raghunath Jha's 14 votes.[56] But the game was not over yet. Lalu Yadav even after getting support from CPI (23 seats) and CPM (6 seats) was short of 11 MLAs required to from the government. Ultimately, he found shelter in the politics of caste and criminalisation. It was a hardened criminal (who got elected as an independent MLA for the first time) Pappu Yadav, who forced 11 other independent MLAs to support Lalu Yadav.[57]

The Politics of Lalu Yadav: 1990–1995

With such a chaotic beginning, the last thing people expected from this government was the improvement in law and order situation. However, in the initial days Lalu Yadav proved this completely wrong. Without losing much time, he started taking concrete and sincere attempts to bring a semblance of law and order in the state and to root out rampant corruption.[58] His first achievement probably was to check incidences of communal violence.

> When post-election violence broke out with clear communal overtones at Nawadah, Jamshedpur and Bhagalpur, he ensured that the first flames of violence were extinguished quickly. During Ram Navmi which had come to be known as 'Danga Navmi' in Bihar, Yadav sternly directed the authorities not to allow processions in sensitive or disputed areas.[59]

Later in the same year, he also stopped L.K. Advani's *rath yaatra* when it reached Bihar. This led to rampant communal violence in several states across the country, but the situation in Bihar was kept under control. Two years later in 1992, when the Hindu nationalist activists demolished the Babri Masjid in Ayodhya, riots broke out in several parts of the country, but the Bihar government once again successfully prevented Hindu-Muslim conflict in the state. Wherever violence broke he ensured that it did not get out of control. He visited all such areas and even went to the extent of camping those places, until peace was restored.[60] In the worst-effected Sitamarhi, he asked the authorities to impose punitive fines in villages and localities where violence occurred. He started a *Sadbhavana Rath* (communal harmony chariot) and appealed to the public to remain peaceful. He also deployed a large posse of paramilitary forces in communally sensitive areas to prevent any untoward incidences.[61] That the year passed without any major flare up of communal riots exposes the collusion of the ruling political elite and the administration and confirms my premise about the failure of the state to be a 'disinterested arbiter' in the past. This made Lalu Yadav a mesiah of Muslims in Bihar. Expressing their sentiments, Muslims until very recently expressed;

> Lalu Yadav started an era of peace for the Muslims in the state. No other government before could achieve that. In fact it would be more appropriate to say that none of the past governments even made any effort in this direction. He stood between peace and communal disturbances for decades and we respect him even now.[62]

Lalu Yadav's second commendable attempt was his concrete steps to free the people from the clutches of corruption. He first targeted the powerful contractor-engineer nexus and gave a free hand to the vigilance department to expose the unaccounted wealth of government officials. He set a time-frame to dispose of the 1,400 pending cases of corruption against government officials, following which the vigilance department conducted several raids and booked more than three dozen senior officers. This included prosecution sanction against some IPS officials as well. In all his efforts Lalu Yadav was well supported by his key ministers such as Jagadanand Singh, Ilias Hussain and Ramai Ram.[63] He also targeted the prevention of the 'March loot'.[64]

The government was very particular towards nailing the irrigation mafia. In 1954 Bihar had only 154 km of embankments, but by the end of 1987–88, the length of embankments touched 3,454 km with a total of ₹ 429 crore spent on their construction. However, the flood-prone area in the state went up from 25 lakh hectares in 1954 to 64.61 lakh hectares in 1988. During the Seventh Five-Year Plan while ₹ 40 crore were spent on construction of new embankments, as much as ₹ 125 crore were spent on maintenance and upkeep of old embankments.[65]

Ironically, as many as 106 breaches took place in 1987 alone. It was this 'maintenance and upkeep of embankments and repair of breaches' which was the source of enormous wealth to the contractors, engineers and their political masters. According to Jagdanand Singh, out of a budgetary allocation of ₹ 400 crore for developing water resources in 1990–91, 50 per cent was siphoned off by local politicians and contractors. Whenever there was a contract, the dons using muscle and fire power hijacked the tenders.[66] Thus, he made up his mind to bring the irrigation mafia to heel which over the years has defrauded the state exchequer of hundreds of crores in the construction, maintenance and repair of flood control embankments.

Lalu Yadav re-established an independent irrigation and flood control ministry and Jagdanand Singh as the minister, stood up against all such practices.[67] He did away with the faulty system of payment and started getting the payment certificates verified. As a result, a set of bills submitted by contractors to the tune of ₹ 200 crore turned out to be fake; and he stopped the payment immediately.[68] A review committee set up to examine the costs of various reservoir projects in its report submitted to the government slashed the estimated cost of the Kadwan reservoir project from ₹ 180 crore to ₹ 115 crore and the cost of the modernisation of the Sone Canal from ₹ 2,000 crore to ₹ 1,400 crore.[69] The biggest blow to the irrigation mafia came, in the form of the government's drive to review the veracity of the construction firms itself. Jagadanand removed several engineers and black-listed many contractors.[70]

These actions of the state government surprised not just the Congress, whose nexus with the mafia was left exposed, but also to a big section of Janata Dal's MLAs. Thus cutting across party lines, all those who had links with the mafias, got together to pressurise Lalu Yadav to oust Jagadanand from the cabinet. The chief minister, although withstood these pressures and fully backed Jagadanand in his fight against the irrigation mafia; he could not save his minister's fate. There was a breach in the western Kosi embankment at Hanumannagar on the Indo-Nepal border, and the whole Assembly, including MLAs from Janata Dal (the only exception was the CPM), stood up against Jagadanand to force him to resign. Certainly the breach of the embankment was not the issue.[71]

> The fact was that the issue of the breach was just a pretext for the legislators, who are on the payrolls of the irrigation mafia, to get rid of an irrigation minister who was fighting to stop the loot of the state treasury in the name of embankment repairs. Year after year hundreds

> of crore were cornered by contractors in the name of repairing the embankments to prevent floods, with the engineers and the politicians sharing the booty. In Jagadanand's reiteration of the pledge to resign in case a breach was caused in any embankment, the contractors' lobby found a golden opportunity to get rid of the errant minister.[72]

However, Lalu Yadav decided to stand by his men and refused to accept his resignation. In addition, Lalu Yadav even initiated significant measures in sectors such as power,[73] and education.[74] On the whole, Lalu Yadav tried to introduce a new work culture in government departments. Ministers were asked to be in their chambers during office hours and actions were initiated against those found absent. He himself used to pay surprise visits to government offices and suspended around 400 officials on finding them absent from or sleeping on duty. Indeed, the improvement in attendance in government departments during that period was noticeable.[75]

However, the herculean task to bring a change and achieve a measure of stability and earnestness in a chronic mismanaged state was not easy to achieve. More especially when it coincided with the implementation of the Mandal commission's report by the same Janata Dal government at the Centre. In reaction to this decision, the upper castes had taken to the streets, rampaging with arson and looting of government property and shops and also property belonging to the Backward Castes. However, it was the active collusion of leaders which turned these stray incidents into organised protests.[76] The urban upper caste students had mobilised themselves under the banner of Anti-Mandal Commission Forum based in Delhi University. Ironically, 17 of its 19 executive committee members were from landowning families from Bihar.[77] Adding strength to their protests were the upper caste bureaucrats and other officers who regarded administration and other service sectors as their monopoly. The Lalu Prasad Yadav government had lodged corruption cases against several of them. In rural areas, the Upper Castes began attacking the Backward Castes, particularly the Yadavs. At some places, they even looted and destroyed shops and other properties belonging to the Yadavs. A backward caste group coming for the October 8, 1990 rally in Patna to be addressed by the prime minister V.P. Singh was attacked by the Bhumihars. The Rajputs too, under the leadership of criminal MLAs like Anand Mohan Singh from Saharasha, were quick to join hand with them. Naturally, the Yadavs also started to retaliate and responded with similar backlashes in various parts of the state led by Backward Caste criminal MLAs like Pappu Yadav in Purnea and several others.[78] This, for the first time led to an open confrontation between the Bhumihar-Rajput alliance and the Yadavs.

Lalu Yadav's actions had already upset a variety of vested interests, both within and outside the party and had created many enemies. Thus, as soon as V.P. Singh was replaced by Chandra Shekhar as the prime minister, all these voices got together to pull down his government and malign his image. With Chandra Shekhar as the PM, Raghunath Jha (whom Chandra Shekhar supported for the chief minister's post in Bihar), Suryadeo Singh (a mafia close to Jha), and criminal MLAs like Anand Mohan Singh and Prabhunath Singh became powerful and started demanding for Lalu Yadav's removal.[79] The PM himself, in a public meeting in Purnea, issued a warning that the Centre would not hesitate to intervene if the law and order situation in the state did not improve.[80] The press predominantly controlled by the upper castes during those days added teeth to their demand.[81]

Pushed continuously into corner by the party dissidents, the opposition,[82] and a hostile press, Lalu Yadav finally was forced to devise measures of survival in politics. He went for a massive cabinet expansion by including 60 more ministers.[83] For the 1991 Lok Sabha elections, Lalu Yadav allotted only 16.6 per cent tickets to the forward castes, comprising Bhumihars (2.7%) and Rajputs (13.5%), and gave 40.5 per cent tickets to the OBCs. Among the OBCs, the Yadavs were given 24.3 per cent, compared to the Koiris (8.1%) and the Kurmis (8.1%).[84] Both the Congress and the BJP, supported by the upper-caste media, tried their best to create an impression among Kurmis and Koeries that the Janata Dal was basically a Yadav party. And to woo the non-Yadav backward votes both the political parties gave a larger share of party tickets to these castes.[85]

It would be interesting to mention the exhibition of the Bhumihar-Rajput alliance shown during the assembly by-election for Vaishali seat held in June 1992.[86] The Congress(I) had fielded Veena Sahi, the wife of slain MLA Hemant Sahi, a bhumihar. The Rajput leaders desperately wanted to bring somebody from the upper/forward caste this time, but they feared that their castemen would not rally behind this bhumihar candidate since she was a woman. It was probably to avoid this that the Rajputs utilised the services of Anand Mohan Singh (who had resigned from the Janata Dal during the anti-reservation stir), and had emerged as a hero of the Rajputs. According to an observer;

> Singh, however, considered it beneath his Rajput pride to support a woman in an election and that too a 'widow'. So he sent his wife Lovely Singh to campaign among the Rajputs at Vaishali. The visit of Lovely Singh to Vaishali proved to be a boon to the Rajput leaders. She not only successfully motivated the Rajput men to support the

'widow' but also sufficiently encouraged the womenfolk to come out of the confines of their home and caste their votes.[87]

During her speech, Rajput don's wife is reported to have said;

> I have come to Vaishali following the order of her 'suhag' who is facing a threat to his life from the state government since he has taken upon himself the task of protecting the "rights" of the upper castes and so the Rajputs must strengthen his hands by casting their votes in favour of Veena Sahi as per his wish.[88]

Leaders like S.N. Sinha, the former C.M. of Bihar, came out openly in support of this kind of caste alliance. This new alliance of Bhumihars and Rajputs, not only wanted to defeat the backward caste-kulak lobby which had captured the political power in the state and was steadfastly spreading its dominance over the political economy, but also to counter the continuing sway of Brahmins over the state politics that the Congress(I) had epitomised under the leadership of Jagannath Mishra. Such unabashed propagation of feudal-patriarchal values in the state was never witnessed before.[89]

With the rising polarisation of the state along the backward-forward divide, Lalu Yadav further consolidated his position by employing populist means. In one such move, the unemployed youth while travelling for any examination or interview for any government institution were given free travel facilities on the state-run buses. Besides, he also promised to remove unemployment in districts, one in each financial year, without analysing where those many jobs would come from.[90]

Although Lalu Yadav himself never claims to belong to the theoretical school that believes in 'knowledge as shared experience';[91] his actions certainly proves so. His approach to cure the anomalies of the society by wrecking the traditional domination at, what Saibal Gupta terms as, the 'Block-Bank-Thana (BBT) level – the power-development tripod'[92], aptly qualifies him to fit him into this theoretical paradigm. In 1993 (more than two decades since the last panchayat elections were held) Lalu Yadav passed a new Panchayati Raj Act under which the traditional power holders lost their space in a big way to the OBCs, SCs, STs and minorities. The Act provided reservations for these marginalised groups on the basis of population strength, and also reserved one-third seats for women at all levels. He also made an attempt to correct the imbalance of these groups in the bureaucracy. Though there were only a few officers from these groups, they had not been given key positions for obvious reasons. He placed these neglected people at the right places, like magistrates, sub-divisional magistrates, etc., in the districts or as secretaries and general managers in important departments at the capital. There was no representation of OBCs in the judiciary even at the district level so far. Mr Yadav reserved 27 per cent of the posts of district judges for the OBCs.[93]

However, Lalu Yadav's estimated scheme of social justice could not bring much change for the most underprivileged, exploited and oppressed sections of the society, viz., the agricultural labourers who were from the lower backward castes and the Dalits. The year Lalu Yadav took over, there was a massacre at Dariyapur in Patna, where the upper backward castes killed five dalit agricultural labourers. In 1991, the upper backward castes again killed 15 dalit agricultural labourers at Tiskhora in Patna. The prime accused in the Tiskhora massacre was Ram Lakhan Singh Yadav. Same year, the agricultural labourers in Deo-Sahiara of the same caste groups were again targeted by the Rajput landlord, Jwala Prasad. He was also the prime accused in the Danwar-Bihta massacre and mass rape in 1984. In 1991 alone, over 50 dalit agricultural labourers were killed at five different places (see Appendix 3). As discussed earlier, even during the 1990 Assembly elections, the Janata Dal had given ticket to the main accused in the Belchi massacre, Bishundeo Chaudhary.

In the 1991 Lok Sabha elections, Lalu Yadav, in fact went a step ahead. He not only gave party ticket to Ramlakhan Singh Yadav, the man behind the Tiskhora carnage, but also solicited the assistance of Jwala Prasad. In many areas, where the dalits stood behind the IPF candidates, they were not allowed to vote.[94] Previously it used to be the upper caste landlords who prevented the dalits from voting but now the new landlords from the middle castes and the Kulak lobby adopted the same techniques.[95] Nowhere in the election campaign did the ruling Janata Dal raise crucial issues like land reforms and payment of minimum wages, concerning the most underprivileged, exploited and oppressed sections of the society.[96]

What went missing from Lalu Yadav's efforts throughout these years was the question of land reforms. The Janata Dal came to power with the support of the Left parties. Therefore, the leaders of the left parties saw this an opportunity to reclaim their lost strength and upbeat their assertive mood. They launched a joint programme, the 'Bhumi Mukti Andolan' (Land Liberation Movement), and identified over 50,000 acres of surplus land in the possession of landlords.[97] But contrary to their expectations, when in August 1991, the Centre decided to create an anti-Naxal paramilitary force, Lalu Yadav played a leading role in its formation. In a detailed report to the Union home ministry in 1991, he identified the ultra-left extremist activities as one of the main causes of the worsening law and order situation in the state.[98] Analysing the deteriorating law and order situation in the state, the report said that the "crumbling of the feudal system and the emergence and assertiveness of the new economic and social forces have added a new dimension to law and order situation resulting into socioeconomic tensions in the state".[99] Soon the police started an exercise 'Operation Agnidoot' in which select areas identified as affected by Naxals-led peasant movements were made targets of intense repression.[100]

Thus, with each passing day, dissatisfaction against Lalu Yadav among the landless kept on increasing. It went to an all time low when the CPI-ML organised a rally on March 18, 1994, virtually appropriating the old JP plank of social revolution of the 70s in the changed context of the 90s – to declare Lalu as the 'illegitimate' product of the 1970s movement.[101] With caste constituting the basis of Mr Yadav's administration, it became an open site of contest for political power. The Janata Dal did not really show any extraordinary sign of causing discomfort to the upper caste landlord lobbies, but the large constituency of marginalised voters which Lalu Yadav brought to his credit, started bothering them. Under the fear that levers of power would slip out of their hands, they started enraging caste rivalries. With such political environment, the state once again failed to respond to public aspirations. It neither could offer anything substantial to the poor by way of land reforms, nor it could achieve any economic growth. Despite all its mineral wealth and resources, the state remained plagued by chronic lack of industrial development and all other evils of economic backwardness. 'Karpoori's real socialist successor would herald the rise of the more entrepreneurial backward classes and speed up development soon', turned out to be an illusion.[102]

However, the reasons of the failing of the state was not monopolized by Lalu Yadav alone. The upper caste dominated bureaucracy worked day and night for the failure of the state government, as they could not tolerate the fact of being ruled by a backward caste leader. The powerful contractor-engineer lobby, which were put under corruption charges by the Lalu Yadav government, the employees associations, which were dissatisfied with the regulation of new work culture, stopped cooperating the chief minister. Between 1991 and 1995, 144 out of 384 IAS officers sought deputation to work at the Centre. Those who remained dutiful to job had to face severe consequences from the mafia dons who wanted to carry their operations with no restrictions. One such heartbreaking case was of the young dalit IAS officer G. Krishnaiya of Gopalganj district, who was shot at and then stoned by a mob led by the Rajput ganglord Anand Mohan Singh, his wife Lovely Anand and another criminal Munna Shukla (for more details, see Chapter 5). Several other incidents followed later.

Nevertheless, against all these heavy odds Lalu Yadav kept growing powerful on the caste plank. On the administrative front, too, he centralised most of the power of the government under his direct control and most of the cabinet ministers were substantially marginalised. Taking lessons from Indira Gandhi's style of 'nothing above politics' (details discussed in Chapter 2), Lalu Yadav also started running the state by his hand-picked bureaucrats. His style became arbitrary and authoritarian. At the party level, too, he started curtailing the powers of other party functionaries. This caused discomfort among the Dalits and the non-Yadav backward castes, and they started expressing their resentment against Lalu Yadav's parochial approach towards his caste men. All this led to widespread disenchantment among the party men and a section of the party revolted under the leadership of George Fernandes and Nitish Kumar. They finally launched the Samata Party (with its major base among Kurmis and Keoris) in 1994.[103] The CPI-ML too, led by Vinod Mishra, angered by Lalu Yadav's failure to curb violence and atrocities against masses and its cadres decided to join hands with the Samata Party for the 1995 Assembly election.

But the case was not that simple. The Janata Dal under the leadership of Lalu Yadav came out victorious in 1995 assembly elections with absolute majority and added 41 more seats to its previous tally of 123 in the 324–member House. The BJP emerged as the second largest party with 42 seats. The Congress was pushed to the third position, losing 29 seats from the previous House. The Left (CPM and CPI), an ally of the Janata Dal, improved its position marginally, and the CPI-ML, which had joined hands with Samata Party, had to remain satisfied with only six seats. The victory of Lalu Yadav in 1995 clearly established what Barrington Moore describes as "the conquest of inevitability": i.e., the social construction of permanence of backward castes in power as a given.[104] This changed the course of politics in the state for ever. A survey conducted by Centre for the Study of Developing Societies (henceforth CSDS) in a representative sample of 16 Assembly constituencies spread across the state revealed that nearly 57.3 per cent of the Muslims and 49.8 per cent of the BCs (primarily the Yadavs) voted for the Janata Dal and its allies.[105] In addition to that, the Janata Dal also had the overwhelming support of the rural poor, primarily Dalits. This may not be easy to explain, considering the steps taken by the Lalu Yadav's government in its first five-year term; but his appeal among the poor came under display during the *'Garib'* rally organised by the Janata Dal in Patna on October 31, 1994. 'About half-a-million rural masses, a good part of them from the lowest depths of poverty and social misery, converged in the state capital in response to the chief minister's call'. The rustic masses, including 'half-fed and half clothed families', to quote one newspaper report, 'tied together to avoid getting separated or lost in the jostling multitudes' came to Patna with some hope of socio-economic uplift.[106] They were aware of the fact that although no tangible economic gain had accrued to them under the Janata Dal dispensation, change had come about in a large number of villages in the shape of increased human dignity for the rural underclass.[107]

> It was the aspirations of the downtrodden *seeking dignity and a decent life free from exploitation and suppression* and not any 'magic wand' in the hands of Lalu or his 'Krishnavatar' which gave the strength, power, and sustenance to the Janata Dal government. *(emphasis added)*[108]

> Sense of acquired *'ijjat'* felt by the poor had inspired them to throw their weight behind the chief minister. *(emphasis added)*[109]

The rift between the Yadavs and the Kurmis, culminating in the formation of the Samata Party under Nitish Kumar and George Fernandes could hardly cause dent in Lalu Yadav's base.[110]

The election process continued for about three months and during that period, Bihar witnessed more violence than in all other states put together. More than 150 people lost their lives, including four candidates and 63 were injured in 1,270 incidents. There were as many as 59 candidates with criminal backgrounds put up by major political parties (see Figure 4.1 below), besides many contesting as independents.

Figure 4.1

Candidates with Criminal Background put up by Major Political Parties in 1995 Assembly Elections

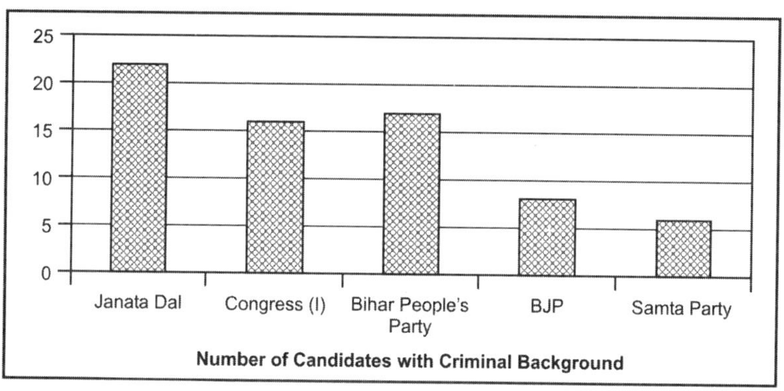

Source: Kanhaiah Bhelari, (1995). 'Blooming Bandits' *The Week*, March 5, p. 31.

The physical manoeuvring of the election process and the last-ditch of rigging on the polling day led the Election Commission to order re-polling in thousands of booths all over the state, not once, but twice. This prolonged process dragged the State Assembly beyond the limit of the five-year term, and created a constitutional crisis. This led to the to imposition of President's rule in the state.[111] The ruling party, as usual, deputed loyal bureaucrats as key election officials in different districts and there were also reports that in some constituencies the number of ballots cast exceeded the total voter strength, indicating a likely rigging by pro-Janata Dal officials.[112]

This happened despite T.N. Sheshan's, (the chief election commissioner), ambitious and effective security arrangement during the polls.[113] Seshan's arrangement was so tough that many looked at him as standing between victory and Lalu Yadav in the state. But perhaps this unprecedented arrangement in the state's electoral history facilitated the rural poor, specially the Dalits, the most backward castes and the women to come out to vote in large numbers and ensured Lalu Yadav's landslide victory. The print media, in chorus with the spokespersons of different political parties, had declared (only initially) that the poll process was less vitiated this time compared to the past.[114]

Politics as 'Lalu Raj': 1995–2005

Lalu Yadav after this triumph in the 1995 Assembly elections was altogether a different man. His earlier techniques to build up his support base by altruism was now replaced by muscle-power and distribution of largesse among his followers to buy their loyalty. Adopting means of eliminating rivals or dissenters physically, as practiced by the traditional political elite, Lalu Yadav reinforced the politics of illegitimacy with the help of his trustworthy musclemen (across caste) to such a level that the state in the days ahead started being defined as a breeding laboratory of 'crime in politics'. The breakdown of the law and order machinery and the cases of crime, kidnapping, social tension and violence was so serious that people were prompted to sarcastically remark Bihar as a synonym of '*jungle raj*'.[115]

A series of scams started unfolding only a year after the election. Nepotism became rampant in all spheres of governmental activities. One such case was the appointment of 1,400 lecturers, most of the positions being cornered by the close relatives of ministers and top administrators, more precisely Yadavs.[116] Large purchases of land were reported by the Income Tax Department in the names of the relatives of the chief minister and some cabinet ministers.[117] But 1.5 lakh government employees of various state enterprises, boards, corporations and educational institutions, who had been working without pay, many many even longer them five years, did not find any relief. Similar was the plight of some 2 lakh teaching and non-teaching employees of unaided educational institutions in the state who had been working without salary for more than 10 years.[118] He rather, stoutly rejected the demand of the agitating teachers to terminate the policy of allowing unaided educational institutions, citing the additional expenditure of ₹ 1,000 crore as impossible for the government to bear. A number of teachers were even reported to have died of starvation or committing suicide.[119]

Although Lalu Yadav after his re-election in 1995 had announced to prioritiese states industrialisation; he never took any concrete step to realise that.[120] Soon Bihar hit the news headlines for one of the biggest scandals in the history of the country. According to reports, the scam, which came to be popularly known as the fodder scam, involved about ₹ 950 crore and the total fraudulent expenditure of the animal husbandry department took place during the period between 1991–92 and 1995–96. It seemed as if almost the entire money spent by the department was stolen. It was also seen that the frequency of the inspection of treasuries by audit had mysteriously declined sharply after 1990. In 1989–90 more than 20 treasuries were inspected; in 1992–93 only two treasuries, and none at all in 1994–95.[121]

While often there was no money to pay the pending bills of the and no money to pay salaries of the starving employees, the state Assembly and the cabinet spent more money on themselves. According to an estimate, while "the neighbouring Bengal in 1995–96 spent a mere ₹ 6 crore on the Legislature, Bihar spent ₹ 26 crore. The expenditure on the Bihar Secretariat alone was ₹ 10 crore, much more than on the entire Bengal Legislature. During the same period, Bengal spent ₹ 1.5 crore on its ministers, while in Bihar it was ₹ 6 crore. More than ₹ 7 crore was given as "advance to ministers and legislators to buy cars, and not a single penny was recovered from this money".[122] Surprisingly even in the departments where the CM and his trustworthy ministers had tried their best to fight corruption in the earlier term (as discussed earlier), the spending was equally reckless. For example, in the "irrigation department, while work expenditure decreased from ₹ 104 crore in 1991–92 to ₹ 44 crore in 1994–95, the salary expenditure went up from ₹ 184 crore to ₹ 262 crore.[123]

In the aftermath of these events, Lalu Yadav got his first setback in 1996 when his party's position was reduced from 31 MPs (in 1991) to

22 in the Lok Sabha. The other setback came during the by-elections to four Assembly seats (held along with the 1996 Lok Sabha elections) where the Janata Dal couldn't win even one. Furthermore, in the by-elections held for 10 seats to the Assembly few months later (after the Lok Sabha elections), it again lost four seats to the BJP-Samata Party combine. There were indications of a new Bania-Rajput-Non Yadav backward castes (BRNY equation) alliance formed between – (a) the forward castes and the tradesmen (usually the Banias) represented by the BJP, (b) a section of the Rajputs represented by the Bihar People's Party, and (c) the non-Yadav middle castes like the Koeris, the Kurmis and the Mahatos under the Samata Party.[124] Lalu Yadav too had such a fear, and he expressed this on several occasions. For example, in Purnea, he preferd caste followership over party ideology. Instead of campaigning for the political alliance partner CPM, he preferred his caste man and criminal politician Pappu Yadav. This was despite the fact that Pappu Yadav was the Samajwadi Party candidate (joined after his rift with Lalu Yadav in 1995). This Yadav trio (Lalu Yadav, Pappu Yadav and Mulayam Singh Yadav) proved to be detrimental to the CPM's vote base in Purnea and Pappu Yadav won by a record margin of 3,16,155 votes. The polarisation along caste (not class) was so strong that the CPM candidate Ajit Chandra Sarkar could not even figure second in the list. It went to R.R. Gupta of the BJP. More than 42 lives were lost and 187 people were injured in 1,226 incidents in that election.[125]

But this did not deter Lalu Yadav and his associates and they continued with their style of politics. A series of incidents indicate the beginning of the tragic fallout of the administrative functioning of the state, which Lalu Yadav had attempted to build six years before, thereby, making a mockery of his own style of social justice. Even the most populist gesture of cutting the hair of Harijan children and bathing them and starting 'Charvaha' schools started losing its sheen in the face of the continued massacres.[126] In fact, the only characteristic that remained common between his two regimes was his 'anti-land reform' image. On July 11th 1996, '21 peasant women and children of Bathani Tola in Bhojpur district were murdered in cold blood'. On March 23rd 1997, the eve of Holi, '10 landless agricultural labourers of the Musahar Tola of Habaspur village in Patna district were lured from their homes, not to be fed but to be massacred'; on April 10th the same year, 'eight lohars, chamars, dhobis, and kahars of Ekwari village in Bhojpur, including four women, were raped and murdered by the Ranvir Sena with the connivance of the local police'.[127] And the list of villages and victims goes on and on 'in a continuing litany of mayhem and killing'. Belaur, Khopira, Chandi, Charpokhri, Patalpura, Nonaur, Narhi and Khanet to name but a few.[128]

Whenever and wherever people agitated for their genuine demands against the feudal oppression and exploitation or the unjust laws of the state machinery; the state instead of listening to their demands resorted to various repressive measures such as police firing, fake encounters, and fake police cases against peasant activists and leaders. The murder of Chandrashekhar Prasad (a student activist from Jawaharlal Nehru University, New Delhi) and Shyam Nandan Yadav (a CPI (ML) cadre who contested the 1990 and 1995 state assembly elections from Siwan) while addressing a meeting on March 31, 1997 in Siwan by the henchmen of Shahabuddin, the local criminal turned MP of Janata Dal (who by then had already accumulated an extensive criminal record in several places, and primarily in the Hussain Ganj police station of Siwan, where he was listed as a "history sheeter type A".[129]) showed signs of the beginning of new era in the socio-political discourse and a paradigmatic shift in the pattern of agrarian violence in Bihar.[130]

According to the CPM's official figures, about 30 of its cadres were killed in Purnea, Darbhanga, Bhagalpur, Kisanganj and other districts during Lalu Yadav's reign. The CPI also had lost a number of its followers in Palamau, Purnea and other places during this period.[131] The system finally proved to be endemic when Pappu Yadav, who played the most important role in making Lalu Yadav the chief minister of Bihar in 1990 (as discussed earlier), masterminded the murder of Ajit Sarkar, the CPM legislator from Purnea (details to be discussed in Chapter 5). Some other famous criminals who reached Parliament from the state on the Janata Dal ticket in 1996 were Mohd Shahabuddin, Devendranath Dubey, and Anand Mohan Singh. Devendranath Dubey was an absconder who faced charges of murder, looting, rape, kidnapping and arson in near about 20 cases. He won as an independent candidate from Gobindganj in the East Champaran district. The details on Anand Mohan will be discussed in Chapter 5.

In the meantime, when the CBI charged Lalu Yadav with several offences and was preparing to arrest him in early months of 1997, a few important party members like Ram Vilas Paswan and Sharad Yadav (the then JD President), openly expressed their disagreement with Lalu Yadav. To everybody's surprise, Lalu Yadav floated his own party, the Rashtriya Janata Dal (RJD). Almost all the Janata Dal legislative members remained with Lalu Yadav and elected Rabri Devi, Lalu Yadav's wife, as the chief minister of the state. The RJD government subsequently became another milestone in the phenomenon of 'criminalisation of politics' of the state. The new cabinet looked more like 'a roll-call of the State's crime branch' with no less than 29 of 74 members being history sheeters in police records.[132] Some of the famous names in the list were:

> Industry Minister, Surendra Prasad Yadav, the Belaganj MLA was a terror in Gaya district. Power Minister, Brij Bihari Prasad was facing a CBI inquiry for irregularities in Combined Engineering Tests and was a mafia in the Muzaffarpur area. The Minister of State for Revenue and Land Reforms, Sarfaraz Ahmaad, was the son of the famous criminal politician Md. Taslimuddin and was convicted in several cases of assault, arson and loot in Araria district. The Relief and Rehabilitation Minister, Dilip Kumar Singh had 53 criminal cases pending against him in Mokamah area. During a raid in the year 1995 at his official Patna residence, a huge cache of illegal and sophisticated arms was recovered; Minister of State for Water Resources, Inderdeo Bhagat was accused in a case of theft of ancient statues and jewels from a famous temple in Gopalganj; Sugarcane Minister, Raghvendra Pratap Singh was charged with raping the wife of a circle officer in Bhojpur who was reportedly beaten up severely by Singh; the Urban Development Minister (Union), Narain Yadav was involved in a sex scandal and (Minister of State) Udit Raj, was a contractor-turned politician who was facing charges of corruption involving crores of rupees and dealing in contraband, including narcotics with the help of his fleet of buses bearing placards '*Vidhayak Udit Raj ka Bus*' (Bus of MLA Udit Raj); another Minister, Ram Vichar Rai had charges of murder of two persons and hanging them from a tree in his constituency. The only woman in Rabri Devi's cabinet, Abbo Devi, needs special mention too. An MLA from Jharia was regarded as the fast-emerging don of the Dhanbad coal mafia and came into limelight when she entered a local police station and assaulted the officer in charge for daring to arrest her bodyguard.[133]

It was a classic example of tyranny of democracy, as discussed in Chapter 2. In such a situation when the criminals were given the power of management of the state affairs, i.e., when law breakers were made the law makers, there was very little that one could hope from the state. The grisly massacre of landless dalits by the private army of the land-owning upper and upper-backward castes continued with the same vigour (see Appendix 3) and the government's 'don't-disturb' attitude towards the police-politician-landlord- criminal nexus went to an all time high.

The Rabri Devi government paid no attention to the socio-political malady afflicting the state. Villages failed to get roads, electricity and drinking water in spite of crores of rupees being spent supposedly on rural development, and landless labourers continued to be forcibly deprived of their right to till the government land in spite of being genuine 'parcha' holders.[134] The education system in the state, that once upon a time used to be world class, was left to be destroyed at the mercy of 'brokers'. Students were allowed to cheat in the examinations openly. There were some centres of examination that were known as 'honeymoon' centres. The men in charge of those examination centres, had close links with either the politicians/ministers in Patna or with the bureaucrats/officers of the Education Board/Councils, and they used to decide the percentage of the marks of students according to the bribe paid to them. Teachers used to take bribes for marking extra-ordinarily in the examination papers. And those who did not spend money were not evaluated.[135] The higher education system was turned into a cruel joke. University degrees and certificates of all kinds were made available to anybody, at any time. Tens of thousands of students started fleeing to Delhi en masse, merely to escape the rot in their home state and to seek academic refuge, but the government remained extremely coy about initiating any action against members of the education mafia who occupied positions in the ministry of both Lalu Yadav and Rabri Devi and others who were close friends, political managers and cheer-leaders.[136] According to the migration data of Census 2001, the migration of students from Bihar increased by 200 per cent from 1991 (see Figure 4.2).[137]

Figure 4.2

Migration Outside Bihar Due to Education

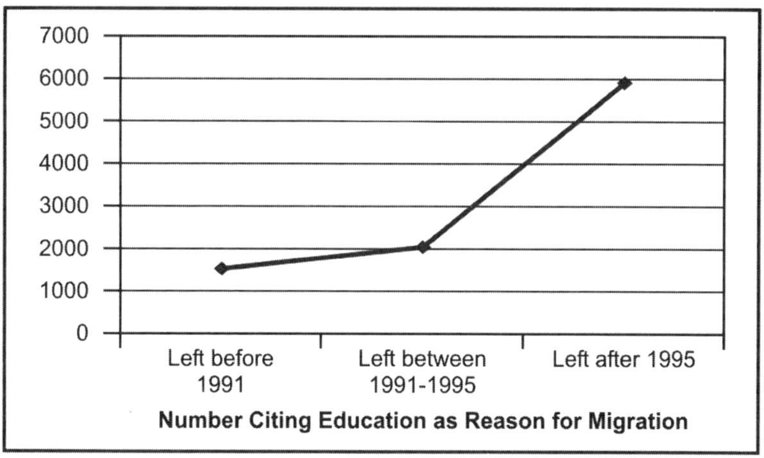

Source: Census of India 2001; URL: http://www.censusindia.gov.in/Census_Data_2001/Census_Data_Online/Online_ Migration/ Reason_ for_migration.as

This happened despite the fact that expenditure on education (at least on paper) was increased significantly (See Table 4.3 below).

Table 4.3

Comparative Percentage Composition of Public Expenditure in Bihar (1985–86 to 1987–88 and 2002–03 to 2003–04)

	1985–86 to 1987–88 (average share)	*2002–03 (actual) to 2003–04 (RE) (average share)*
General Services	**23.3**	**43.0**
Services	**32.3**	**34.3**
Education	16.8	24.2
Health	8.0	4.0
Welfare Programmes	4.8	3.7
Others	2.7	2.4
Economic Services	**37.0**	**15.6**
Agriculture	6.8	2.2
Rural	9.9	5.8
Irrigation	13.4	4.7
Power	0.7	0.1
Transportation	3.6	1.8
Others	2.7	1.0
Grant-in-aid	0.3	0.0
Net loans by state	7.1	7.1

Source: World Bank, Bihar (2005:40)[138]

Bihar's literacy level at 48 per cent in the 2001 census was the lowest in the country, (the national average was 65 per cent). Bihar was the only state where primary enrolments fell by 2 per cent between 1993–94 and 1999–2000.[139] However, what is more important is that, in a situation where the legitimate economy was stagnant and the only 'growth sector' was crime; access to education and degrees continued to be taken from outside the state.[140] What was assured, primarily, under Lalu Yadav was that the Yadavs gained an added vantage in all spheres of lives. According to Das,

> With Lalu as the 'raja' and Rabri Devi as the 'rajmata', the Yadavas have felt themselves to be part of a Praetorian Guard led by the likes of the regal brothers-in-law, Sadhu and Subhash Yadav. The real or imagined or assumed proximity to the court has also enabled the Yadavas to try to bully others. This has been particularly evident in the relationship between the landholding sections of this caste and the Dalits. ...

> Neither Lalu Yadav nor his chief minister spouse Rabri Devi gave any evidence of developmentalist perspective, administrative acumen or visionary politics. The state of Bihar languished as public finances were squandered if not looted outright; institutions collapsed; construction and even maintenance activities were stalled; lawlessness was encouraged; the infrastructure had decayed and there was a general social and political fragmentation.[141]

With such kind of the rule of 'raja' and 'rajmata', anything done by anybody close to the duo was no surprise. The most heinous of all crimes surfaced in the year 1998 when Champa Biswas, wife of a senior IAS officer B.B. Biswas, claimed that Mrityunjay Yadav, the son a former RJD MLA and the then chairman of the State Women's Welfare Board – Hemlata, raped her in connivance with his mother. After all, Mritunjay had penned Lalu Yadav's biography. Surprisingly, Champa's ordeal had started right back in September 1995, soon after Lalu Yadav started his second term as the CM. 'Mritunjay continued to torture her over the next two years and even compelled her to have sex with his friends'. Champa kept mum, as usual, 'fearing for her family and her own honour'. When the matter came into the knowledge of Mr Biswas, he took it to the home secretary and director-general of police only to invite further threats from Hemlata 'to be killed' if he 'pursued the case'. The family ran away from Patna in order to save their life and 'changed houses more than 20 times'. The case was registered only at the behest of the National Human Rights Commission and the Bihar Governor, after the family approached them. The matter came into public knowledge when the opposition leader revealed it at a press conference.[142]

But nothing could make any dent in the political fortunes of Lalu Yadav and his criminal associates. In 1998, Lalu Yadav (read the RJD) once again emerged as the single largest party in the State with 24 Parliamentary seats and 25.2 per cent of the popular votes. The original Janata Dal could get only 8.3 per cent votes and one seat (of Ram Vilas Paswan) as compared to the 31.9 per cent of votes and 22 seats during the 1996 Lok Sabha election. Its alliance partners, the CPI and the CPM, could not win even a single seat and polled as low as 3.1 and 2.1 per cent votes respectively. The BJP-Samata Party alliance got 29 seats (improving its tally of 24 in the 1996 Lok Sabha election) with each party getting 23.1 per cent (19 seats) and 15.8 per cent (10 seats) votes respectively.[143]

However, a year later Lalu Yadav got its first electoral shock when in the 1999 Parliamentary election his party could win only 7 out of 54 seats in the state. Even the Muslim-Yadav (M-Y) equation on which

Lalu Yadav had built his electoral base was left shaken. The CSDS survey of the 1999 Parliamentary Election showed that the BJP-Samata Party combine which in 1998 had gained virtually no Muslim support; in 1999 under the BJP-JD(U) banner secured 19 per cent of the Muslim votes.[144] The JD(U), under the influence of leaders like Ram Vilas Paswan was able to transfer the traditional Dalit vote base of Janata Dal to the BJP-JD(U) alliance (see Table 4.4).[145]

Table 4.4

Voting Pattern along Caste in Parliamentary Election 1999 in Bihar

Caste	*RJD-Cong*	*BJP-JDU*
Rajputs	8	92
Other Upper Castes	13	86
Kurmis-Koeris	19	79
Yadavs	79	20
Lower OBCs	27	55
Dalits	49	43
Muslims	79	19

Source: 'Emerging Pattern', *Frontline,* op. cit.

Nevertheless, Lalu Yadav's charisma continued even in the 2000 Assembly election and his party once again emerged as the single largest party in the state. Some of the candidates with criminal charges in the 2000 Assembly election were:

> Surajbhan Singh, an independent from Mokama, supported by the RJD, was in jail during the election and had more than 26 cases including murder, kidnapping and extortion pending against him; Ramkishore Singh a JDU candidate from Mahnar had over 25 cases pending against him; Munna Shukla from Lalganj was one of the co-accused in the murder of the IAS officer G. Krishnaiya and many more murders; Dhoomal Singh, an Independent candidate from Baniapur, was wanted in more than 175 cases of murder, kidnapping and several other heinous charges not only in Bihar but also in the neighbouring MP and MP and the far-flung Delhi and Maharashtra; Rajan Tiwari, another Independent from Govindganj was the prime accused in the murder of CPM MLA Ajit Sarkar and another criminal-turned politician Brij Bihari Prasad and won the election from behind the of the Beur jail; Sunil Pandey of Samta Party from Peerowas the main accused in several massacres and kidnappings in central Bihar; Malkhan Singh of BJP from Ichagarh; Bachha Singh of Samajwadi Party contesting from Mothihari was in jail during the election; Shakuni Choudhary of the Samata Party from Khagaria was

accused in about six criminal cases; Prabhunath Singh of Samata Party from Maharajgan was released from jail only a couple of months before the elections as he had about 40 cases against him for murder, kidnapping, robbery, etc. He was also the main accused in the murder of Janata Dal legislator Ashok Singh. Awanesh Kumar Singh of BJP from Sitamarhi was an accused in a murder case and was lodged at the Kanda Chainpur police station in East Champaran district in 1989. He was also chargesheeted in three other cases. In an FIR lodged against him in Pathahi, Singh was booked under Section 27 of the Arms Act; Kali Pandey of the Jan Congress from Gopalganj; Vijay Singh of the Congress from Singhbum was convicted for murder by a trial court. RJD president Lalu Yadav was accused in fodder scam case; JD president Sharad Yadav from Madhepura was tainted in *hawala* scandal; Chandra Rao Prasad Verma, another accused in Hawala scandal, contested from Arrah; Jharkhand Mukti Morcha's chief Shibu Soren was accused in several cases including murders, for details see Chapter 2); Ram Lakhan Singh Yadav of the Jan Congress from Arah was chargesheeted in the urea scam; Devendra Prasad Yadav of the JD from Jhanjharpur was the main accused in Congressman Upendra Yadav's murder; and Jakir Anwar of the BSP from Forbesganj was in the jail during the election for allegedly murdering his earlier mentor Bhagwan Yadav.[146]

Some even managed to send their wives to the State Assembly:

> Lesy Singh (wife of a Rajput don Buttan Singh on a Samta Party ticket from Dhamdaha in Purnea; Bima Bharati (the wife of another dreaded criminal and gang-leader Avdhesh Mandal of the Faizan Party won as an Independent from Banmankhiin, Purnea; and Aruna Devi (wife of another don Akhilesh Singh) from Varisliganj.[147]

During the 2000 Assembly elections it seemed as if political parties and the castes were competing against each other to bring the highest number of criminals in the Assembly. However, what's important to note is that despite Lalu Yadav's RJD emerging as the single largest party, the verdict unambiguously denied absolute power to Lalu Yadav and showed that his political patronage had 'limited encashability'.[148]

At the local level, invariably, the upper-castes continued to exercise domination at different sites. In 2001, when the state government decided to go for the long awaited (since last twenty three years) Panchayat elections, the upper castes captured nearly 35 per cent of the seats. The only non-uppercaste candidates in all the three positions, viz., *mukhia* (village chief), members of *zila parishad* (district councils) and its chairman, were yadavs (see Table 4.5).

Table 4.5

Caste wise distribution of Mukhias, Members of Zila Parishads and Chairmen of Zila Parishads after 2001 Panchayat Elections

Caste	*Mukhias (in %)*	*Members of zila parishads (in %)*	*Chairmen of zila parishads (in %)*
Upper Castes	34	25.3	35.2
Brahmin	7.7	5.0	8.2
Bhumihar	12.1	9.1	13.5
Rajput	13.4	10.3	13.5
Kayastha3	0.8	0.9	—
OBCs	45.7	42.1	45.9
Yadav	24.2	24.2	35.1
Kurmi	5.8	4.1	2.7
Koeri	6.3	5.2	—
Bania/Vaishya	3.6	4.4	5.4
EBC (Annexure I)	3.9	3.5	2.7
Scheduled Castes	1.06	16.9	—
Scheduled Tribes	0.5	0.6	—
Muslims	15.6	13.0	16.2

Source: Shaibal Gupta, (2002).[149]

Though official accounts have tried to prove that the elections held in the state were free, fair and peaceful;[150] the fact remains that the 19–day panchayat elections held for 8,452 panchayats in 29 districts in six-phases in the month of April were swathed in blood. At least 100 people were killed and thousands injured in the war between the old masters from the upper/dominant castes and the newly empowered lower castes, primarily Dalits.[151] There were 1,30,563 candidates for mukhia (panchayat head), 2,28,995 for seats in the panchayat committee and over four lakhs for membership in the *zila parishads.* The Election Commission was unable to prevent the spread of violence in spite of taking preventive measures such as the arrest of 40,000 people with criminal records, the closure of a number of mini gun factories and the seizure of illegal arms.[152]

The ruling party of the state and the cabinet ministers made an open mockery of the democratic practices. According to some news reports,

> In Salar Kalam Panchayat in Gopalgunj district from where Shiv Prasad Chowdhury, father of Rabri Devi contested for the post of mukhia was "fiercely fought" ... Chowdhury's younger son Subhas Yadav, a member of the State Legislative Council, was present in the

panchayat with jeep-loads of supporters and security personnel, intimidating voters. In his native Phulwaria block, Laloo Prasad's younger brother and nephew contested the panchayat polls. The wife of Animal Husbandry Minister Aditya Singh contested from Nawada, while former Minister Vijay Krishna's wife contested from Mokama. The brother and nephew of the Member of Parliament from Saharsa, Dinesh Chandra Yadav, also contested the polls.[153]

Thus, with the centralisation of power in the hands of primarily Yadavs (among the OBCs) and Rajputs (among the Upper castes) (as shown in Table 4.4), there emerged three types of polarisation that became instrumental to a large degree in increasing the incumbency against Lalu Yadav and his spouse chief minister Rabri Devi.

First, there started a higher degree of mobilisation against Lalu Yadav, primarily in the form of non-Yadav backward castes. Later they were also supported by dalits, landless, and other depressed sections of society. Secondly, several leaders of the erstwhile JP movement, who were ignored by Lalu Yadav finally came together and floated a new party, Janata Dal-United. Thirdly, the more the state was growing illegitimate, the more the people's aspirations were rising. All this was happening, perhaps, due to the growing politicisation of the masses by a highly competitive politics and thus, was making Lalu Yadav's failure more and more apparent.

Between 2000 and 2005 there were over a dozen caste massacres in which more than 100 lives were lost (see Appendix 3 for more details). There was also a sharp rise in general criminal offences in the state. The share of Bihar in the national crime graph showed a sharp spurt especially in dacoity, murder, kidnapping and abduction and even rape, and activities of the armed criminal gangs, big and small, became a hard reality. Between 1992 and 2005, the criminal gangs carried out a reported 30,000 kidnappings in the state.[154] This led to a very peculiar situation where the state, already a 'non-performer', now seemed to be 'non-existing' in all spheres.

In the meantime, the Patna High Court in a petition filed by an organisation, People's Watch, in 2004 passed an order that 'persons behind bars cannot contest elections'. But unfortunately, on the ground that the High Court had passed the order during the course of the election process, the Election Commission obtained a stay order on this judgement from the Supreme Court.[155] A year later when the state was to face another Assembly election in 2005, all the parties put together fielded about 28 per cent candidates with criminal charges that included murder, extortion, kidnapping and robbery.[156] In simpler words, cutting across party lines, one out of every four candidates in the fray had a criminal record. Every party has its own share of *bahubalis* (strongmen) and those who could not buy a ticket from any political party fought as independents.[157] Some of the important highlights of the results of the Bihar Assembly Election held in February 2005 were:[158]

- At the Rupauli Assembly seat in Purnea district the fight was held between the Lok Janshakti Party candidate Shankar Singh, the chief of the North Bihar Liberation Army, who had 26 cases of cognizable offences – including murder, conspiracy and dacoity pending against him and sitting independent MLA Beema Bharati, wife of Awadesh Mandal, leader of a dreaded Faizan gang, accused in several murder cases. The third candidate was Jai Kishan Mandal, who was locally known as the "father of all dons," contesting as an Independent.
- In the adjacent Dhamdaha constituency of the Purnea district again, the RJD's candidate, Dileep Yadav, was listed in seven cases and was charged under IPC and Arms Act. The prime rival was Lesi Singh, the wife of another history-sheeter Madhusudan Singh (Buttan Singh), who was killed in a gang war, on the JD(U) ticket.
- In Mokameh in Patna district, the battling dons were the JD(U) candidate Anant Kumar Singh, who while filing his nomination paper provided the details of his cases in a separate annexure due to lack of space; the RJD's Shyam Sunder Singh, against whom cases have been registered under several IPC Sections.
- In Bhabhua, there was Ramesh Tiwari, charged under Sections 307, 465 of the IPC among others, as an Independent candidate.
- Another well-known gangster Chitaranjan Singh, jailed in Jehanabad was fighting independently from Makhumpur. He had at least five murder charges and four attempts to murder pending against him, apart from other criminal cases.
- In Piro, the JD(U) had given its ticket to dreaded gangster Narendra Kumar Pandey, alias Sunil, jailed on charges of murder and kidnapping.
- In Nautan, alleged kidnapping kingpin Bhagariya's son, Amar Yadav, was contesting on the RJD's ticket.
- In Chanpatia, the BJP had picked the strongest muscleman in the area – Satish Chandra Dubey, who has listed four cases including murder.
- In Govindganj the LJP's selected Rajan Tiwari, who was the prime accused in the murder of the CPI (M) legislator Ajit Sarkar from Purnea. He had 10 other charges including murder.

- The LJP candidate Vijay Kumar Shukla, alias Munna Shukla, was listed in 17 cases including those of murder. Brother of dreaded north Bihar don Chotan Shukla, Munna was an accused in the murder of former Bihar Minister Brij Bihari Prasad and along with Rajan Tiwari and Suraj Bhan Singh, figured in several other cases in Bihar, including the murder of CPI (M) legislator Ajit Sarkar.
- The LJP had also fielded Ranjit Don from Hilsa in Nalanda, who was then in Beur Jail for leaking the CAT question-papers.
- From Siwan RJD MP Sahabuddin's protege Awadh Bihari Choudhury contested on a RJD ticket.
- Dhumal Singh, an LJP candidate was lodged in Buxar jail in the murder of Dhanbad's coal mafia kingpin Suraj Deo Singh. He was also accused in a number of extortion and murder cases, mostly in Jharkhand.
- Rama Kishore Singh, who was specialised in keeping kidnapping victims in safe custody and had links with kidnapping rackets across states was yet another LJP candidate who was contesting from Mahnar constituency.
- BJP nominated another *Bahubali* Nityanand Rai, from Hajipur.

Ram Vilas Paswan's Lok Janashakti Party (LJNSP) alone accounted for five of them. Except Rajan Tiwari – the prime accused in the murder of Ajit Sarkar, the CPM legislator from Purnea – all of Paswan's new recruits had qualified to be lawmakers in the state.[159] These numbers may seem less, but their participation in the election on nearly every political party's ticket and even independent, displays enough of the tyrannies of democracy. Lalu Yadav was defeated, but his style of politics continued.

Six months later, when the political situation of the state forced another assembly election, some of these dreaded criminals, including that of the LJNSP, switched sides and the opposition parties accepted them heartily. A galaxy of don-turned-politicians even brought in their wives into the political field keeping in mind the winnability factor.[160] All the winning criminal candidates were re-nominated.[161] Aruna Devi, wife of jailed gangster Akhilesh Singh and the sitting LJNSP MLA from Warsaliganj in Nawada district, was made a Congress nominee. The LJNSP, who was then left with less muscle power, brought in the new faces such as Punam Dev, wife of notorious criminal, popularly known for sharp shooting, Pappu Dev whose very name spells terror in Kosi region of north Bihar, from Bihpur. The victory margins of all these criminal-politicians remained very high.[162]

Even the President's rule in the state for a brief period in 2005, during which nearly 12,000 absconding criminals were arrested, could achieve anything substantial.[163] Officials continued to perform their duties not as a public-servant but only as puppets in the hands of their criminal-politician masters. Such was the situation in 2005 that an observer, after the Jehanabad jailbreak, remarked,

> A striking example of the state of governance ... is the regular occurrence of massacres, especially of Dalit agricultural labourers and other marginalised people. Almost all massacres become major headlines, but are soon forgotten ... . The Jehanabad jailbreak is a spectacular victory ... against the State. Besides drawing our attention to the ineptitude of the administration in Bihar ... it can be seen as a symbol of protest against an anti-poor system.[164]

In Sum

It is a little known fact that the powerful peasant movement in India that had its base in Bihar Provincial Kisan Sabha was actually the product of the efforts of Yadav peasants of Bihar. In 1927, they pleaded Sahajanand Saraswati to aid them in their struggles against the bhumihar-brahman zamindars of Masaurhi.[165] However their attempt to build a mass movement could not stand before the 'accommodation' strategy of the Congress.[166] It was thus, only in the 1970s that there emerged a backward class movement under the leadership of Ram Manohar Lohia and Karpoori Thakur in the state and Yadavs became the principle beneficiaries. Lalu Yadav came into power nearly a decade after that period built his social base on the foundations of this explosion. This was so strong that he became the unquestioned leader of the backward castes/classes in the state. He proved this not merely by words but by actions. Bihar saw the most dramatic rise of the backward caste MLAs and MPs in the post-Independent India only during his regime (see Figure 4.3). He also gave proportionate representation to the OBCs and SCs/STs in his ministries (see Table 4.6 below).

Table 4.6

Caste Composition (in percentage) of the Ministries in Bihar: 1990–2000

Year	*C.M.*	*Upper Caste*	*UBCs*	*LBCs*	*Muslim/ Bengali*	*SCs/ STs*	*Others*
1990–5	Lalu Yadav	27	35.2	11.3	11.3	15.5	0
1995–7	Lalu Yadav	n.a	n.a	n.a	n.a	n.a	n.a
1997–2000	Rabri Devi	17.1	51.31	6.58	11.84	13.16	—

Source: Jose J. Nedumpara, (2004). op. cit. p. 66; C. Jaffrelot, (2003). op. cit. p. 358; S.N. Choudhary, (1999). op. cit. pp. 219, 251.

Figure 4.3

Caste Background of Members of the Bihar Legislative Assembly: 1952–2005

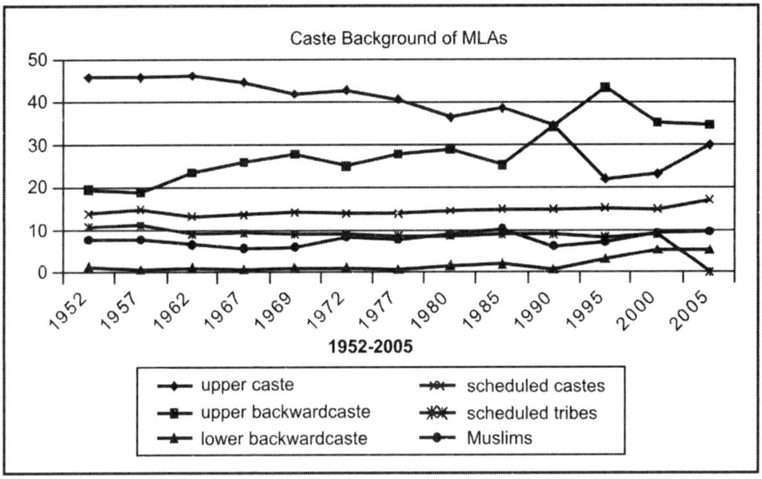

Source: Cyril Robin, (2009). op. cit. p. 100–1.

With the widespread support from these marginalised groups, Lalu Yadav made his electoral base appear insurmountable. He found and established the credible notion of "ijjat" closer to social justice than development. It was primarily for this reason that during the first term of his government, a popular JD slogan was "*vikaas nahin, samman chahiye*" (we want dignity, not development). Lalu Yadav, unlike many other OBC leaders, came from a family of near-landless cultivators, and he openly claimed to represent the the lower castes. In addition to that, Lalu Yadav, to further consolidate his position, promoted several lower backward caste leaders, and also increased the quotas for EBCs (officially termed 'Annexure I' castes within the system of reservations implemented by Karpoori Thakur in 1977) in government jobs from 10 per cent to 14. By consolidating his core support from the backward/lower caste groups, Lalu Yadav produced a formidable electoral alliance. In the expressions of V.P. Singh;

> The inexorable process of transfer of power to the deprived has begun ... Now the bid by the deprived sections in not for mere jobs or any other benefits of power, but to operate the levers of power itself. Nothing less. This represents a change in the very grammar of Indian politics ... . Bihar was my lab experiment of social justice. And under Lalu Yadav, it has been a success.[167]

Lalu Yadav also emerged as the most popular and trusted face of the anti-communal politics among Muslims against the venom of communalisation being spread by the BJP.

An important characteristic of Lalu Yadav's scheme to mobilise supporters, however, was that it was based more on identifying himself personally with their concerns than on initiating policies and programmes. More importantly, the state had hardly witnessed any effective governance. The Congress party in the state was engaged only in de-institutionalising the state apparatus and Lalu Yadav had no magic wand. By the time Lalu Yadav came to power, the state had become so obscured by the cliches of poverty, backwardness and de-institutionalisation that even significant initiatives ultimately proved insufficient for its economic transformation.

However, this cannot justify what Lalu Yadav's politics, or as this study refers to, 'politics as *Lalu Raj*' finally became known as. After all Lalu Yadav was elected for three consecutive terms and he therefore owes larger answers than anybody else. The political change that started in 1990 finally culminated into statelessness, polarisation along the caste lines and ultimately into a worse form of, to borrow Tilly and Tarrow's term, 'contentious politics'.[168]

Figure 4.4

Percentage of MLAs (Caste wise) among the Backward Caste Groups of the Bihar Legislative Assembly 1952–2005

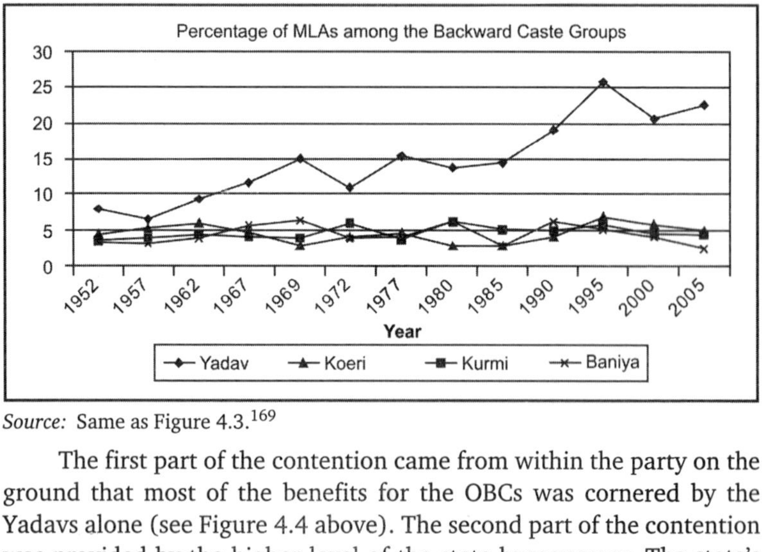

Source: Same as Figure 4.3.[169]

The first part of the contention came from within the party on the ground that most of the benefits for the OBCs was cornered by the Yadavs alone (see Figure 4.4 above). The second part of the contention was provided by the higher level of the state bureaucracy. The state's IAS officers primarily came from the four upper caste groups. One can imagine the upper caste domination in the highest level of the bureaucracy from the simple fact that despite the one and a half decades of the so-called "Yadav Raj" nearly 60 per cent of the IAS officers, until as recently as 2002 was from the four upper castes (See Table 4.7 below). Since Lalu Yadav threw an open challenge to the upper caste domination in society, the bureaucrats from these groups created an atmosphere of administrative non-cooperation. As discussed earlier, the extent of non-cooperation went so deep that between the 1991 and 1995, 144 out of 384 IAS officers sought Central deputation. Most of them did not work seriously and some even joined hands with the opposition and passed not only official secrets but also a good deal of disinformation to the press to harm the regime. Thus, Lalu Yadav was forced to use his discretionary powers. He started placing his own men in key districts as district magistrates. In 1995, while the upper castes were brought to work (in the state Secretariat in 110 out of 113 positions), 30 out of 50 IAS from the OBCs, Muslims, or SCs were given postings in the districts.

Table 4.7

Caste Break-up of Bihar IAS Cadre in 2002

Caste	*Total*	*From Bihar*	*Other States*
Kayasthas	54	47	7
Brahmins	60	38	22
Rajputs	22	17	5
Bhumihars	7	6	1
SCs	25	8	17
STs	7	0	7
Banias	15	4	11
Muslims	10	9	1
Yadavs	4	4	0
Kurmis	3	3	0
Christians	3	0	3
Sikhs	2	0	2
Jains	2	0	2
Backward	9	4	5
Unidentified	21	—	—
Total	244	—	—

Source: Source: Witsoe (2006:23).[170]

In the meantime, the movement of the landless under the banner of Naxalism grew more and more violent in response to the barbarity of the upper/dominant caste armies. With the state power on the latter's side, a widespread conflict became inevitable.

Lalu Yadav's astute political commitment to 'grass root democracy' by adopting people's language without confirming to the 'rule of law' brought the state closer to a reign of 'participatory autocracy'. He succumbed to his self-defined political acumen and failed to learn and listen to the demands of the movements from below that actually had shaped up in his initial years, when his revolutionary élan was still high. Instead, it favoured the use of increasing participation merely as a means to legitimise the illegitimate. Lalu Yadav failed to understand that in the age of 'hegemonic modernism' his notional interpretation of social justice alone could not survive for long.

Figure 4.5

Contentious Politics of Bihar

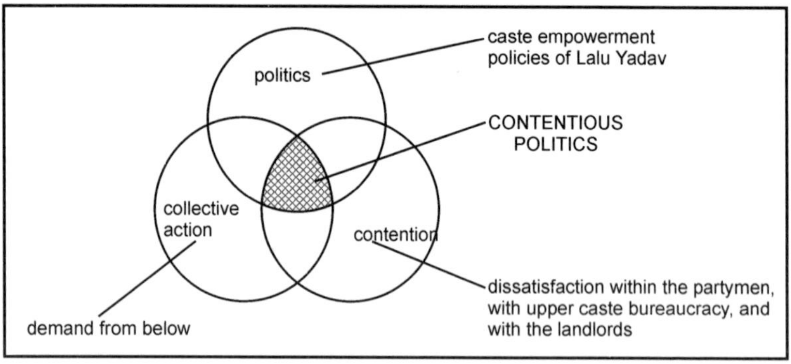

The contentious environment opened up more and more space for crime and affected the governance of the state adversely, culminating ultimately in a 'tyranny of democracy'. The practice of using criminals for booth-capturing and bullying on election-day for career-politicians had become very common since the early days of the Republic, but criminals choosing politics as a means to avoid punishment, now became the order of the day. Thus, as argued in Chapter 2, although the phenomenon of criminalisation of politics and the uncoupling of the crime-punishment link started as early as the days of *zamindari* abolition days, the new marriage between crime and non-punishment was sanctified only in the post-1990 era. With the state failing to have created an atmosphere of security and development and to have satisfied the growing needs of the increasing population from different caste and categories, the masses lost interest in continuing to operate in accordance with the rule of law, and started parading behind the criminals, voting them to power to get their demands fulfilled outside the state's institutional structure, thus making crime a political necessity and the 'tyranny of democracy' beyond repair. The socially injurious and parasitic elements in politics, finally led the non-performer state give way to being 'non-existent'.

In the words of dalit/lower backward caste labourers who spoke to me during an informal group discussion in Purnea,

> *Isme koi shak nahi hai ki Lalu ji ne hume ek aisi 'ijjat ki ziandagi' di jo humare dada-pardadaon ne kabhi socha tak nahi tha. Vo hum sabo ke liye lade. Unke aane se hum sab me ek umeed jagi. Unhone humse bahut se vaade kiye aur bahuto ko pura karne ki koshish bhi ki. Lekin yeh sub keval ek tarfa nahi tha. Humne bhi Lalu ji ko 15 saal tak raj karne ka mauqa diya. Par jeevan keval vadon par nahi tika reh sakta. Ijjat ki zindagi ke saath saath hume roti bhi to chahiye tha. Unhone na to hume zameen ka koi haq dilaya na hi koi rozgaar. Lalu ji un 15 salon me bhool gaye ki vo keval Yadavo ke neta nahi the, humne bhi unko utna hi samman diya tha. Par galti shayad humari hi thi ki humne unpar andha vishwas kiya. Pandrah saal me sab jadav Brahman ban gaye. Humare jaan-maal ki suraksha tak ki koi guarantee nahi rahi. Oonchi jati ke Zamindar logo ki chalti to band ho gayi, par rangdar, chahe vo kisi bhi jati ka ho, unki chalti badhti chali gayi. Prashashan ke naam par keval gundaraaj reh gaya.* (There is no doubt that Lalu Yadav provided us with a life of dignity which our forefathers did not ever imagine. He became a voice for each of us. He gave us hope, made promises and even tried to fulfil many of those. But it was not a one sided affair. We also gave Lalu ji an opportunity to rule the state for fifteen years. But life is not all about hopes and promises. What did we ultimately get? Lalu ji, in all these 15 years forgot that he was not representing Yadavs alone. We too had shown equal respect for him. But perhaps the mistake was ours that we trusted him blindly. In the last fifteen years all the Yadavs have turned into Brahmins. We lost even our right to live safely. Though the upper caste landlords lost their power, they were taken over by the ganglords, of whichever caste they belong to. On the name of administration there remained only the rule of the mafias)

Notes

1. *Constituent Assembly Debates,* Vol. IX, New Delhi, Lok Sabha Secretariat, p. 979.
2. See A.N. Das, (1992). op. cit. pp. 34–6. In 1989, when A.N. Sinha's son, S.N. Sinha became the chief minister, the son of the Kursela Raja, Dinesh Singh was given important political positions. Thus, speaking on land reforms was out of bound.
3. See Ramashray Roy, (1995). 'Bihar' in Sadhna Singh (ed.), *Caste Politics in India,* New Delhi, Mittal Publications, pp. 91–117.

4. For more details see, A.N. Das, (1992). op. cit. p. 36.
5. K.S. Narayanan et al. (1998). 'A Commission a Day', *Outlook,* April 13, URL: http://www.outlookindia.com/article.aspx?205351, accessed last on April 15 2008.
6. In 1967, Congress had been reduced to minority in as many as nine states (all northern Indian states) including Bihar, for details see Chapter 2.
7. See Cyril Robin, (2009). 'Bihar: The New Stronghold of OBC Politics' in Christophe Jaffrelot and Sanjay Kumar, *Rise of the Plebians? The Changing Face of Indian Legislative Assemblies,* New Delhi, Routledge, pp. 65–102.
8. See Atul Kohli, (1992). op. cit. p. 215–6.
9. Arun Sinha, (1977). 'Violence Against the Poor', *Economic and Political Weekly,* Vol. XII, No. 15, p. 5.
10. For a deeper analysis, see Rajni Kothari, 1988a. 'Democracy and Fascism in India' in his book *State Against Democracy,* New Delhi, Ajanta Publications, pp. 282–98.
11. In recorded statements in the court of a munsif magistrate; as cited in Arun Sinha, (1977). 'Violence Against the Poor' op. cit.
12. Ibid.
13. The continuing spree of landlord-police nexus over the landless during Karpoori Thakur's regime has been well documented by Arun Sinha by his various writings during those years, some of which are. 'Landlords on Rampage in Champaran', *Economic and Political Weekly,* Vol. XII, No. 39, (September 1977), p. 1671; 'Police, Politicians and Hoodlooms', *Economic and Political Weekly,* Vol. XII, No. 40, (October 1977), p. 1605; 'Police to Landlord's Aid', *Economic and Political Weekly,* Vol. XII, No. 49, (December 3, 1977), pp. 1999–2000; 'Murder of a Peasant Leader', *Economic and Political Weekly,* Vol. XII, No. 31, (December 10, 1977), p. 2098; 'The Killing Continues', *Frontier,* (October 15–20, 1977); 'Bajitpur: Landlord's Violence' *Economic and Political Weekly,* Vol. XIII, No. 50, (16 December 1978).
14. As expressed by the people during the field work.
15. Ibid. However, there existed a sub-classification among the OBCs and the reservation was decided in such a way that those backwards scheduled in 'Annexure I' were allotted 12 per cent of the posts; those under 'Annexure II" were allocated 8 per cent, 3 per cent to women of any group, and 3 per cent to those who were 'economically backward'.
16. See Christophe Jaffrelot, (2003). *India's Silent Revolution: The Rise of Lower Castes in North India,* London, Hurst and Company, p. 317.

17. For a seminal analysis, see Harry W Blair, (1980). 'Rising Kulaks and Backward Classes in Bihar: Social Change in the Late 1970s', *Economic and Political Weekly*, Vol. 15, No. 2, January 12, pp. 64–74.
18. Harry W. Blair, (1980). op. cit. The reason perhaps, Blair suggests, was embedded in the caste affiliations of Indira Gandhi and the Emergency period chief minister of Bihar, Jagannath Mishra, both of whom were Brahmins. The voters in some sense held the Brahmins responsible for the 'excesses' committed. The backward castes specially the Yadavs by 1977 had become the second largest group in the Assembly, next only to the Rajputs.
19. For details on caste of the chief ministers see Appendix 2.
20. Ibid.
21. See Arun Sinha, (1978). 'Politics of Panchayat Election', *Economic and Political Weekly,* Vol. XIII, No. 24, pp. 982–983. Initially the high caste group had opposed the Panchayat elections tooth and nail. Hundreds of writs were filed in the Patna High Court to stall the elections. In fact, the Patna High Court had stalled election in 500 out of 11, 740 panchayats and ordered that in view of a large number of petitions pouring in, a division bench be constituted to examine the whole matter. However, the government, a day before the polls were to begin, held an extraordinary meeting and decided to promulgate an ordinance prohibiting people from rushing to the courts to get the elections stayed.
22. See M.L. Majumdar, (2005). *Emerging Grassroots Power: A Critique on Elections to the Panchayats and the Municipalities in Bihar,* New Delhi, Concept Publishing Company, pp. 66–92.
23. For details see Correspondent's story, (1978). 'Towards Village Autocracy' in *Economic and Political Weekly,* July 22, Vol XIII., No. 29, pp 1166–67.
24. Indu Bharati, (1989d). 'Decay in Gram Panchayat', *Economic and Political Weekly,* January 7, pp 18–19. Bharati writes that the situation of panchayat has come to such a pass that even to dig a tube well in a village it was the MLA and not the panchayat authorities who decided its place of installation.
25. See Sankarshan Thakur, (2000). *The Making of Lalu Yadav: The Unmaking of Bihar.* New Delhi, Harper Collins Publishers India, pp. 65–7.
26. Atul Kohli, (1992). op. cit. p. 223.
27. A.N. Das, (1992). op. cit.
28. A.N. Das, (1986). 'Landowners' Armies Take over 'Law and Order", *The Economic and Political Weekly.* January 4, pp. 15–8.
29. Atul Kohli, (1992). op. cit. p. 224. Kohli further writes that in 1986 when the civil rights groups were protesting against the poor

handling of the Arawal massacre, the government unleashed a police terror on them and arrested nearly 30,000 people in a day.

30. Dalits/agricultural labourers were holding a meeting to demand the release of one of their men in Arwal police station. But the police surrounded the assembly and opened fire on the unarmed innocent people. Scores of people got killed and hundreds were left injured. As informed by informants during my fieldwork at several places in the state.
31. For more details, see Indu Bharati, 1989d. op. cit. p. 19. Bharati writes, 'As late as in May 1988, a senior member of the Jha cabinet Bhisma Prasad Yadav, announced that the panchayat polls would be held before the end of November 1988. It went even a step further to announce that his government was intended to empower the gram panchayats to collect the full amount of land revenue instead of giving them a share of 6.25 per cent as was practiced then. However, in early November the same year, Yadav announced that the polls could not be held.
32. Ibid. The Bihar government, headed by Bindeshwari Dubey, a year before had got promulgated an Ordinance seeking to reserve the posts of *Mukhiyas* for SCs and STs. The Ordinance was challenged in the Patna High Court which then declared it unconstitutional. Consequently the government moved a writ petition in the Supreme Court challenging the High Court judgment. Since the matter was sub-judice, the government declared that the polls could not be held.
33. Ram Darshanachari, the president of the Bihar Rajya Panchayat Sewak Shangha, as quoted in Indu Bharati, 1989d. Ibid., Indu Bharati, (1989b). 'Making Up with the Mafia', *Economic and Political Weekly* October 14, pp. 2290–91.
34. Ibid.
35. Ibid. They secured bail and stay orders against most charges levelled against them and challenged the Ordinance in the Patna High Court.
36. Indu Bharti, (1989b). op. cit. Bharati writes: 'at the Congress Legislative Party meeting it was declared that Azad had to resign and S.N. Sinha, the nominee of the high command, would takeover. Jagannath Mishra, the former CM also advised the members to honour the wishes of the high command, since the main demand for removal of Azad was conceded. Azad then proposed Sinha's name as the new leader of the CLP. No other proposal naturally was put forward and the 'unanimous' election at the "orders of Rajiv Gandhi" was done. It would be pertinent to point out here that since an overwhelming majority, 140 out of the total of 189 Congress MLAs had demanded Azad's ouster as early as in January, Azad should himself have resigned the moment it became known that he did not

enjoy the majority support. In such a situation, going by the constitutional provisions and requirements of parliamentary democracy, a simple meeting of the CLP was all that was needed to elect a new leader. But, the Congress style of democracy does not permit these democratic practices.'

37. Indu Bharti, (1989b). op, cit. A cabinet minister in the state from 1961 to 1967, Sinha declined to go with Indira Gandhi and preferred to remain in the Congress-O. In 1977, however, when the Congress-O merged with the Janata Party, he became the state Janata Party president grooming his desire to become the chief minister. But when the Janata Party won the 1977 Assembly elections, Karpoori Thakur became the CM. Sinha walked over to the Congress once again in 1983.
38. Ibid. The four petitions were listed by the chief justice of the High Court Justice D.K. Sen, for hearing before a division bench comprising the C.J. himself and two other judges. The C.J. then went on leave and was scheduled to return in April. But in an unusual move the acting chief justice, S.K. Jha referred the petitions to a bench of three judges on March 29 and ordered that they be listed for hearing the very next day – March 30, just a day before chief justice Sen was to resume his duties. Justice Jha's explanation for this was, that the C.J. was to retire very soon (at the end of April) and that the petitioners were making daily pleas for quick hearing.
39. Ibid. See Indu Bharti, (1989c). 'Bihar Crisis: Making of a CM', *Economic and Political Weekly*, April 8, pp. 715–16.
40. The BJP's performance has been an unprecedented one, as the BJP and the erstwhile Jana Sangh had never been able to secure more than 2 seats. In 1984 it had lost all the seats it had contested and secured second position in six constituencies, all of which it won this time. Source: http://www.eci.nic.in
41. The Left parties had never secured more than five seats, normally all by the CPI. This time the CPI improved on its 1984 performance. The MCC (Marxist Co-ordination Committee) leader A.K. Roy, won from Dhanbad. The two constituencies, Arrah and Nawadah, were given to the Indian People's Front and the CPM respectively, and both won their respective constituencies.
42. For details see Indu Bharti, (1989a). 'Rearranged Political Mosaic', *Economic and Political Weekly* December 9, pp. 2698–2701.
43. A.N. Das, (1992). op. cit.
44. Indu Bharti, (1989a). op. cit.
45. Ibid.
46. For details, see Indu Bharti, (1990c). 'Election-Eve Promises', *The Economic and Political Weekly*, February 17–24, pp. 372–73. In 1956,

the state government had imposed a nominal educational, health and agricultural cess on big industrial houses. But the Tata Iron and Steel Company (TISCO, now Tata Steel) and other establishments of the Tata group did not even pay a single penny on this count. However, the Mishra government, after coming to power not only waived the entire amount accruing to the state exchequer from the Tatas, but also freed them forever from this nominal cess. Though Mishra had said that the due cess, which was waived, was only ₹ 5 crore, according to some knowledgeable sources quoted by Bharati, this was a gross underestimate and placed the actual waiver to be of the order of a few hundred crores. Apart from this, Mishra announced several other concessions to his industrial friends. Priority was given to private units establishing industries in the state. Letters of intent issued to and the approval given to public undertakings for establishing industries was transferred to the private sector and it was decide that they would be provided 15 to 20 per cent capital grant by the government. While giving these big concessions, Mishra had entirely forgotten how one big house had been robbing Bihar of hundreds of crores in sales tax and did not deem it fit to impose a condition on the big houses to stop such robbery. In a big boost to the transport mafia Mishra decide to abolish the system of permits for operating buses.

47. Ibid.
48. Ibid.
49. Ibid.
50. Ibid.
51. Indu Bharti, (1990b). 'Bihar Elections: Violence Inevitable', *Economic and Political Weekly*, March 3, p. 429.
52. Ibid.
53. Ibid.
54. In a total of 324 assembly seats Janata Dal got 122 seats, Congress won 71, BJP bagged 39 seats, CPI won 23, CPM won 6, JMM won 19 seats and independents got 30.
55. As informed by Arun Kamble in a personal interview to the author in New Delhi.
56. As informed by Arun Kamble in a personal interview to the author in Mumbai.
57. Ibid. Also see Ajit Sahi, (2009). 'The Gangster Last Gamble, *Tehelka Magazine,* Vol 6, Issue 20, Dated May 23. URL: http://www.tehelka.com/story_main41.asp?filename=Ne230509the_gangster.asp
58. Indu Bharti, (1990a). 'Bihar: New Government, New Hope' *Economic and Political Weekly* June 30, pp. 1373–4.

59. Ibid.
60. Ibid.
61. Faizan Ahmad, (1992). 'Riot Force Rushed to Sitamarhi' October 10. accessed at URL: http://www. indiarightsonline.com/Sabrang/relipolcom81–90.nsf/5e7647d942f529c9e5256c3100376e2e/68cebf5 139 e22c90e5256d500034a95c/$FILE/ced04822.pdf
62. In a personal interview in April 2008.
63. Indu Bharti, (1990a). op. cit.
64. It was an established practice that on the last month of each financial year, unspent amounts used to be gobbled up by the officials and contractors through juggling of accounts. Ibid.
65. See Indu Bharti, (1990a). op. cit
66. See Indu Bharti, (1991a). 'Fighting the Irrigation Mafia in Bihar', *Economic and Political Weekly,* September 21, pp. 2185–87. For instance, the Kosi project: Every year ₹ 5 crore was being paid to the contractors to carry out just the desiltation work and a few crore more for the repair of the embankments. But hardly any work was ever done. As a result, the Kosi barrage always stood as a threat. If the water flow was increased the barrage was endangered and if it was decreased the siltation got increased. The embankment had a capacity to sustain the pressure of 9 lakh cusecs of water, as was seen during the devastating floods of 1964–65. But the case of breach in 1991 showed that it could not sustain even the pressure of 1.5 lakh cusecs of water. The irrigation capacity of the Kosi project, which was supposed to revolutionise agriculture in north Bihar, was reduced from 8 lakh hectares to 2.5 lakh hectares. And yet, year after year this sordid charade of desiltation and repairs continued to be kept on and on. For more details on the embankments in the river Kosi, see Chapter 3.
67. A tradition begun by Jagannath Mishra. It is widely alleged that Mishra perfected the business of percentages and transfer/postings of engineers (already discussed above). 'There was a perfect system of percentages in which there was a share for everyone that mattered right from the minister to the junior engineer. The actual expenditure never exceeded 30 per cent of the budgeted cost and after doling out the fixed percentages, the contractors were able to pocket as much as 25 per cent of the sanctioned amount. A part of this was used to finance their pet politicians so that they would get the next projects as well. Thus the cycle went on. The contractors' bills were paid without verifying them. The same lot of boulders and craters were shown as freshly purchased year after year and the government exchequer was duped of crores. Many of the desiltation, repair and maintenance works shown to have been completed were never done at all and yet payments were made all in advance'. See Ibid.

68. Ibid. He ordered the seizure of boulders, crates and other flood fighting materials at the sites. The contractors used to mint money by showing the same material to have been supplied year after year. More than 4 lakh sqft of boulders were seized in the process. He also started reviewing the work being done by the contractors and ongoing projects, which were loaded with unnecessary details and specifications just for the sake of minting money.
69. Ibid. There were several such cases. But one such case that needs special mention was Durgawati project. The estimated cost for this project was slashed by about two-thirds. Even for a minor job like dewatering the small Ajay Barrage was shown to cost as much as ₹ 44 lakh, for which the contractors got full payment even before the completion of the work. Similarly, another contractor specialising in drought works had submitted a bill of ₹ 52 lakh for no reason and had already been paid ₹ 12 lakh. The minister stopped payment of the remaining amount.
70. Ibid. Jagdanand in his effort to break the engineer-contractor-politician nexus started looking at the postings of the engineers. Though rules said that after three-year stint in 'works', an engineer has to be posted in a non-works job for the next three years, Jagdanand found that several engineers continued to be posted in 'works' for more than 10 years. Postings of some 5,000 engineers were found to be in contravention of the rules. Jagadanand transferred all these engineers as per the rules. For sanctioning fake bills without the completion of work, he dismissed, one chief engineer, 11 superintending engineers, 43 executive engineers and 251 assistant engineers. To break the monopoly of the irrigation mafia Jagadanand started enforcing the gradation system for award of contracts. Big contractors registered in the grade of ₹ 5 crore used to bag contracts of even of ₹ 50,000. Jagdanand stopped this practice. He established a system where a contractor could try for a contract just one grade below his classification. Through a move to renew the registration of the contractors in the water resources, it was found that as many as 1,510 contractor firms were fake. These firms had been bagging contracts for the last 15–20 years and were being run on paper by big contractors for cornering all contracts. All these firms were duly black-listed. Besides as many as 20 of the biggest construction companies were also black-listed on charges of misappropriation of crores of public money.
71. For details, see Indu Bharti, (1991a). op. cit.
72. Ibid. "Contractors of the Balua Bazar family (close to Jagannath Mishra's family) were also gunning for Jagadanand as, he not only had refused to pay fake bills submitted by them but also got show-cause notices served on them to explain their position in the

light of the existing rules which debarred foreign citizens from undertaking contract works in India, unless a specific global tender was floated for some work. Some of the contractors, namely, Tripti Narain Jha, Tula Nath Jha, Kalanand Jha, Upendra Jha, Shyam Sunder Prasad, Badri Narain Yadav, Sharda Prasad Giri and owners of H.S. Construction, Anand Construction, Gaurishankar Construction and Taishiv Constructions were Nepali citizens of Indian origin, and had been doing contract work in the Kosi project in Bihar for years. However, Lalu Yadav decided to stand by his man and refused to accept Jagadanand's resignation.

73. Indu Bharti, (1990a). op. cit. When his government took over in April 1990, only 250 MW was being generated out of an installed capacity of 1,310 MW in the state. In just two months, the power generation in the state got more than doubled. It also detected another malpractice which was causing the state exchequer a loss of ₹ 60,000 daily. The Bihar government had an agreement with the Damodar Valley Corporation (DVC) that 66 per cent of the power generated by the DVC would be supplied to the state and the rest to others. The DVC had agreed to supply power to the government at the rate of 70 paise per unit, and the government sold it at ₹ 1.20 per unit to commercial consumers to recover the establishment and distribution costs. However, due to the collusion of the Congress leaders, officials and the DVC, Tisco was getting power from the DVC at the rate of 70 paise per unit, thereby defrauding the government of ₹ 60,000 daily. Lalu Yadav government not only rescinded the previous government's decision to write off the cess due from Tisco (now Tata Steel) but also scrapped its exemption from paying the cess in the future.
74. Ibid. Hundreds of illegal appointments were detected in the Bihar School Examination Board and that led to the arrest of its chairman. Another 700 illegal appointments were detected in the state Intermediate Council and an enquiry was ordered against its chairman. The VCs were told either to improve the functioning of the universities or to resign. Technical institutions, run by the powerful education mafia who were mostly Congress heavyweights, were banned. The action of the Mishra government to run six universities as the sub-centres of the existing universities was ordered for a review and all budgetarys were cancelled.
75. Ibid.
76. Indu Bharti, (1991c). 'Survival against Heavy Odds', *Economic and Political Weekly,* January 19, pp. 91–3.
77. *India Today*, 31 October, 1990.
78. For more details see, Chapter 6. Also see Indu Bharati, (1991c). op. cit.

79. Ibid. However, "the chief minister instead of indulging in backroom manoeuvring decided to take the bull by the horns and lost no time in getting 10 Janata Dal MLAs including Jha and Singh expelled from the party for anti-party activities."
80. See Editorial, (1991). 'Bihar Drama', *Economic and Political Weekly*, May 11, p. 1187
81. Indu Bharati, (1991c). op. cit.
82. Ibid. Mishra held three meetings with the Prime Minister Chandra Shekhar to persuade him to dismiss the Lalu Yadav's ministry. However, Lalu Yadav once again decided to accept this challenge head on, and asked the governor to convene the Assembly so that he could prove his majority on the floor of the House. The house was convened on November 22, 1990 and he won the vote of confidence with a comfortable majority of 202–108 (BJP abstained from voting). But this was not enough for the Mishra-Jha combine. On 21st November 1990 when V.P. Singh was to reach Patna, they took to some nefarious tactics. They orchestrated stone-throwing at their own residences during V.P. Singh's visit and started demanding for imposition of President's rule citing the deteriorating law and order situation. The arrangement was so cleverly managed that two Union ministers visited the state and said that the "Centre was considering the imposition of President's rule in the state".
83. Lalu Yadav had started with only 11 ministers in the cabinet.
84. For details see Ravindra Kumar Verma and Nihora Prasad Yadav, (1991). 'Caste and Candidate Selection: Lok Sabha Poll in Bihar', *Economic and Political Weekly*, June 1–8, pp. 1376–8. "The overall caste-wise examination of the candidates showed that the largest share for any single caste was that of the Yadavas followed by Rajputs. Of the candidates of these parties 17.5 per cent belonged to the Yadava caste and 13.6 per cent to the Rajput caste. These two castes accounted for nearly half the candidates of their respective caste clusters or groups. The population of Yadavas in Bihar at that time was 14.6 per cent and that of Rajputs 5.9 per cent. Of the total candidates belonging to the forward castes group, Brahmins constituted 8.7 per cent, Bhumihars 7.8 per cent and Kayasthas 3.9 per cent compared to the 13.6 per cent share of Rajputs. Among the other backward castes group other than Yadavas-Kurmi, Koiri, Bania, Mallah, etc., were the major constituents. While only the Yadavas' share in the tickets was 17.5 per cent, that of the non-Yadavas, all together was16.3 per cent only."
85. Ibid. The Congress allotted 38.9 per cent of its tickets to the forward castes, of which 11.1 per cent had gone to Brahmins, 13 per cent to Bhumihars, 13 per cent to Rajputs and 1.8 per cent to Kayasthas. It had provided 25.9 per cent of tickets to the OBC group, of which 9.3

per cent had gone to Yadavas and 16.6 per cent to non-Yadav OBCs. It also had provided 14.8 per cent tickets to scheduled castes and 9.3 per cent to scheduled tribes. The Congress Party had given 11.1 per cent of its tickets to Muslims. A big chunk of Congress nominees were from the forward castes, mainly Brahmins, Bhumihars and Rajputs. However, the party could not avoid giving a substantial share to the Yadavas. Like the Congress, the BJP too had provided the largest chunk of tickets to the forward castes (44.4%). Out of the total, 14.8 per cent tickets had gone to Brahmins, 13 per cent to Bhumihars, 11.1 per cent to Rajputs and 5.5 per cent to Kayasthas. The share of the OBC group in BJP candidates amounted to 31.5 per cent, the largest share of which had gone to Yadavas (14.8%) followed by Banias (7.4%), Koiris (5.5%) and Kurmis and Mallahs (1.9% each). The BJP had allotted 14.8 per cent seats to the scheduled castes and 9.3 per cent to the scheduled tribes. It is notable that the BJP did not provide any ticket to the Muslim community, though the party gave one ticket to a Christian nominee.

86. During the 1990 Assembly elections this seat was won by the Janata Dal candidate, Ramsunder Das. However, Das was subsequently elected to the Lok Sabha, and had to leave his Vidhan Sabha seat. In the November 1991 assembly by-election, Congress(I) fielded Hemant Sahi, the son of a veteran Congress leader L.P. Sahi. Mr Sahi, with the support of his lumpens, had proved to be more resourceful and skilful in booth capturing than his rivals and won the election very comfortably. However, he was killed in March 1992, in a fight over procuring a contract for one of his men. For more details on the murder of Sahi, see Vikas Kumar Jha, (1996). *Bihar: Criminalization of Politics*', (translated in English by Ruby Roy), Patna, Srishti Prakashan, p. 97–100.
87. See Krishna Chaitanya, (1992). 'Emerging Upper Caste Alliance', *Economic and Political Weekly,* July 25, pp. 1595–6.
88. Ibid.
89. Ibid.
90. Indu Bharti, (1991c). op. cit.
91. A post-modern school, which argues that it is not impossible for those who occupy non-marginalised positions to become part of the process and help understand a critical consciousness with respect to the effects of power structures on epistemic production.
92. For details see R.K. Yadav 'Ravi', (2004). op. cit. p. 77.
93. Ibid. pp. 74–8.
94. This was particularly in those villages of central Bihar where the IPF had put up a commendable performance in the 1989–90 elections.
95. Indu Bharati, (1991). Lok Sabha Elections: Message from Bihar, *Economic and Political Weekly,* August 17, p. 1896.

96. Ibid.
97. Mukul, (1992). 'Bihar's Land Liberation Struggles', *Economic and Political Weekly* August 22, pp. 1780–81. This evoked on the ground, several land struggles, some of them, even bloody. Thousands of sharecroppers were evicted by landlords and an activisation of landlords' armies and mafia started taking place. One important example was that of the Kahalgaon subdivision of Bhagalpur district, where the movement had taken its own course, different from the struggle over agricultural land. In Chetharia Peer, another place near Kahalgaon town, where the displaced villagers from Bakia diara, Toffir diara and Jatooya diara 'liberated' one acre of land in 1991 and built more than 40 houses, the landlord, a businessmen, conspired and the whole new basti was burnt to ashes in 1992. In Sulaiman Pahar too, when the landless liberated the 2.5 acres of Bihar government land grabbed since long by a local businessman, they started terrorising the villagers. Near about 300 houses were built there in a short span of three years. The land liberation movement took quite an organised form with the active party support. One successful event supported the other and a series of demonstrations, rallies, dharnas started being organised to challenge the onslaught of businessmen, landlords and the police.
98. The other causes mentioned in the report were communal situation arising out of the Ram Janmabhoomi-Babri Masjid issue, tribal unrest stemming from the demand for a separate Jharkhand state and the situation on the Indo-Nepal border.
99. Krishna Chaitanya, (1991). 'Social Justice, Bihar Style', *Economic and Political Weekly*, November 16, p. 2612.
100. Harish Dhawan, (1991). 'Letter to the Editor: "Landlord-Police Nexus in Bihar"', *Economic and Political Weekly*, April 20, p. 1006.
101. Amaresh Misra, (1994). 'Changing Peasant Struggle', *Economic and Political Weekly*, May 7, pp. 1111–12
102. Ibid.
103. Christophe Jaffrelot, (2003). op. cit. p. 381; also see Indu Sinha and Arvind Sinha, (1996). 'Setback to Political Arrogance' *Economic and Political Weekly*, June 29, pp. 1650–52
104. Barrington Moore Jr., (1978). *Injustice: The Social Bases of Obedience and Revolt,* New York, Sharpe.
105. For a seminal analysis see Sanjay Kumar, (1999). 'New Phase in Backward Caste Politics in Bihar, 1990–2000', *Economic and Political Weekly,* 34 (34–5), August, pp. 2472–80.
106. See Editorial, (1994). 'Aroused Aspirations', *Economic and Political Weekly,* November 5–12. p. 2889.
107. Ibid.; also see Indu Sinha and Arvind Sinha, (1996). op. cit.

108. Indu Sinha and Arvind Sinha, 1996. op. cit.
109. Tilak D. Gupta, 1995. 'Elections with a Difference', *Economic and Political Weekly, April 15, pp 789–792.*
110. Editorial, 1994. 'Aroused Aspirations', op. cit.
111. Saroor Ahmad, 2000. 'The Cost of an Election in Bihar: Few Score Lives', *Rediff News,* Patna, URL: http://www.rediff.com/news/2000/feb/07bihar.htm, accessed last on 22nd January 2009. Also see Mammen Mathew, 1995. 'Don-Sayers on Mat' *Hindustan Times,* Patna, April 3, (Monday extra); and S.K. Sinha, 1995. 'Bihar, Poll and Seshan' *Hindustan Times,* (Patna), April 3; S.K. Ghosh, 2000. 'Elections: Mafia Gangs and the Guns', in his book *Bihar in Flames,* op. cit. pp. 47–53.
112. Ibid.
113. T.N. Seshan introduced the concept of a Voter-id card in India in 1995.
114. Tilak D. Gupta, (1995). op. cit.
115. For a seminal analysis, see Alakh Narayan Sharma, (1995). 'Policy Economic of Poverty in Bihar', *Economic and Political Weekly,* Vol. 30, No. 41/42, Oct. 14–21, pp. 2587–2602. Sharma and some other observers use the expression 'withering away of the state' to indicate its dysfunctional nature. But because this expression has a specific Marxist connotation and has its origin in a completely different political context, I have tried to avoid using this expression in my work. The author owes this suggestion to Professor Suranjan Das and Professor Manoranjan Mohanty.
116. See S.N. Choudhary, (1999). *Power-Dependence Relations: Struggle for Hegemony in Rural Bihar,* New Delhi, Har Anand, p. 262.
117. See Editorial, (1996). 'Covering Up Corruption', *Economic and Political Weekly',* December 28, p. 3341.
118. Victor Das, (1991). 'Bihar Teachers' Struggle for Rights', *Economic and Political Weekly',* January 5–12, p. 22.
119. Ibid.
120. A.K. Roy, (1995). 'Industrialising Bihar: The Options', *Economic and Political Weekly,* July 29, pp. 1902–03. The government never came out with a white paper on industries in Bihar giving all the relevant information so that proper guidelines could be framed. According to Roy, 'mere announcing an ambitious target of securing investment of ₹ 15,000 crore in the state by industrialists could not had brought change in reality. The fact was that the JD government in its rule since 1990, never made an attempt to get a report about the number of industrial units running in the state and those lying sick or closed, the causes of sickness, the amount of capital blocked and the number

of persons unemployed as a result .... A report in 1996 said that out of 325 big and medium industrial units in Bihar 67 had been referred to the BIFR and of these 17 had been recommended for sale, including Heavy Engineering Corporation (HEC) of Ranchi. But these 67 apart, the condition of the other units was not known. Similarly, out of 1,66,000 small-scale, including handicraft, units, about 49.000 were lying closed. Generally, South Bihar was known for industry and north Bihar for agriculture. But, even in north Bihar, industrial estates had been established in every district with Muzaffarpur, as the headquarter. Thousands of acres of land were acquired and crores of rupees of loans had been advanced. But these 'industrial gardens' had withered away and the industrial units were lying closed. For prescribing the correct economic and political remedies the condition of the patient must be known .... Lalu Yadav without even thinking on these lines had decided to embark on a foreign tour to attract capital ... this decision of Lalu Yadav was far from reality ... . There were 59 industrial units in the state public sector with a capital investment of ₹ 3,000 crore, apart from land and other immovable properties. There were also outstanding loans of ₹ 1,200 crore to them. The losses of these public sector units till then had exceeded ₹ 1,000crore. The sick public sector industrial units included the prestigious Sindri superphosphate factory, the electrical equipment factory in Ranchi, the scooters projects and the silk mills in Bhagalpur and the Rohtas Industries of Dalmianagar producing many things of public utility. The government was looking for buyers or, more appropriately, scrap dealers to dispose of these units without exercising its mind over rehabilitating them. In the government's ₹ 2,500 crore Plan budget there was no mention of any spending on those'.

121. See K.P. Joseph, (1997). 'Lessons from Fodder Scam' *Economic and Political Weekly*, July 12, pp. 1686–7
122. Ibid.
123. Ibid.
124. Binoy S. Prasad, (1997). 'General Elections, 1996: Major Role of Caste and Social Factions in Bihar', *Economic and Political Weekly*, November 22, p. 3021–28
125. Saroor Ahmad, (2000). op. cit.
126. Editorial, (1996). 'Covering Up Corruption', op. cit.
127. Walter Hauser, (1997), 'General Elections 1996 in Bihar: Politics, Administrative Atrophy and Anarchy', *Economic and Political Weekly*, October 11, pp. 2599–2607.
128. Ibid. For more details on this see Appendix 3.

129. Type A indicates criminals who are beyond reform. He in fact was also made the minister of state for home in the H.D. Deve Gowda government at the Centre. Later, he was forced to be dropped only after the media highlighted his criminal cases. See Balbir K. Punj, 2003. 'Ojha and the Lord of Misrule' *Pioneer,* December 19, available online at URL: background. http://www.indiafir stfoundation.org/ARCHIVES/articles/arc_bkp/2003/December1903.htm, last accessed in January 2009.
130. Walter Hauser, (1997), 'General Elections 1996 in Bihar: Politics, op. cit. Also see the documentary *'Ek Minute Ka Maun'* produced by Chandrasekhar Aandolan Samiti.
131. See Editorial, (1997). 'Two Faces of Bihar'. *Economic and Political Weekly*, May 3, pp. 919–20.
132. See S.K. Ghosh, (2000). 'Criminal Cabinet' op. cit. pp. 79–81.
133. Ibid. Also see 'Tainted Flock' *Outlook,* August 13, 1997 URL: http://www.outlookindia.com/printarticle.aspx?204001
134. See Editorial, (1997). 'Land Question', *Economic and Political Weekly* December 6, p. 3105.
135. As shared by several respondents across the state during my fieldwork.
136. Arvind N. Das, (1998). 'India in the Image of Bihar', *Economic and Political Weekly,* December 5, 3103–4.
137. Another measure to estimate the flow of students coming out of the state was the significant movement of capital out of the state. A World Bank report puts that Bihar's credit/deposit ratio fell from 40 per cent in 1991 to 21 per cent in 2002 (note: Bihar was divided by this time). That means that for every rupee deposited in Bihar, only 21 per cent was extended as credit in Bihar. Families, even with no employment security or a fixed income sent their children out for education. Most of them sold their land to meet the cost of education. See World Bank, 2005. *Bihar: Towards a Development Strategy,* Washington D.C., op. cit.
138. World Bank, (2005). op. cit.
139. The net primary enrolment rate for Bihar in 1999–2000 was 52 per cent, compared to 77 per cent nationally. Indicators for women were worse than men, with an enrollment gap of 14 per cent (58% for men versus 44% for women) and a literacy gap of 26 per cent (60% for men and 34% for women). Net primary enrollment and literacy rates among women in Bihar were much below the national average of 73 per cent and 54 per cent respectively.
140. Arvind N. Das, (1998). op. cit.
141. Arvind N. Das, (1998b). 'Para Democracy in Bihar', *Economic and Political Weekly,* November 21, pp. 2159–60.

142. Kanhaiah Bhelari, (2002). 'Champa Biswas Case: Justice in Parts', *The Week,* March 24; URL: http://www.the-week.com/22mar24/events3.htm. The case was so clear that both mother and son was booked within an year and three years later on February 26, 2002 the Patna district and sessions court sentenced Mritunjay Yadav to 10 years rigorous imprisonment. However, the Court let off the co-accused Hemlata, taking into account the three years she spent in jail pending trial. Surprisingly, the case of the suspected was being presented by a special public prosecutor, who asked the court to take a lenient view in Hemlata's case. Mritunjay Yadav's appeal before the High Court was heard eight years later on 21 May 2010, and the Court surprisingly, acquitted them on the ground that the relationship between the two (Champa and Mrityunjay) was of consensual in nature'. See 'Twelve Years On: HC Relief for Rape Victim', *Times of India,* (May 22, 2010), URL: http://articles.timesofindia.indiatimes.com/2010–05–22/patna/28310206_1_ias-officials-champa-biswa s-convict
143. For more details see Sanjay Kumar, (1999). op. cit.
144. The Samta Party in 1998 merged with the original Janata Dal that was left with only two popular faces: Sharad Yadav and Ram Vilas Paswan after Lalu Yadav formed his own political party Rashtriya Janata Dal (RJD), and together they renamed it as Janata Dal (United).
145. See CSDS Team, (1999). 'Election Analysis: Emerging Patterns-Sharp Polarisation in Bihar', *Frontline,* Vol. 16, November 27–Dec. 10. URL: http://frontlineonnet.com/fl1625/16250360.htm.
146. Information gathered from various news reports of newspapers, news channels and also collected during the visit in several parts of the state. Also see various issue of the journal *Samkaleen Tampan,* published from Patna, especially Vibhesh Trivedi, (2000). 'Vote, Bihar aur Bahubali' (Hindi), *Samkaleen Tapmaan,* March, pp. 16–22, and columns 'Kal ka Don, Aaj ka MLA' in issues from March-December, 2000.
147. Information collected during my field work. For details on Buttan Singh and Avdhesh Mandal, see Part-III).
148. Arvind N. Das, (2000). 'Electing Another People in Bihar', *Economic and Political Weekly,* February 19–26, pp. 603–604
149. Shaibal Gupta, (2002). 'Subaltern Resurgence: A reconnaissance of Panchayat election in Bihar', *Crisis States Programme, Working Paper,* 8. Development Research Centre, London School of Economics, January (although total number of elected *mukhias* were 8348, the information presented here is only for 7120 Mukhias for which the caste data was available); also see Ashok Kumar Pankaj and M.P. Singh, 2004. 'The Changing Socio-political Profile of Local Political

Elites (Mukhias) in Bihar', *Contributions to Indian Sociology*, Vol. 38, No. 1–2, pp. 43–71.

150. See M.L. Majumdar, (2005). op. cit. pp. 66–92. Mr Majumdar was the State Election Commissioner of Bihar during 2001–2003. He conducted two general elections – Panchayat elections and Municipal elections – within a year.
151. For details, see Kalyan Choudhary, (2001). 'Violent Elections in Bihar', *Frontline,* Vol. 18, Issue 10, May 12–25. URL: http://www.thehindu. com/fline/fl1810/18100380.htm, last accessed in May 2008.
152. Ibid.
153. Ibid.
154. See Crime in India, 1980–2005. Although presented as dramatic and exaggerated, a depiction of the condition of the state in Bihar during this period can be sensed in movies such as *Apharan* (directed by Prakash Jha) and *Shool* (directed by E. Nivas).
155. The issue is still pending before the Supreme Court for final disposal and the Government of India till date has hardly bothered to consider this issue seriously; See SLP (No. 9204–05/2004– ECI Vs. Jan Chowkidar (Peoples Watch) and Ors.) For more details see Chapter 2.
156. Ibid. see Table 2.1.
157. Swatantra Bhattacharya, (2005), 'One in Every Five Hoping to make it to Bihar House', *The Indian Express,* New Delhi, February 22.
158. Based on several newspaper reports and personal interviews.
159. The Lok Jan Shakti Party (henceforth referred as LJP) was formed by Ram Vilas Paswan after a split from JD(U) in 2000 and was contesting the Bihar Assembly election in alliance with the Congress.
160. Varghese K. George, (2005), 'Paswan's fistful' Indian Express, March 2, accessed at http://www.indianexpress.com/oldStory/65681/The names who won the election for Ram Vilas Paswan were Dhumal Singh (lodged in Buxar jail, accused in a number of extortion and murder cases, mostly in Jharkhand); Rama Kishore Singh (was in jail during the election, Kishore's crime record says he specialises in keeping kidnapping victims in safe custody and has links with kidnapping rackets across states); Munna Shukla (along with Rajan Tiwari and Suraj Bhan Singh, Shukla figured in the murder of CPM MLA Ajit Sarkar. However, Shukla was out on bail during the elections); Shankar Singh (who won the Rupauli seat in Purnea district, heads the North Bihar Liberation Army, Shankar Singh was also lodged in Buxar jail during election, but he defeated RJD's Bhima Bharati, wife of Avdesh Mandal, who was the head of another private army called the Faizan Party).

161. 'Dons Set to Flex Muscles in Bihar Poll Arena', *PTI news,* October 9, 2005; Accessed online at http://www.dailyexcelsior.com/web1/05oct10/national.htm#11. The report said, "The NDA gave tickets to Vijay Kumar Shukla alias Munna Shukla and Manoranjan Singh alias Dhumal Singh, who had deserted LJP leader Ram Vilas Paswan to root for Nitish Kumar after the February polls, from Lalganj and Baniapur constituencies respectively. Both had been elected twice from these seats. Anant Singh, a dreaded ganglord of Barh-Mokama area, who had won the last poll defeating Lallan Singh, a cousin of LJP Lok Sabha member Surajbhan Singh from Mokama, is in the fray once again on a JD(U) ticket and so is Narendra Kumar Pandey alias Sunil Pandey from Piro. Both Singh and Pandey have dozen criminal cases pending against them."
162. Ibid. Lesi Singh, wife of slained Rajput don Buttan Singh was re-nominated by JD(U) to contest from Dhamdaha, while Lovely Anand, wife of former MP Anand Mohan Singh was put in fray from Barh on JD(U) ticket and so was Punam Yadav, wife of Ranvir Yadav, a ganglord, who was serving life sentence. Punam had won from Khagaria on LJP ticket in the last election, but later switched to JD(U).
163. Ibid. Rama Singh triumphed by a whopping 42,597 votes in the last assembly polls, Munna Shukla won by 48,604 votes, Anant Singh by 35,783 votes, Sunil Pandey by 54,767 votes, Dhumal Singh by 32,724 votes and Shanker Singh by 25,777 votes.
164. An action carried out by the CPI (Maoist)'s in the name of "Operation Jailbreak" freed nearly 389 prisoners from the south Bihar town of Jehanabad on November 13, 2005. The main objective of the action was to free "communist revolutionaries along with activists and supporters of the peasant movement ... and to give 'mrityudand' (capital punishment) to those notorious killer-leaders of feudal-goonda army Ranveer Sena guilty of various massacres who were safe in the jail." It also denounced the corrupt and oppressive system of which the police, the judiciary and the jails were a part. See Bela Bhatia, (2005b). 'Jehanabad-I: Jailbreak and the Maoist Movement', *Economic and Political Weekly,* December 17, pp. 5369–71.
165. Walter Hauser, (1997), 'General Elections 1996 in Bihar: Politics, Administrative Atrophy and Anarchy', *Economic and Political Weekly,* October 11, pp. 2599–2607.
166. See Francine Frankel, (1989). 'Caste, Land and Dominance in Bihar' in F. Frankel and M.S. Rao (eds.), *Dominance and State Power in Modern India: Decline in Social Order,* Vol I, Oxford University Press, Mumbai, pp. 84–85.
167. V.P. Singh, 'Power and Equality – Changing Grammar of Indian Politics', Lecture delivered at Harvard University USA.

168. Charles Tilly and Sidney Tarrow, (2006). *Contentious Politics,* London, Paradigm Publishers. Henceforth referred as T&T. T&T defines contentious politics as the convergence of collective action, contention, and politics, as the area of their overlap have destructive – and potentially dangerous – properties.
169. Also see Prasann Kumar Chaudhary and Shrikant, (2001). *Bihaar Me Samaajik Parivartan Ke Kuchh Aayaam,* New Delhi, Vani Prakashan, p. 326.
170. Jeffrey Witsoe, (2006). 'Social Justice and Stalled Development: Caste Empowerment and the Breakdown of Governance in Bihar', Spring, Philadelphia, Centre for Advance Study of India, in the series *India in Transition: Economics and Politics of Change,* (ed.) Francine Frankel.

5

Where Life Meets the State

From Landlords to Ganglords

> Na zahar khao, na mahur khao. Marna hai to Puraniya jao.[1]
>
> (Don't take poison. Don't eat *mahur* (a poisonous fruit). If you want to die, go to Purnea).
>
> —Sir John Houlton

In the previous chapter we have discussed how Bihar with its feudal character 'deeply embedded in caste' has failed to evolve as a disinterested arbiter over the years and endorsed a 'politics of contention'. With a strong desire for maintaining the status quo among the traditional ruling elite and equally powerful upsurge among those traditionally oppressed and exploited, this process rather seems natural, inevitable and sometimes even necessary. However, it would be unfair, if we do not analyse this transition at a level where the state meets and affects the everyday life of the individuals and vice-versa. This chapter makes an attempt to analyse the phenomenon of criminalisation of politics at a more micro-level in Purnea district of Bihar.[2]

Caste, Land and the Political

This ominous proverb (written at the top) about Purnea, a place in the Eastern part of northern part of Bihar,[3] may have a very different context at its origin, but it remains the most relevant explanation of the condition until sometimes before. Caste and class, although conceptually different, have run along the same line in Bihar, and Purnea is no different. According to Buchanan;

> the highest castes *Brahmans, Rajputs, Kayasthas* among Hindus; *Seikhs, Pathans* and *Moguls* among Muslims had the largest holdings and paid the lowest rent, as well as having a host of other privileges, some of which were traditional and others of which were usurpations ... most of the larger *zamindaars* were themselves Brahmins and hence caste linkages worked to provide concessional treatment to caste brethren. (from the Raj Darbhanga, as they themselves were Brahmins)[4]

The Yadavs, at least some of them, were at par or even better-off than the higher castes, but as a class they could never emerge as politically significant (due to their low caste status).[5] The other lower castes like Kurmis, Koeris, who had land holdings of inferior kinds, were marginal and inferior than the Yadavs. They were forced to pay higher rents and were subjected to numerous *abwabs, (*extra-legal cess) by the upper caste *zamindars* and their henchmen, and sometimes even forced to quit their independent peasant status and become share-croppers and agricultural labourers.[6] At the lowest rung of the ladder were placed Dalits, who seemed to have lost their right to freedom to the higher castes and sometimes even to those other backward castes, who had the power of land, grain and money.[7]

A comparison of the distribution of landholding in Purnea with that of the state and the country in the 1950s makes it amply clear that the degree of inequality in Purnea was greater than anywhere else (see Figure 5.1).

Figure 5.1

Comparative Distribution of Land Holdings in Purnea, Bihar and India

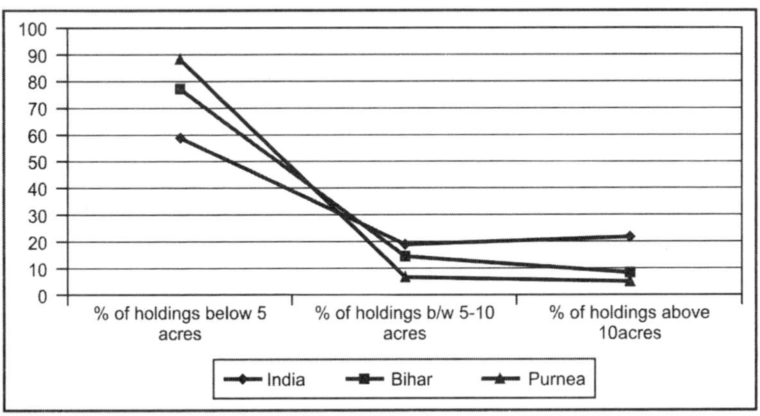

Source: Graph prepared from data provided in Yadav (1990: 74).[8]

Stories of wealthier upper/dominant caste commanding immense power with their own aerodromes, private planes and armies continued to remain the defining characteristics of Purnea.[9] Nothing substantial could change even after the Bihar Land Reforms Act 1950 or the two amendments made subsequently in 1954 and 1959. In fact, it was the landlords of Purnea who forced the first Constitutional amendment in 1951 (for details see Chapter 2 and 3), and even later they kept stalling the process of land reforms, whatsoever the state initiated. A Planning Commission report on 'Implementation of Land Reforms in Bihar' that reviewed the progress of land reforms in 1964 mentioned that about 40,000 appeals have been filed by landlords before the civil courts in Purnea.[10] By March 1989, the total land under dispute at the state level was nearly 70,766 acres in which Purnea had a major share.[11] In addition to that the landlords had also adopted several tactics to escape the land ceiling laws.[12] Lands were transferred in favour of wives, minor daughters, minor granddaughters, minor grandsons, relatives, servants and sometimes even their pets.[13]

The administrative and judicial set-up provided enough loopholes to the landlords to keep control over their mammoth sized landholdings. They were challenged only when officials, deeply committed to the goal of social equity, were posted as the district collector, occasionally. When J.M. Lyngdoh,[14] posted as Collector in Purnea, took on the notorious landlords of the region, he was awarded transfer by the then chief minister Karpoori Thakur in just 10 months and 29 days.[15] Raising this issue, the commissioner of the Kosi division, P.S. Appu, expressed his disagreement with the state government's decision and in a letter to the state chief secretary, K.P.J. Menon wrote:

> In the past, the big landlords of Purnea invariably had cordial and friendly relations with men in charge of the district administration. When they found that the District Magistrate (read J.M. Lyngdoh) and the Sub-Divisonal Officer (read Tarkeshwar Prasad) were fearless men who would uphold the majesty of law even at the risk of incurring the wrath of powerful vested interests, the big landlords of Purnea came to the conclusion that they should spend all their energies towards getting these officers transferred and having pliable men posted in their place. Intensive lobbying started at Patna with results which are by now well known. The land owners did not rest there. The D.M. being a member of the IAS, they knew that not much could be done to him except getting him transferred. So they decided to go all out for the blood of the S.D.O., who, being a member of the State Civil Service, did not enjoy the same degree of security of the

> service as the D.M. ... Government should look into the matter and take appropriate action ... . My purpose ... is not to seek to persuade the government to reconsider its decision to transfer Lyngdoh from Purnea. His greatest reward lies in the high esteem and affection in which he is held by all but high and mighty and their minions. Deprived of the just and fair treatment they received at his hands, the hapless share-croppers of Purnea may find themselves again at the complete mercy of the predatory landlords. But then, that will be no new experience for them. I have little doubt that their future will continue to be bleak until they build up a militant organisation capable of successfully fighting for their rights. Administrative efforts, at the best, can only be palliatives.[16]

The blatant belligerence of landlords during those days, was also reported the Working Group on Land Reforms of the National Commission on Agriculture:

> Landowners ... are organised and aggressive ... With an obliging administration on their side; they are definitely not going to give up an iota of their rights, privileges and economic dominance without a stiff fight ... No law, however, good it may be in conferring on paper rights, title and interest on the *bataidars,* will have the slightest chance of success unless the bataidars have a strong and militant mass organisation of their own, capable of not only defending their own rights given by the law but also capable of mounting counter-action to prevent and forestall any direct attack on them.[17]

Thus, the administration provided every favourable condition to the landlords in order to keep social justice for the landless and poor a distant dream. Together they created a class that was ignorant, slothful, devoid of abilities and therefore, looked upon the land not as a productive asset that could maximise their per-capita income, but essentially as power and social status. Even during the period of Green Revolution, Bihar, and especially Purnea, remained reluctant to accept the process of monetisation.[18] Phanishwar Nath Renu, the author the famous novel, *Maila Aanchal,*[19] who was from Purnea, in an interview to a national news magazine *Dinman,* published from New Delhi, in 1975 said:

> The story of the Purnea region is the story of the landless peasantry. So many rich landlords in Purnea have two aeroplanes each. These landowners form the second class; landowners of the first class are misers. They do not buy aeroplanes; they buy far too much land. They are not *kisans* (farmer landowners), but they are better off than *Zamindars*. There are *Zamindars* who own only 50 *bighas* and there are also *Zamindars* who own only 3 acres. They are not *praja* (the

> subjects). So, on the one side there is the large group of landless peasantry, and on the other there are the farm owners.[20]

Majority of the agricultural workers were landless.[21] Official surveys even after nearly four decades show that Purnea had 210 landlords with over 200 acres each (nine of them having more than 1,000 acres each).[22] According to a senior administrative service officer posted in Purnea in the late 1980s, the family members of the landlords, who could not get into either politics or bureaucracy, had very purposefully selected law as their profession and used it as a potential weapon against the large non-literate landless mass;

> Even when some of the officers posted in the district tried to bring a change in the situation, they were confronted by local lawyers who were kith and kins of the upper-caste landlords. The legal processes on the land issues were already very lengthy as it had to cross many stages between DCLR (Deputy Collector Land Reforms) and the Land Reforms Board. These lawyers used to manage the officers, involved in the judicial or quasi-judicial process, to commit some mistake so that orders issued at any level get quashed at the last stage and the whole process would begin again from the start. This provided them ample time to use, sell and regain their status on the lost land. Thus, it further enhanced the periodic violence.[23]

All this clearly show that accumulated in the hands of a few upper castes, land as a resource remained neglected. With no monetisation of economy, the exploitation of agricultural labourers remained at its peak.

Resistance and Protests

This is not to indicate that this power relation was not met by any resistance. The struggle of the dominant castes for climbing up in the ladder of caste hierarchy or the status order in this territory has been remarkable. Way back in 1925 a special report titled, *'Subject: Serious riot between Babhans and Goalas at Monghyr, Lakhochak Riots'* by the Political Department, Government of Bihar and Orissa noted that,

> The Goalas (read the Yadavas) had very strongly objected to the caste order and often vented their frustration. In the early 20th century, this frustration sometimes even took the shape of physical confrontation between the landed elite (viz., Bhumihars) and marginal cultivators (the Yadavs). Official police reports of the 1920s describe in substantial detail the tension and occasional violence between the Goalas forwarding a Yadav-Kshatriya identity and the landed elite who felt threatened by that new identity. This threat was perceived as

> economic as well as social, in as much as the systemics of *varna* provided the cultural justification for the agrarian perquisites demanded of cultivating tenants. While the Muslim elite also challenged the Yadav-Kshatriya identity, they did so, on purely economic and not religious grounds, and Yadav-Kshatriyas responded in kind. These tensions culminated with the threat of serious blood-letting on May 27, 1925, when a group of three thousand Goalas (Yadav-Kshatriyas) and an equal number of heavily armed "Babhans" (Bhumihar Brahmins) faced each other at Lakho Chak village near Lakhisarai town, Monghyr district, in central Bihar.[24]

Later Santhals also had started a struggle against their principal landholders to establish their rights as full-fledged tenants on the lands they cultivated in 1938, but its momentum was somewhat checked by the Quit India Movement.[25] But these unresolved tensions between the landholders and their *bataidars* could not remain quiet for long and emerged again on the agrarian scene in Purnea soon after Independence. The non-*adivasi bataidaars,* under the leadership of Nakshtra Malakar, revolted against this caste-class nexus during 1952–60. However, they also could not produce a long sustained movement.

A decade later in the early 1970s the Communist Party of India (Marxist) and some Socialist leaders[26] started a 'Land Grab' movement. However, in the early years, the movement remained only symbolic and could not really mount an attack on the iniquitous land structure in the state.[27] The Congress had openly chosen to anchor the interests of the landlords, and the Janata Party also could not bring any significant change. Under such socio-political climate, the landless of Purnea came under the influence of the ultra-leftist outfit, the CPI (M-L). Unfortunately, the leader of the movement, Afsar Ali, was killed very soon.

The landlords, however, under no restrictions from either the political class or the state administration, uleashed an era of terror and the state witnessed its first massacre on November 22, 1971. An armed mob attacked the village Chandwa-Rupaspur in the Dhamdaha revenue circle (one of the Santhal settlements) and set it on fire. Since the attack took place in the afternoon, most of the residents were away harvesting paddy. Those at home, when attempted to run were shot down. Ten Santhals were shot dead and four were burnt alive.[28] The chief perpetrator this carnage was the nephew of Lakshmi Narain Sudhanshu, a senior Congress leader who had served as the State Assembly Speaker between 1962 and 1967. Surprisingly, the chief minister Bhola Paswan Shastri[29] was also form Purnea. A month later, similar confrontation took place at Sabdalpur village between the Mohammadia Estate and the *bataidars*.[30] The prime suspect for this massacre was another high profile leader Hasibur Rehman, the former law minister in the Mahamaya Prasad Sinha cabinet.[31]

In the later years, the CPM under the leadership of Ajit Sarkar and with the support from underground cadres of CPI-ML got itself organised and waged many more struggles against the landlords. Explaining the struggle, a senior member of the district committee CPM, said:

> Our struggle was focused around three most important issues. The seizure of the surplus land; land possessed illegally; and the *benami* lands in occupation of the big landlords and rich peasants and its distribution among the landless and poor peasants. In the late 1980s and early 1990s, we carried out hundreds of such operations, more or less, in all parts of the district, but, primarily in the Dhamdaha revenue circle. We got success in some but many of them were still blocked by the landlords at one stage of the other.[32]

Some of the noted land struggles under the banner of various outfits of the Left leadership, other than those discussed above were: (i) a ten-month long wage strike in 1987–88 against six notorious landlords including the family of Sitaram Singh, one of the killers of CPM leader Brajesh Thakur (Thakur was killed in 1986 and to avenge his death, Sitaram Singh was also killed on June 7, 1986); (ii) the land struggle against a notorious Congress MLA from Dhamdaha, Amarnath Tiwari, during 1988–93; (iii) the land struggle against the Bhishna estate in Rupauli in 1988–89; and (iv) the land struggle against Tirthanand Mandal, a relative of the Barahari estate family who was denounced by the peasantry as the most cruel landlord of the district.[33]

When, during my field work in the area, I inquired about the cases in which Lyngdoh had taken actions (mentioned in Appu's letter discussed above), I found that the landlords in 1984 had organised massacre of santhals at Haldiwari Kamat Tola, (located 2km from Dibra village, the place mentioned in Appu's letter) under the leadership of Kameshwar Singh (another migrant landlord from Hajipur Kumarkol) and, burnt down 50 houses killing several of them. All these activities were actively supported by other big landlords and political personalities, viz., L.N. Sudhanshu (already figured earlier in the discussion), Kameshwar Chaudhary (district Congress president) and Shivnandan Singh (a landlord in Dumra).[34] In all these years, the district administration, quite contrary to their raison-detre-function, remained inert, inactive and in many cases even a party to these conspiracies.

CPM's presence under the leadership of Ajit Chandra Sarkar (who was popularly called the 'Messiah of the landless') no doubt, had kept the landlords under some restraints; but Sarkar was killed in 1998 on the behest of a criminal-politician prom Pappu Yadav (details discussed later). The landlords saw this as a golden opportunity to take the land back from the landless labourers. One such incident took place on December 14, 1998, where the landlords of Nikhrel village under the Baisi sub-division went to their 20–year-old disputed land, and began ploughing the field. The Santhals, however, even after the death of their leader, did not lose their courage and went ahead to stop the landlord from doing so. The landlords who were ready to confront them with their musclemen surrounded the village and set the houses on fire. Running helter-skelter most of the male members of the house managed to escaped, but several women and children were burnt alive.[35]

Politics: From Landlords to Ganglords

The electoral victories in Purnea for the first three decades after Independence remained controlled by the powerful and mighty landlords, who were known as the *'maliks'* (master), of the Congress Party (see Table 5.1). The 1970s brought in some change in its nature, but it remained only temporal. The 'maliks' regained the majority of seats in the 1980s and continued with their own style of politics and status quo. Conflict started only in the later years when the backward castes started to assert for greater representation and equal opportunity. This created such a vicious cycle of conflicts in Purnea that crime started making a heady brew in the politics. The polarisation of the society between 'maliks' and 'landless' started traversing towards a polarisation on the basis of caste.

It was mere a coincidence that when the Central government constituted a Backward Class Commission, it appointed Bindeshwari Prasad Mandal as its chairman, who hailed from Madhepura, a part of the Kosi region. But this provided the criminal elements such as Anand Mohan Singh (a Rajput from Saharsa district of Kosi division) and Pappu Yadav (a Yadav from Madhepura district from Kosi division) an opportunity to become the self-proclaimed caste leaders and the political manipulators of the area. During the late 1980s and early 1990s, these two high-priests of casteism clashed so frequently in the area that it started looking almost like a civil war between upper and backward castes in general and between the Rajputs and the Yadavs in particular. However, this did not happen in a day, month or even a

Table 5.1

Winners of Various Assembly Constituencies from Purnea District, 1951–1971

Year	Constituency	Party	Winner
1951	Bhagalpur-cum-Purnea	INC	Anup Lal Mehta
	Purnea North East	INC	Mohammad Islamuddin
	Purnea Central	INC	Phani Gopal Sen Gupta
1957	Kishanganj	INC	Md. Tahir
	Purnea	INC	Phani Gopal Sen Gupta
	Katihar	INC	Awdhesh Kumar Singh
1962	Kishanganj	INC	Md. TAhir
	Purnea	INC	Phani Gopal Sen Gupta
	Katihar	PSP	Priya Gupta
1967	Kishanganj	PSP	L.L. Kapoor
	Araria	INC	T.M. Ram
	Purnea	INC	P.F.S. Gupta
	Katihar	INC	S. Keshari
1971	Kishanganj	INC	Jamilur Rehman
	Araria	INC	T.M. Ram
	Purnea	INC	Md. Tahir
	Katihar	BJS	Gyaneshwar Pd. Yadav

Source: Election Commission of India; INC: Indian National Congress; PSP: Praja Socialist Party; BJS: Bhartiya Jan Sangha.

year. It got shaped over several years. The presence of a high degree of inequality and non-availability of the monetised economy further added to the accumulation of wealth through illegal means and the place of landlords soon went under the control of the ganglords.

The Transitional Phase (1984–1987)

In the 1980s while the state was witnessing the 'politics of intrigue' (discussed in chapter 4), Purnea was rapidly becoming a centre of notoriety of the musclemen of the landlords and criminals, viz., Pramod Singh, Pankaj Singh, Buttan Singh, Siya Yadav, Shyambihari Yadav and Arjun Yadav. While Buttan Singh, Pankaj Singh and Siya Yadav were acting as the musclemen of the local landlords; Pramod Singh, Arjun Yadav and Shyambihari Yadav were simply dreaded criminals. However, important to notice is that there was hardly any caste antagonism among various criminal groups as they made friendships across the caste groups. In 1984, due to some personal animosity, Pankaj Singh killed Pramod Singh (both from the same caste (Rajput) and same village (Sarsi)). Taking revenge of Singh's death, Arjun Yadav and Shyam Bihari Yadav killed both Pankaj Singh and Siya Yadav. Three years later Buttan Singh, (a Rajput friend of Pankaj Singh), killed both Arjun Yadav and Shyambihari Yadav. These killings although took place only as a result of the personal enmity between the criminal youths; the context of the politically charged atmosphere of the state, and that specially of the Kosi region, pushed this towards a phenomenon of caste war.[36]

Institutionalisation of the Caste War (1987–1990)

By the time Arjun Yadav was killed, Pappu Yadav had already acquired notoriety and established himself as the junior Arjun Yadav in the area.[37] Arjun Yadav's murder in 1987 provided Pappu Yadav an opportunity to proclaim himself as the 'uncrowned king of the crime world'. He challenged Buttan Singh and projected himself as the 'only saviour of the Yadavs'. Two years later, when there was an anti-reservation stir by the upper-castes, Pappu Yadav, took the ladership of the Yadav offencive against the upper-castes in the region and went on a rampage. It was then that the district magistrate (DM) of Purnea put him behind bars under the National Security Act. However, Pappu's activities did not stop even after that. Talking to me in a personal interview, the then DM of Purnea said;

> Even when he was put behind the bars in the Purnea jail under the NSA, his activities did not stop. He kept operating from inside. The administration, therefore, procured an order to transfer him to the Bhagalpur jail. However, Pappu Yadav than very cleverly managed to open all the cases registered against himself for hearing in Purnea, and failed us in our plan. There were so many cases registered against him that he had to appear in the court daily. The travel from Bhagalpur to Purnea, in those days, was not that easy, as it was separated by river Ganga with no bridge over it. Thus, crossing the river on the steamer daily and producing him in the court under police protection on time became very challenging. He pleaded the same in the court and was brought back to the Purnea jail on a judicial order.[38]

The jail superintendent of the Purnea jail during those days expressed similar views:

> When Pappu Yadav, by an order from the office of IG, Bihar was sent to the Bhagalpur central jail, he managed to influence the jailer and the doctor of the jail and asked them to pressurise me to keep him in the Purnea jail against the order passed. But I did not succumb to their pressure. However, soon I had to bend before the orders of the

legal luminaries when they passed a judicial order to keep him in the Purnea jail, as he had to appear in the Purnea court almost daily.[39]

Pappu Yadav's notoriety in the area kept growing continuously. He allegedly once tried to run a car over an inspector who had once arrested him in Dhamdaha. At another time, he allegedly set afire a shop whose owner had objected to being extorted.[40] Pappu had once forcibly shaved of the moustache of policeman Ram Parvesh Paswan of the Banmankhi Police Station. The police were so annoyed with him in this area, added the DM, that;

> Many a times they (*read police*) even planned for encountering Pappu after arresting him. However, I did not allow the police vent their frustration and warned them of dire consequences in any such case.[41]

In the meantime, the Buttan Singh gang got connected with Anand Mohan, who like Pappu Yadav had declared himself as the saviour of the upper castes'. Some 35 cases were registered against him in several adjoining districts by early 1990s. Anand Mohan too was kept behind bars several times under the National Security Act, the Maintenance of Internal Security Act, the Crime Control Act and the Arms Act. The gangs of these two self-proclaimed caste leaders clashed at several places in Purnea and the adjoining districts and created a civil war like situation in the Kosi region.[42]

Sharing his experience, the then Superintendent of Purnea Jail said;

> The worst days of my service period were spent in Purnea. The two caste leaders Buttan Singh and Pappu Yadav had made our life hell. Being a jail superintendent my job was to ensure the safety and well-being of the prisoners, whatsoever charge they might be carrying on their head. However, the caste enmity was so deep in their mind that they even divided the jail into two wards – the Rajput ward and the Yadav ward.
>
> One day, as I reached my home after the office, I heard the emergency siren from the jail. I had to rush back instantly. When I reached inside the jail I saw both Buttan and Pappu fighting with each other along with nearly 50 members on each side. The floor of the jail was red with blood. Some were hit in their heads, some left with broken hands and legs and some were even dying. Looking at the situation, I could not control my anger, and vented my frustration on both the gang leaders. The basic fight between the two caste-leaders was to gain superiority over the other.[43]

Adding edge to this criminality in the region was another ganglord Md. Taslimuddin, who by now had already won an Assembly Constituency (Joki Haat) on a Janata Dal ticket and later the Purnea Parliamentary seat by defeating Madhuri Singh of the Congress.[44] A report submitted by the All-Party Bihar Assembly House Committee in 1988 provided details of his alleged involvement in several heinous cases of kidnapping, robbery, rioting, assaulting public servants, and attempt to murder, etc.

Political fortune, however, still favoured the upper castes. The Rajput gang leader Anand Mohan Singh managed to get a ticket from Janata Dal from the Mahinsi constituency in Saharsa district, but Pappu Yadav could not find any taker in the 1990 Assembly polls. He therefore, decided to contest independently from Singheshwar in Madhepura district. Both Anand Mohan and Pappu won the elections as caste antagonism between these two castes was at its peak. However, soon after the elections Pappu Yadav gained prominence over Anand Mohan Singh as Lalu Yadav turned to his caste-brethren to get the necessary support of 11 MLAs to form his government (for more details see chapter 3). Anand Mohan Singh soon parted ways with Janata Dal on the issue of the implementation of the Mandal commission report. This only added to the explosion of caste war in the Kosi region. The air got filled with popular slogans like, *"BHURA BAL saaf karo"* (clean up the BHURA BAL: literally meaning 'finish BHU (Bhumihar), RA (Rajput) BA (Babhan, i.e., Brahmins) and L (Lala, i.e., Kayasthas) – the four castes that constitute the forward group). The Rajput gang used to wear head scarves which had "I am Anand Mohan" printed over it.[45]

While some simply blame the leadership of Lalu Yadav for spreading this vicious caste antagonism and creating a backward-forward divide in the state; this study, as discussed earlier rejects all such claims. It was the local context and condition that went on to become so vicious. Lalu Yadav's rising higher and higher on the waves of caste was not something that he planned meticulously; it was merely the pressure that the local conditions forced upon him during that particular period.

Post 1990 Phase

The fight between these two gangs became a day-to-day affair in the 1990s. Murders were being carried out in broad daylight and in major public places such as court compounds, markets, bus terminals, railway stations. The criminals roamed around freely as the police either chose to keep quiet or, on most of the occasions, became a party to the fight of these gangs.[46] The situation went to such an extent that it became difficult for the common man to disclose his identity. In an interesting case found during my field trip, an upper-caste man was shot (but he survived) by an upper-caste gang because he out of fear, identified himself to be a Yadav.[47]

Both these gangs were ready to kill people for no reason, but to prove their superiority over the other. This hostility between caste leaders gained full vigour during the 1991 Parliamentary elections in Madhepura and Purnea. Pappu Yadav created a record of capturing nearly 70 per cent of the polling booths in Purnea. The election was boycotted by all political parties and finally countermanded.[48] In Madhepura, the election was countermanded due to the murder of an independent woman candidate, Raj Kumari Choudhary, in which Anand Mohan Singh was named as the prime accused.[49]

The situation was so serious that the chief minister, Lalu Prasad Yadav, had to declare:

> *"Un dono choohon ko hum jaldi hi pakad lenge. Ye dono vidhayak, Anand Mohan Singh aur Pappu Yadav, apne apne jati ke liye koi masiha nahi hain. Ye to bas choohen hain."* [These two rats will be caught. These two legislators Anand Mohan and Pappu are not the Robin Hoods of their respective castes, they are only rats.][50]

After this announcement Pappu Yadav went underground, and Anand Mohan Singh challenged the state government to arrest him 'if they can'. He also declared that he would remain in open and would not surrender until Pappu Yadav was caught. On December 7, 1991, he organised a mini rally to display his support and remained present at the rally himself, throughout. However, the police failed to arrest him! When Lalu Yadav made a personal appeal to Pappu Yadav, he surrendered in a dramatic way at his official residence in Patna. But Anand Mohan was still out of reach of the police. Pappu Yadav saw this as his insult and escaped from police custody. He was later arrested only to be released on bail.[51]

The number of cases against Anand Mohan in the next few years increased up to 67. A reward of ₹ 25,000 was announced and even shoot-at-sight orders were issued in three cases against him.[52] However, in 1994 his political career got a major boost when he ignited a mob, that he was leading along with his wife Lovely Anand, Munna Shukla (the younger brother of Chhotan Shukla) and Akhlaq Ahmad (Anand's Mohan's associate) near Khaabra village on National Highway No 28 on December 5, 1994, to kill G. Krishnaiya, the Collector of Gopalganj district.[53] Krishnaiya, a 1985 batch IAS officer of Bihar cadre, was a dalit. He had spearheaded land reforms and was very popular among the poor and the oppressed. He was first shot at and then stoned by the mob. Anand Mohan's popularity soared so high after this incident that the Parliamentary by-election on Vaishali seat was won by his wife Lovely Anand (an independent candidate) against the Janata Dal.[54] Since then, there is no political party (be it JD, SAP, SJP[55], RJD, BJP or the Congress) in the state that did not provide support to this Rajput don. He formed his own party (Bihar People's Party – BPP), and contested the 1995 Assembly elections on his own. However, this did not bring him any good luck, and out of the 259 seats contested, his party could win only one. Anand Mohan himself, contested from three seats, but could not win even at one.[56] Later he merged his party with the Samta Party (SAP) and became the chief of Yuva Samta. He entered the Lok Sabha in 1996 from Sheohar as a Samata Party member. He won the seat again in 1998 as an All-India Rashtriya Janata Party (AIRJP) candidate, but lost in 1999.[57]

By 1995, Pappu Yadav too had more than 60 serious cases registered against him, including cases of murder, but that still could not fetch him a Janata Dal ticket in the 1995 State Assembly election. He contested from Purnea on a ticket of the Samajwadi Party of Mulayam Singh Yadav. However, victory did not come his way this time, and Pappu Yadav was defeated by the CPM leader Ajit Chandra Sarkar. It was a very close fight as the margin of victory was only of 2000 votes (see Table 5.2). Soon the position reversed in the Parliamentary by-election held in Purnea, the same year (since it was countermanded in 1991). Pappu Yadav emerged as the clear winner despite contesting as an independent. A year later during the Lok Sabha elections in 1996, contesting on a Samajwadi Party ticket, he increased his victory margin by over 4,00,000 votes. Ajit Sarkar this time could get only 9.78 per cent of votes polled against 65.98 per cent cornered by Pappu Yadav (see Table 5.3). This elevation in political life with no fear of punishment further elevated Pappu Yadav's confidence in crime and he increased his criminal activities in the area manyfold.

Table 5.2

Votes Polled to Top Three Candidates in the 1995 Assembly Election in Purnea

Name	*Party*	*Votes*	*% Votes*
Ajit Chandra Sarkar	CPM	35,167	30.57
Rajesh Ranjan	SP	33,552	29.17
Panchanand Yadav	BJP	17,571	15.27

Source: www.eci.nic.in.

Table 5.3

Votes Polled to Top Three Candidates in 1996 Parliamentary Election in Purnea

Name	*Party*	*Votes*	*%Votes*
Rajesh Ranjan	SP	4,43,119	65.98
Rajendra Prasad Gupta	BJP	1,26,956	18.90
Ajit Chandra Sarkar	CPM	65,678	9.78

Source: www.eci.nic.in.

Buttan Singh too in the 1995 Assembly elections, instead of supporting his landlord mentor, decided to try his luck in politics. But he was defeated by Dilip Yadav, another criminal contesting on the Janata Dal ticket. While Buttan Singh got 21.05 per cent of votes contesting as an independent candidate, Dilip Yadav managed to get 29 per cent of votes. Amaranth Tiwari, the sitting Congress MLA, without the support of his muscleman, Buttan Singh could get only 7.65 per cent of the votes and was pushed to the fourth position.[58] Buttan Singh had 21 cases registered against him that included eight murder charges; and Dilip Yadav had criminal charges under sections 302, 364, 201, 144 and 379 of the IPC and sections 34 and 27 of the Arms Act.[59]

All these incidents kept adding fuel to the caste antagonism and both the Yadavs and the Rajput gangs went on a rampage to claim superiority over the other by creating fear in the masses. Although the pattern and style of the fight remained uncertain, there developed few sites where their contestations became an inevitable day-to-day affair. The Purnea bus terminus was one among such sites. Both these gangs scripted a bloodbath to gain control over the site, as it was considered to be a pot of wealth.

The dominating gang used to collect *rangdari* tax (extortion money) from the bus terminus and use the buses at their whims. The *rangdari* tax collected from the bus terminus was so high (according to some estimates it was around ₹ 5 lakh a month) that they soon started created their own business empire. Such examples from both the gangs were Jaipreet Travels (owned by Buttan Singh and Laddoo Singh: 8–10 buses plying between Purnea and Raniganj) and Pappu Travels (owned by Pappu Yadav: 10–12 buses plying between Purnea-Saharsa and Purnea-Patna). The peculiarity of their system of working was such that once their bus/jeep/mini taxi started plying on a route, no other agency was allowed to ply in that route. Thus, travelling in those days by bus, by no means, was simple. Seats were not occupied inside the buses according to the availability, but one's proximity with the criminal owners or their supporters. The buses did not even stop at villages that did not have population of the caste group (backward or forward) of the bus owners. There were several instances when the rival caste group vented their frustration on the bus and the bus staff.[60]

Another such disputed site was the local wholesale market, Gulabbagh *Mandi*. This *mandi*, one of the biggest *mandis* in the country, was also a site for an annual cultural and trade fair. The famous feature film, *Teesri Kasam,* starring Raj Kapoor and Waheeda Rahman was shot at the same place.[61] However, this collapsed as criminals began to invade and loot it at will.[62] According to the information gathered during the fieldwork;

> Vishwanath Aggrawal, a businessman dealing with fertilizers was asked to pay a *rangdari* tax of ₹ 10 lakh by the Pappu gang. But Aggrawal could manage only ₹ 5 lakh. Therefore, the gang kidnapped his younger brother Ramu Aggrawal. They even shot dead Ramu's friend Rangu Singh, who tried to save Ramu from them. The same was the fate of Jagdeesh Trading and several other prominent trading families of Gulabbagh. Many of them either paid lakhs and lakhs of rupees in ransom or else lost their kith and kin. As a result, all the big traders of the *mandi* stopped doing their businesses and left Purnea. Gulabbagh also used to have a flourishing plywood industry. But, with the surge in crimes against them, more than 90 per cent of the industries downed their shutters.[63]

The third important site of violent contestation was the Katihar railway syndicate. The Katihar Railway division alone used to get the annual construction work of nearly ₹ 30 crore. There were many syndicates that were being run under protection of politicians. The contract was won by the person who had greater muscle power. Thus, both these gangs started providing the muscle and gun power to these syndicates. It was an established norm that whosoever won the contract had to pay 10–15 per cent of the contract amount to these gangs. Also, once the contract was won, they also provided an easy route for these gangs to carry out the smuggling of the wood from Rulauli, Bhawanipur area and in return purchase new arms from the border areas. There were several occasions when both the gangs clashed head-on over the issue. However, it was the Buttan gang that used to dominate over the war on all such occasions.[64]

The easiest and most common of all the activities of these gangs mentioned above was kidnapping for ransom and killing them in case of non-recovery. Their prime targets were engineers (to secure all the contracts being passed in the Purnea and the neighbouring districts), doctors and businessmen. Looting bikes and crops from the field was also a usual story. All this led to an enormous increase even in the general crime graph of the area in the decade of 1990 (see Table 5.4). The number of murders and attempt to murders that were only 54 and 40 respectively in 1990, reached to 98 and 125 in 1993 and 109 and 207 in 1996, respectively. Cases of kidnapping that were 43 in 1990, reached to 91 by 1997. Cases of robbery, burglary, and theft also increased at alarming rates.

Table 5.4

Incidence of Crimes (IPC) in Purnea

1	*2*	*3*	*4*	*5*	*6*			*7*	*8*	*9*	*10*	*11*		
					6a	*6b*	*6c*					*11a*	*11b*	*11c*
2005	113	35	6	39	60	7	53	38	6	95	72	218	34	184
2004	128	41	6	62	138	62	76	6	4	144	82	242	64	178
2003	99	74	12	50	102	50	52	12	2	131	72	231	78	153
2002	96	75	4	46	94	46	48	17	7	114	86	174	38	136
2001	104	89	10	39	103	39	64	23	5	97	100	227	27	200
2000	114	101	5	91	96	14	82	46	1	111	79	262	32	230
1999	109	114	9	60	92	21	71	58	5	83	74	222	45	177
1997	102	227	7	75	91	39	52	72	11	74	162	283	—	—
1996	109	207	14	69	54	22	32	61	7	74	150	282	—	—
1994	86	84	9	65	69	21	48	120	4	126	233	355	—	—
1993	98	125	8	60	60	19	41	84	2	79	215	392	—	—
1990	54	40	4	36	43	17	26	83	1	68	189	471	—	—
Total	1,212	1,212	94	692	911	357	554	620	55	1,196	1,514	3,359		

Source: Ministry of Home Affairs, Govt. of India, URL: http://www.indiastat.com/india/state.asp?stid=05&secid=153&ptid=2&level=3Columns: 1–year, 2–murder, 3–Attempt to Commit Murder, 4–C.H.Not Amounting to Murder, 5– Rape, 6– Kidnapping and Abduction, 6a–Total, 6b–Of Women and Girls, 6c–of others, 7–Dacoity, 8–Preparation and Assembly for Dacoity, 9–Robbery, 10– Burglary, 11–Theft, 11a–Total, 11b–Auto Theft, 11c–Other Thefts. Abbr.: CH: Culpable Homicide; IPC: Indian Penal Code.

Growing clever over the years, these criminal politicians also began to use their influence to develope the image of a Robin Hood. Several supporters of Pappu Yadav, while speaking to me in the field expressed;

> "Purnea used to live in darkness before Pappu Yadav came. He managed to provide us uninterrupted supply of electricity. He brought the bureaucrats to kneel before the public demand. He did even beat up corrupt officers. He forced the doctors to treat the poor patients at a low fee, sometimes even free. He managed to make roads even in the interiors of the district."

Murder of the CPM Legislator

By the time of the 12th Lok Sabha elections in 1998, the political equation of the state had changed drastically. Purnea, by now had become a battle ground for many old and new *bahubalis* (musclemen). In the fray were the sitting MP Pappu Yadav of the SP, Dilip Yadav of the RJD, Jaikrishna Mandal of the BJP,[65] and Pappu Singh of the

Congress.[66] Interestingly the CPM had decided for a pre-poll alliance with the SP in the state, and therefore, the party was supposed to support the SP candidate Pappu Yadav in Purnea. But the CPM MLA from Purnea, Ajit Sarkar decided to defy the party high command and instead supported the Congress candidate Pappu Singh. Ajit Sarkar was pitted against Pappu Yadav since the early 1990s, and they had clashed with each other on several occasions. Even in 1998, they faced each other on a land issue in Budhali village.

> The CPM cadres had captured and distributed 200 acres (to nearly 200 families of landless Mushars (SCs) and Dhangars (STs) of Lallu Miyan, a landlord of Budhali village who owned more than 800 acres in the area. Pappu Yadav, who till now had also established himself as a saviour of the Bhumihar landlords of Purnea was approached by Lallu Miyan to clear the encroachment. Pappu readily accepted the task. One day, he came along with several gunmen and asked the people living on that land to vacate it. When the local CPM cadres objected to Pappu's action, they shot dead two of them. The case is still going on and Pappu Yadav has been asked to appear before the court.[67]

Pappu Singh was from the landlord family of Maul Babu of the Manchand Estate against whom Sarkar had led a big fight since his early days in politics. Notwithstanding the ideological differences. Sarkar, however, preferred a landlord over the ganglord for the election. The party high command, upset with Sarkar's decision suspended him from the party but Sarkar maintained that his support to Pappu Singh was justified by the party central committee's line of fighting criminals, corruption and communalism.[68]

All these made the election in Purnea bloodier. While Sarkar could not collect enough votes for Pappu Singh, he made the task of Pappu Yadav's very difficult. As a result, Jai Krishna Mandal of the BJP won the polls (see Table 5.5). Pappu Yadav saw it as a big humiliation. His anguish over Sarkar was so high that he, allegedly masterminded the murder of the legislator.[69] Rajan Tiwari, a famous sharp-shooter, killed Sarkar and two of his associates, a few kilometres away from his house on June 14, 1998 when he was returning after a visit from Harda block nearby.[70] The matter was handed over to the CBI and Pappu Yadav was arrested soon on charge of political assassination and sent to Beur jail in Patna. However, his spirits remained high, and he once again won the Purnea Parliamentary seat in 1999 contesting from jail as an Independent candidate with a record margin.[71] He continued to coordinate his operations from behind the bars.

Table 5.5

Votes Polled to Top three Candidates in 1998 Parliamentary Election in Purnea

Name	*Party*	*Votes*	*%Votes*
Jai Krishna Mandal	BJP	2,65,096	37.96
Rajesh Ranjan	SP	2,29,279	32.83
Uday Singh	INC	10,297	14.65
Dilip Kumar Yadav	RJD	5,825	8.34

Source: www.eci.nic.in

Rise of Faizan Party and North Bihar Liberation Army

While all this was happenning, there came into existence another gang that was supported by the backward caste (Kurmi) landlords of the Brahmagyani and Barhari estates in the Rupauli Assembly constituency.[72] The Rupauli Assembly constituency, politically represented by the CPI; had gone under the control of the Naxals (CPI-M-L) who remained underground, and had waged a war against the landlords.[73] The most effected among the landlords of the area were the backward caste (Mandal) landlords of the Barahri and Brahmgyani estates. To fight with the Naxalites, they therefore, created a gang under the leadership of Avdhesh Mandal (of the Gangota caste, an OBC).[74] The other prominent members of his gang were Gidra Mandal (of Gangota caste) and Ashok Rai (a Kurmi). This gang created such fear in the area that it started being known as the Faizan Party.[75]

Soon due to the existing backward-forward divide, the Faizan Party also started identifying itself with the gang of Pappu Yadav. They together started carrying out brutal attacks on the Rajput villages such as Sirsia, Dumra, Kasmara and Madhukarchak. However, during my field work, when I asked people from these areas about the incidents, they replied that;

> The daughters of the lower castes were allowed to marry only after they were raped by the Rajputs of the area. It had become an established norm. In Dumra village, when Rajputs raped the daughter of a Gangotri Mandal in broad daylight, the administration did not take any action. Thus, the lower castes were left with no option but to take such retaliatory steps.[76]

Soon there were about 43 criminal cases against Mandal including 15 murder charges. To meet the increasing influence of the Faizan Party, the Rajput gang under Buttan Singh, made another gang in the form of a caste army named as North Bihar Liberation Army (NBLA). Tolva Singh, the next in command after Buttan was made the NBLA chief and soon they attacked the villages dominated by Gangota caste (caste of Avdhesh Mandal), viz., Bhittha and Parvatta.[77] Though, Buttan, Singh was defeated in the 1995 Assembly election from the Dhamdaha constituency, his search for space in politics did not stop. His ambitions to reach the Bihar Assembly grew stronger day-by-day. Thus, even when Tolva Singh was projected as the NBLA chief, Buttan remained its *de-facto* controller.

However, after the murder of Ajit Sarkar in 1998, the equation of crime and politics took an unexpected turn and the two caste leaders made the situation very complex. Pappu Yadav, who was then imprisoned, felt that winning the 1999 Parliamentary elections from behind the bars, especially due to people's anger against him over the murder of the mass leader Ajit Sarkar, would almost be impossible. Thus, he invented a compromise formula with his arch rival Buttan Singh. In return, however, he assured that he would help him during the Assembly election, due next year. Buttan, too, saw a political future in this compromise formula and readily accepted it.

Thus, during the 1999 Parliamentary elections Buttan helped Pappu Yadav win the Purnea seat. Pappu made similar promise with Avdhesh of the Faizan Party. Thus, Avdhesh, also helped the Pappu camp. It was probably, this powerful support from both Buttan and Avdhesh that Pappu Yadav despite being lodged in the Beur jail, managed to capture over 60 per cent of the votes. He fought as an independent and defeated the sitting BJP MP Jaikrishna Mandal with a huge margin (See Table 5.6).

Table 5.6

Votes Polled to Top three Candidates in 1999 Parliamentary Election in Purnea

Name	*Party*	*Votes*	*%Votes*
Rajesh Ranjan	IND	4,38,193	63.17
Jai Krishna Mandal	BJP	1,85,627	26.76
Abdul Khalil Ahmad	CPM	29,799	4.30

Source: www.eci.nic.in

Subsequently, Pappu helped both Buttan (who made his wife Lesi Singh contest on from Dhamdaha Assembly seat on a Samta Party ticket), and Avdhesh Mandal (who made his wife Bima Bharati to contest as an independent from the Rupauli seat) win the Assembly elections in 2000.[78] However, Buttan could not live long to enjoy the benefits of being the husband of an MLA wife. His decision to compromise with Pappu Yadav was not accepted by the other members of his gang and many of them revolted against him openly. To suppress the dissenting voices, Buttan Singh even got killed some of his own men (Sugra Singh was killed inside the Purnea jail), but he was soon shot dead by unidentified gunman (allegedly his own caste/gang men) in the Purnea court premises in broad daylight on April 19, 2000.[79]

A balance sheet of the argument presented so far looks something like this. Purnea was initiated into a situation of caste war by the selfish interest of individuals like Pappu Yadav and Buttan Singh (supported by Anand Mohan Singh), and the society got split into backward-forward divide. Soon both of them were coopted in the political field (Pappu Yadav in 1990 and Buttan Singh in 1995). Pappu Yadav, later, in order to fulfil his greater political ambition, i.e., to secure his entry into Parliament, it is alleged, got the CPM mass leader Ajit Sarkar killed in 1998. He also compromised with Buttan Singh. In return, Pappu Yadav helped Buttan Singh's (wife's), reach the Assembly in 2000. However, Buttan's decision to compromise with the rival was not accepted by the other Rajput gangsters and he was shot dead by his own caste men. In the meantime, there came into existence a new gang named Faizan Party under the leadership of Avdhesh Mandal. Though, it was primarily a creation of the backward caste landlord-politician Jaikrishna Mandal, it soon got out of the control of its mentor and joined hands with Pappu Yadav. The Rajput gang headed by Buttan Singh, too, had created a new group called North Bihar Liberation Army.

Purnea in Flames: 2000–2005[80]

After Pappu Yadav's arrest and Buttan Singh's murder, Purnea became a battle ground of the NBLA and the Faizan Party and together they created a mayhem in the region.[81] This also proved to be a turning point in the caste equations. Sensing a vacuum in the leadership, both Anand Mohan Singh and Md. Taslimuddin,[82] started interfering in the day to day criminal affairs of the land. Anand Mohan, after the death of Buttan Singh, wanted to clain the leadership of the Rajputs. However, Taslimuddin making a clever judgement started supporting the NBLA.[83] To facilitate NBLA's activities, Taslimuddin even manipulated the administration. He managed to create a network of officers in Purnea, who could work at his whims. During my field work in the area, people named several officers, including IAS and IPS who were primarily working for Md. Taslimuddin and the NBLA. An IPS officer who was sent to Purnea as a trainee, was promoted as an Assistant Superintendent of Police and few months later, though unusual, was also appointed as the

Superintendent of Police (SP) of the same place. In fact, many respondents said that his predecessor was transferred early because he could not restrict Pappu Yadav from winning the Parliamentary elections in 1999, as Taslimuddin had wished.[84] A close look at the succession list of the SPs in Purnea shows that between January 7, 2000 and November 28, 2000; Purnea saw three SPs (see Table 5.8).

During this period, the people of Purnea allege, the NBLA chief travelling in the official vehicle of the collector for demanding '*rangdari tax*' (extortion money) from the market had become very common. "With all such help, it easily made up to ₹ 50 lakh every year".[85] Though most of the businessmen at Gulabbagh M*andi* had already left the town by the mid 1990s, the NBLA made life hell for whosoever stayed there. NBLA also started extorting money from smaller *mandis* in other parts of the district. Marwari businessmen of Barhara Kothi M*andi* near Dhamdaha also had to meet with a similar fate. Complaining about the situation, poor labourers in that area said;

> There were near about 50 Marwari businessmen in Barhara Kothi. We used to get some work from them to earn a livelihood. But due to the extortion threat and *rangdari* tax of the NBLA, majority (nearly 40) of them left this place. Only the smaller ones are left and we have no place for work now.[86]

Kidnapping for ransom also increased at an alarming rate. The NBLA kidnapped the sons of several businessmen and doctors. In case of non-payment they even killed some of them. "In just two-three years", said the Purnea Merchant Association president, "We had to face about 40 cases of extortions and kidnapping by the criminal gang."[87] Soon the number of criminal charges against Shankar Singh reached 58, including 35 related to murder.[88] The administration maintained its ineffective character all throughout this damaging disorder.

All this was taking place under the political protection of Taslimuddin, who had a larger political plan. His support to the NBLA was primarily intended to reduce the influence of Pappu Yadav. It was widely known that like Lalu Yadav, Pappu Yadav also had built his electoral base on the M-Y equation. Taslimussin's target was to break the alliance of Muslims and Yadavs and new alliance of the Muslims and Rajputs (M-R equation) in this region.

When the state government decided to hold panchayat elections in 2001, criminals from each gang, jumped into the electoral battle. No common man could muster courage to contest against these dreaded criminals. Whosoever dared was threatened either to withdraw or face dire consequences.[89]

This brought the hidden confrontation between Pappu Yadav and Taslimuddin wide and open, and Taslimuddin displayed his acumen by causing great damage to the M-Y equation. To everybody's surprise, all the 34 seats of the Purnea Zila Parishad were captured by candidates who had support from either of the two gangs.

Taslimuddin working successfully on his Muslim-Rajput formula defeated Pappu Yadav in the final run for the posts of chairman and vice-chairman in the *Zila Parishad.*[90] Similar incidences were witnessed during the municipal elections in Purnea, a year later. However, Pappu Yadav, despite being lodged in a jail, this time managed to place his man on the chairman's post.[91]

After the panchayat elections, the criminals-turned *mukhias* started carrying out their activities more vigorously and openly and scripted another reign of terror – of loot, *rangdari,* kidnapping and murder. In one such event on August 11, 2003 the NBLA reminded the people of Purnea of the Rupaspur massacre that had happened 20 years ago. Residents of Kasmara-Jaitola, a small hamlet in Dhamdaha block of Purnea and populated by nearly hundred families of tribals, saw the most barbarous day of their life. The NBLA encircled the hamlet early in the morning and started their killing spree which continued till the evening. This cost more than a dozen precious lives including women and children besides a long list of those injured seriously.[92] Several eye witnesses told me during the interviews that;

> People running for their lives were brutally shot or thrown alive into the flames emanating from their own houses as almost all the houses were set on fire by the killers. Moreover, the killers, who came to the village on jeeps and motor bikes in the morning, continued the massacre for a whole day while police in the nearby Dhamdaha police station, with full knowledge of this crime, not only remained passive but also kept threatening a large number of people who somehow managed to go to the police station with the hope that police will save them.
>
> The incident happened for restoring the illegal possession of 85 acres under the possession of local landlords Premjit Singh and Ajit Singh. The killers had assembled in the house of the *mukhia* of the village Buchhan Yadav, a day before the incident, and fearlessly carried out the massacre.[93]

Shankar Singh's fortune soon reached new heights when the Lok Janashakti Party (LJNSP) chief Ramvilas Paswan made him the district president of the LJNSP. Later he won the Assembly election from the Rupauli constituency on an LJNSP ticket, in February 2005 by defeating Bima Bharati, the wife of Avadhesh Mandal who had contested on an RJD ticket. Lesi Singh (the sitting MLA and widow of Buttan Singh) too won the Dhamdaha seat on a JD(U) ticket.[94] However, the political equation changed very soon when the Assembly was dissolved and elections were held again in October the same year. Both Shankar Singh (LJNSP) and Lesi Singh JD(U) were defeated by the RJD candidates Bima Bharti and Dilip Yadav respectively.[95]

In the 2004 General Elections, Pappu Yadav, contesting the Purnea Parliamentary seat on an LJNSP ticket, lost at the hands of Pappu Singh, who now had left the Congress and embraced the BJP. However, supporters of Pappu Yadav, who considered him as Robin Hood, had something else to explain for his defeat;

> Nobody could ever defeat Pappu Yadav in Purnea. However, he was very unfortunate during the 2004 Parliamentary elections. He lost the election because many people had got confused between the election symbol – 'Bungalow' of Pappu Yadav fighting on a Lok Janshakti Party ticket and that of *'Lifafa'* (envelop) of an independent candidate Jeevachh Paswan. Both looked similar and therefore Jeevachha Paswan got 58,000 votes, which even he himself had not expected. Pappu was defeated by Pappu Singh of the BJP on a paltry margin of 9,000 votes – a margin much lesser than the votes gained on *lifafa*. If he contests the election again in 2009, he will certainly win.[96]

Table 5.7

Votes Polled to Top Three Candidates in 2004 Parliamentary Election in Purnea

Name	*Party*	*Votes*
Uday Singh alias Pappu Singh	BJP	2,44,426
Rajesh Ranjan	LJP	2,31,543
Jeevachha Paswan	IND	57,021

Source: www.eci.nic.in

The supporters of Pappu Yadav although might have found consolation in the reason explained above, but in reality, he seemed to have lost his ground in comparision to his position during the earlier elections (4,43,111 votes during 1996 and 4,38,193 during 1999). Taslimuddin may not have succeeded in creating a feasible M-R equation, but the M-Y equation had certainly reached an all time low. However, Pappu Yadav's support among his caste men in the Yadav dominated seat of Saharsa remained intact and he managed to bring his wife, Ranjita Ranjan, into Parliament on an LJNSP ticket in 2004.

The Role of the Administration

From the discussions made above, it is clear that the politics at Purnea was very far from what we understand as democratic and representational in character. But equally surprising is the fact that the district administration too was nowhere close to the 'rule of law', and facilitated and escalated this undemocratic practice of criminalisation of the public life. There came into existence a system of law that was neither fair nor impartial and people's trust on the bureaucracy and the police was put at stake. When during my field work, I asked people to name some of the administrative or police officers posted in the district in the last 20 years, whom they could identify as upright, nobody had names more than one or two. Their complaint was that although there came some good officers, they were not allowed to stay for a longer period. They were brought in only when law and order situation used to reach to its worse and were removed immediately after that.

To understand the growing ineffectiveness of the administration and its role in the face of increasing criminalisation, I interviewed some of those officers who were named by the people as upright. These officers, at the condition of assuring their anonymity, provided valuable insights on the working of the system. One of them expressing his grief over the condition, said;

> Criminals get popular only when the administration creates a vacuum. I do not say that there was no crime during my days in the district, yet I can assure you that no criminal ever dared to overpower the administration. Law makes the administrators very powerful, and thus allows them to restrict those who overpower the law. But in the later years, neither the administrators paid any respect to the law, nor did the state require such persons. Policies were made to favour the administrators rather than the administration and thus the administrators lost their competence, integrity and brought discredit to the whole administrative machinery.[97]

One of the officers pointing towards the working of the district administration of all the border districts in the 1990s, said;

> A closer look at the policing of the border districts shows that during these years the promoted officers from the state service had remained the first choice of the government of the day. The IPS officers were called in only when the situation went out of control. If not, then the IPS officers were transferred so frequently that no officer was allowed to stay for more than six months at one place. They were never allowed to settle at one place and were transferred even before they could understand the law and order situation.[98]

Pointing out this differentiation is not to suggest or suspect the integrity and competency of all the officers in the state services; it is simply an analytical tool to look at the working of the government during those days. Only those IPS officers (including those among the promoted officers) who chose to remain in the favour of the ruling party were allowed to settle.

Purnea fits in best to explain this theory. Throughout the period between 1989 and 2004, Purnea remained a place for majority of those officers, who according to the public perception used to function as the puppet of the government or the politicians concerned. People openly mentioned the names (withheld here) of several such officers. That the average service span of an officer in the district reduced from two years (between 1947 and 1989) to mere nine months in the 1990s (see Table 5.8).

Table 5.8

List of SPs posted in Purnea District 1989–2004

Name of the SP (source of recruitment)	*From*	*To*
M.K. Jha (IPS)	13.05.1988	16.04.1990
Rajiv Kumar (IPS)	16.04.1990	25.03.1991
VACANT	25.03.1991	18.04.1991
A.K. Seth (IPS)	18.04.1991	18.04.1992
Rajesh Ranjan (IPS)	23.04.1992	21.08.1992
B.C. Verma (promotee)	22.08.1992	14.06.1993
Jagdish Raj (IPS)	18.06.1993	16.12.1993
R.R. Verma (IPS)	16.12.1993	10.05.1997
P. Hayat (IPS)	10.05.1994	23.06.1996
K.K. Bhatt (promotee)	11.07.1996	01.01.1997
A.S. Rajan (IPS)	01.01.1997	28.07.1997
Ajay Kumar Singh (IPS)	28.07.1997.	25.06.1998
R.S. Bhatti (IPS)	15.06.1998	28.04.1999
M.S. Majid (promotee)	28.04.1999	07.01.2000
Ramanand Parsad (promotee)	07.01.2000	09.06.2000
B. Sriniwasan (IPS)	10.06.2000	24.09.2000
A. Choudhary (IPS)	24.09.2000	22.11.2000
K.C. Surendra Babu (IPS)	28.11.2000	10.10.2002
A.K. Verma (IPS)	12.10.2002	22.12.2003
K.K. Verma (promotee)	23.12.2003	10.12.2004
Sudhanshu Kumar (IPS)	10.12.2004	–2007

Source: http://purnea-police.bih.nic.in/download.pdf

Between 1988 and 2004, the number of SPs posted in the district nearly equalled the number of postings (27) during the 40 years since Independence (1947–1987).[99] Thus, in all these years, the police lost their objective of being impartial and started acting on behalf of one or the other criminal politicians. Professionalism was put at stake. Whosoever (among the policemen) dared to challenge the criminals was taught lessons by the criminals. In 2000, the officer in-charge of the Sarsi police station was brutally murdered inside the police station when he took strict action against some of those. With such deteriorating situation and the rising graph of all types of crimes in all parts of the district, the people of the area in 2004 became so furious that they locked the Superintendent of Police along with other policemen inside the Khajanchi Haat police station and put it on fire. Finally they were rescued by the Pappu Yadav gang.[100] The administration looked hapless.

Concluding Observations

Thus, the discussions on the changing pattern of political domination in Purnea district, in essence, revolved around three contentious issues:

(i) The interest of the upper castes to maintain their status quo by keeping as much land in occupation as possible and the struggle against this casteist-feudal hierarchy by the Scheduled Castes, Tribes and some of the lower backward castes.

(ii) The selfish-interest of few individuals in a politicaly charged atmosphere turned out to be a caste war between the forwards and backwards (between the Rajputs and the Yadavs primarily), which later turned out to be a struggle for political domination between these two groups, and

(iii) The domination of criminal gangs in public offices to become the uncontested king of the land.

The functional distinctions drawn here, however, were not rigid. The boundaries between the three were often blurred and the differences between them, subtly hidden. Whatever may be at the level of ideology, practically all of them had used violence as their easy and preferred means to settle scores against the other. The values, ethos, and the morality of democratic politics, therefore, had been compromised equally, by all concerned. They had broken and adjusted the configurations and alignments according to their personal interest as and when suitable. No ideology or practice could be marked as neat boundaries between crime and politics in the area since the very beginning.

Caste and class, despite being conceptually different, have run along more or less the same line. There has been a strong, but imperfect interrelation between the two, and it continues to be so, even today. In the class of *zamindars,* there existed although a few from the dominant backward caste groups; it was primarily the upper-caste *zaminadars* who held the sway over political matters.

They continued to maintain their ability to secure intervention of various arms of the state to advance their interests, and brought the state in such a state of mismanagement that the 'rule of law' lost to be anybody's concern.

The most important reason, however, has been the lack of a disinterested arbiter in the form of a state. The police, the administration and the courts in the name of social justice left the landless, the poor and the less educated, simply, at the mercy of unscrupulous landlords who chose to ruin them by litigation. Through their caste kinship, illegal gratification and networks of corrupt officers, politicians and local judges, they legitimised the dominance of the rich and the powerful landlords. Although movements under the Left-wing parties and other organisations attempted to challenge the status quo, the upper-caste landlord politicians repressed it brutally with their social, economic and political power. They did not allow monetisation of the economy and consequently, pushed it into the hands of ganglords. There emerged a peculiar political class that was concerned only with grabbing as much power as possible to become the uncontested king of the land. With the passage of time this process accelerated from criminalisation of politics to politicisation of criminals to politicisation and criminalisation of the bureaucracy, and ultimately, the venom spread to every walk of life.

Notes

1. Sir John Houlton, (1949). *Bihar: The Heart of India*, Calcutta, Orient Longman. "Even in our times a transfer to Purnea was sometimes regarded almost as a censure. Purnea is [sic] an alluvial plain, the western part of which is profoundly affected by the vagaries of the Kosi ... for many generations have been the cause of great suffering and devastation." With annual floods come epidemics, *malaria* and such heavy silt that "it takes one, or even two, generations to get the land back to fertility. The rate at which the sand is deposited is almost incredible. Within four years an indigo factory was buried in sand so that only the chimneys were visible".
2. The analysis in this chapter, unless otherwise specified, is based on my personal experience and through various interviews and group

discussions conducted during the several visits between 2005 and 2011 as a part of this study.

3. Historically Purnea was part of the *Zamindar*i of Raj Darbhanga. With not many officials agreeing to administer the region during the British time, the area reached a state of utter mismanagement, corruption and exploitation and also became a haven for bandits (dacoits) and autocratic colonial planters. At the time of Independence, Purnea gained importance because a Muslim League conference held in 1942 at Kishanganj under the leadership of Raja Gaznafar Ali passed a resolution to include Kishanganj along with all the Muslim populated areas of Bihar and Bengal into Pakistan. See Ratneshwar Mishra, "Land, Labour and Power: Pargana Dharmapur of Raj Darbhanga under the Permanent Settlement," *IHC: Proceedings, 65th Session,* 2004, p. 474; Sir John Houlton, 1949. op. cit. Ganga Prasad Choudhary and Ashok Kumar, 1999. 'Seemanchal Rajya Ki Maang Kyon?' *Samkaleen Tapmaan,* Patna, May, pp. 53–55.
4. Francis Buchanan, 1928 (1986). *An Account of the District of Purnea in 1809–10,* Bihar and Orissa Research Society, reprint Usha Publications, Delhi. The work of Buchanan between 1809 and 1813 is one of the most detailed sources for the social and cultural history of Purnea in the early 19th century.
5. Manoshi Mitra, and T. Vijayendra, (1982). 'Agricultural Labourers and Peasant Politics: Rural Proletarianisation in Purnea, Bihar' in A.N. Das, (ed.) *Agricultural Movements in Twentieth Century Bihar",* London, Frank Cass and Company. pp. 88–118.
6. For further details see Kalyan Mukherjee, (1979). 'Caste-Class Polarisation in Bihar: A Case Study of Bhojpur, *Public Enterprises Centre for Continuing Education,* New Delhi; and W.W. Hunter, 1877. *A Statistical Account of Bengal, Vol. XV. Monghyr and Purnea,* London. As cited in Mitra and Vijayendra, 1982. op. cit. pp. 93–4.
7. Francis Buchanan, 1928 (1986). op. cit. p. 230–248.
8. N.P. Yadav, (1990). *Land Reforms and Agricultural Development: A Study of their Impact on Small Farmers,* Delhi, Commonwealth Publishers, pp. 69–94.
9. Some of the prominent names among them (mentioned here, with most probability, in accordance to their hierarchical status) are Vir Narayan Chand alias Moul Babu of Dhamdaha, Banmankhi and some parts of Madhepura (Chausa); Raghuvansh Narayan Singh of Kursela; Ramghulam Sahu of Parvatta; Hasibur Rehman of Mohamadia Estate; Md. Bux Chaudhary of Narkatia Kothi (also known as Sharifganj Kothi); Laxmi Narayan Sudhanshu of Rupaspur-Chandva; Prithwi Chand of Dhamdaha; Balbhadra Narayan Singh of Khagra; Bateshwar Singh of Bhawanipur and

Purnea; Pulkit Narayan Singh of Dibra and Purnea; P.C. Lal of Purnea City, Raghuvar Mandal of Barahri; Biranchi Mandal of Brahmagyani; Bansbain Roy and Bankhandi Roy of Chunapur and Domin Chaudhary, Jagdish Chaudhary and Hari Chaudhary of Rupaspur; Ghero Choudhary and Chhatradhari Roy of Parora; Kashi Singh of Akbarpur; Kashi Singh of Dumra; Chandra Mohan Jha of Tulsia; Kali Prasad Mahto of Baniapatti; Ruddi Mahto of Kajha Kothi; Surya Narayan Singh Yadav of Deori; Mahant Raghav Das of Chainpura Estate (Jankinagar-Murliganj border); Vibhuti Tiwari of Barhara and Vishwa Mohan Sah of Champavati-Damaili. Some among them, for example, the Manchand Estate of legendry Moul Babu, owned nearly 22,000 acres in various blocks of Purnea district and the Kursela Estate of Raghuvansh Narayan Singh had nearly 19,000 acres in different parts of the district and were said to be the largest landholders in the entire country. The others like Hasibur Rehman of Mohamdia Estate with 10,000 acres and Md. Bux Choudhary with 12,000 acres were not far behind. Jagdish Choudhary and Prithvi Chand too had over 10,000 acres each, while Rudi Mahto had 4,000 acres in possession. See Mitra and Vijyendra, 1982. op. cit. p. 92; also see K. Gopal Iyer, 1993. op. cit. pp. 87–116; and C. Rajeswara Rao, Bhowani Sen and Y.V. Krishna Rao. 1970. *Problems of India's Agrarian Sector*, New Delhi, Communist Party Publication, p. 16.

10. The report was discussed in the Implementation Committee of the National Development Council on June 26, 1965. Source: http://planningcommission.nic.in/reports/publications/pub1966land.pdf (last accessed on 11th Nov, 2008).
11. K. Gopal Iyer, (1993). op. cit. p. 97.
12. See Subhash Chandra Mishra, (1993). 'Problems in Pursuing Land Ceiling Cases: A Case Study of Purnea District, in B.N. Yugandhar, *Land Reforms in India-Volume 1: Bihar-Institutional Constraints,* New Delhi, Sage Publications, pp. 216–243. Mishra in his study elucidates how Moul Babu's family, which was one of the biggest landed aristocracies in the state with considerable political clout and positions in the Bihar Legislative Council, Purnea District Board, the Indian Civil Services, Bihar Civil Services and even Parliament, claimed exemptions from the court, adopted various delaying tactics and employed methods to circumvent ceiling laws and exploited legal loopholes to retain the land.
13. In a very interesting case, I found that the landlord family mentioned above had transferred their land on the name of some Moti, who was actually their pet elephant. As told by a senior CPM activist during a personal interview in Purnea.

14. He later went on to become the Chief Election Commissioner of India.
15. J.M. Lyngdoh, *"Babu Samjho Ishare," Tehelka, Feb 11, 2006,* http://www.tehelka.com/story _main 16.asp?filename=In021106Babu_samjho_14.asp
16. See P.S. Appu, (1996). 'Appendix V-2', in his book *Land Reforms in India: A Survey of Policy, Legislation and Implementation'*. New Delhi, Vikas Publishing House, pp. 339–45. In a letter sent earlier to the Chief Secretary of Bihar, K.P.J. Menon, Appu after listening to the rumours of the transfer of Lyngdoh had written, 'it will, indeed, be a great pity if the vested interests (of the landlords to get the transfer order of the Lyngdoh) are allowed to have their way. Lyngdoh's premature transfer form Purnea will utterly demoralise the upright officers who discharge their duties fearlessly in strict conformity with the law ... i still hope the rumour is baseless. I am, however, bringing these facts to your notice so that the government may not be in dark in the case Lyngdoh's transfer is under construction'.
17. National Commission on Agriculture, Working Group on Land Reforms, 'A Field Study: Agrarian Relations in Two Bihar District', *Mainstream,* 11 (40) June 2, 1973, p. 14, *quoted in* Nirmal Sengupta, (1982) Agrarian Movements in Bihar,' *The Journal of Peasant Studies,* 9(3), pp. 15–39.
18. The term 'monetisation' means the expansion and commercialisation of the restricted home market. It also refers to the improvement of agricultural standards. See, Gerry Rodgers and Jenine Rodgers, (2001). op. cit.
19. As the title suggests (*Maila Annchal:* a soiled end of a sari), this novel is about Purnea's backwardness and the cruelty the landlords practiced over the landless poor.
20. As cited *Dirty Regions,* n.d. on http://dspace.vidyanidhi.org.in:8080/dspace/bitstream/2009/1014/4/UOH-2003–240–3.pdf.
21. S.R. Bose and P.P. Ghosh, (1976). *Agro-Economic Survey of Bihar,* Patna, as cited in Mitra and Vijayendra, (1982). op. cit. p. 102; Gerry Rodgers and Jenine Rodgers, (2001). 'A Leap Across Time: When Semi Feudalism Met Market Economy in Purnea', *Economic and Political Weekly* June 2, pp. 1976–83; Praveen Jha, (2004). 'Continuity and Change: Some Observations on the Landscape of Agricultural Labourers in North Bihar, India', *Journal of Agrarian Change,* Vol. 4 No. 4, October, pp. 509–531;
22. People's democratic Revolution in India and Land Problem, *CPI (ML) Approach Paper – New Democracy,* presented at the convention on July 4th 2007 at Hyderabad. URL: http://www.cpimlnd.org/on-new-democratic-revolution-and-land-problem/peoples-de

mocratic-revolution-in-india-andland -problem.html; also see K. Gopal Iyer, 1993. *Evaluation of Land Ceiling Measures in Bihar,* in B.N. Yugandhar, *Land Reforms in India-Volume 1: Bihar-Institutional Constraints,* New Delhi, Sage Publication, p. 97.

23. In a personal interview in June 2009.
24. 'Letter from Y.A. Godbole, Esq. I.C.S., D.O. of Purnea, to the Commissioner of the Bhagalpur Division, 15 July, 1925' as cited in *Special Section, file no. 171 of 1925,* pp. 105–6. The report also carries a lengthy note written by Purnea SDO Phanindra Nath Mukherji in 1925 to his superior YA Godbole on a similar kind of situation. Reproduced from Hetukar Jha, (1977). 'Lower-Caste Peasants and Upper-Caste Zamindars in Bihar (1921–1925): An Analysis of Sanskritization and Contradiction between the Two Groups', *Indian Economic and Social History Review* 14, no. 4, pp. 550–4, for extended extracts from this file, see *Report: The Goala Movement, its Causes and Character.* No. 108 Con. from S.A. Khan, Dist. Officer, Bhagalpur, to the Commissioner of Bhagalpur Division. 7 July, 1925. (I, hereafter, refer to the entire report reproduced by Jha and Pinch as *PDS File no. 171 of 1925*). Also see, William R. Pinch, 1996. 'Culture, Conflict, and Violence in Gangetic Plane', in his book *Peasants and Monks in British India.* Berkeley, University of California Press. Accessed online; URL: http://ark. cdlib.org/ark:/13030/ft22900465/
25. See Anand Chakravarti, (1986). op. cit. p. 1847.
26. The socialist leader like S.M. Joshi who was one of the senior most Samyukt Socialist Party leaders of Maharashtra and had come to Purnea district to work in the Rupauli block.
27. Indradeep Sinha, (1970). 'Land Liberation Movement in Bihar', *Mainstream,* October 20.
28. Anand Chakravarti, (1986). op. cit. p. 1847.
29. He was the first Scheduled Caste chief minister of Bihar as a leader of the Progressive Legislator's Party, supported by the Congress.
30. The two leaders who headed the movement were Mohan Sharma and Buddhinath Shah.
31. Mahamaya Prasad Sinha was the CM of Bihar between March 5, 1967 and January 28, 1968.
32. In a personal interview in Purnea in June 2008.
33. Comrade Prabhat Choudhary, (1997). 'Bihar Bulletin',*Liberation: Central Organ of CPI(M-L),* February. URL: www.cpiml.org/liberation/year_1997/february/report.htm
34. As told by the residents of the area during the several group discussions.

35. See L.K. Advani, 1998. XII Lok Sabha debates, *Session III, (Winter)* Monday, December 21. (Accessed at http://parliamentofindia.nic.in/lsdeb/ls12/ses3/0521129801.htm on January 7, 2009); also see Arun Srivastava, 1998. 'Mob sets 4 tribal women; 2 children ablaze in Purnea', *The Indian Express,* December 15.
36. Information gathered from the residents of Sarsi village (from where Pankaj Singh, Pramod Singh and Buttan Singh hailed) during my visit in April 2008. Though some of them remained tightlipped on the issue, many came forward with clear answers to all my questions.
37. Unlike Arjun Yadav, he did not spare even petty crimes such as extortion from rickshaw-pullers and shopkeepers. He used to sell cinema tickets in black and even loot the commuters at night. He soon made up a gang and started bullying merchants for free goods. Once, when Pappu along with two of his supporters tried to bully a shopkeeper for giving them free 'cut pieces', the shopkeeper thrashed Pappu well. In one such case when Pappu was arrested in Dhamdaha, the police placed a plaque around his neck that read, "I am Pappu Yadav, a thief" and paraded him around the town. Information gathered during interview with several respondents of the Purnea town (names withheld). Also see Ajit Sahi, 2009. 'The Gangster's Last Gamble', *Tehelka,* Vol 6, Issue 20, May 23. URL: URL: http://www.tehelka.com/story_main41.asp?filename=Ne230509the_gangster.asp
38. During a personal interview in June 2009.
39. During a personal interview in September 2008.
40. Ajit Sahi, (2009). op. cit.
41. During a personal interview in June 2009.
42. As told by respondents in Banmankhi that is located on the Purnea-Murliganj road.
43. In a personal interview in Delhi in Sep. 2008.
44. Madhuri Singh was the daughter of one of the biggest landlords of Purnea, Mol Babu and had represented Purnea twice in the Lok Sabha.
45. Ajit Sahi, (2009). op. cit. Information collected during interviews in Purnea.
46. Sanjay Chauhan, a member of the Rajput gang was killed by the Yadav gang in broad daylight in the Purnea court compound soon after the 1990 Assembly polls. Ramakant Singh, the chairman of the Katihar Municipality was killed by the Yadavs and the Rajput gang, in revenge shot Anil Yadav. See *Samkaleen Tapmaan,* (henceforth referred as ST) 2000. Patna, May, pp. 35–39.
47. During a personal interview in Purnea in June 2009. The gang members in order to deceive their enemies had dressed up in

"yadav's attire". He also added "when the gang members came to know my real identity, they brought me to the hospital in Purnea and bore all the expenses of my treatment until I recovered completely". He didn't file any case against them.

48. Ashish Chakrabarti, (1998). "Here Fight is for Booths, not Votes", *Indian Express,* May 19. Bombay.
49. As described by people in Purnea and also during my visit to Saharsa in 2007.
50. Vikas Kumar Jha, (1996). op. cit. p. 103.
51. As expressed by people in during the interviews in Purnea.
52. Kay Benedict, (1996). 'Crime and Politics Inextricably linked in Bihar', *Indian Express* (Kochi), 23 March.
53. Chhotan Shukla was a famous criminal of Vaishali region against whom several cases of murder, dacoity and arsons were registered. He was earlier with the Congress, but in 1994 he joined Anand Mohan's BPP and was projected as the BPP candidate from Vaishali for the next assembly election in 1995. However, before he could fulfill his political ambitions, he was murdered by the rival gang, allegedly of Braj Bihari Prasad. This was his funeral procession. Information gathered during the field work in Muzaffarpur. Also see *ST,* 2000, March, p. 19.
53. Webindia, 'Anand Mohan gets death sentence for IAS officer's lynching', Patna, October 04. URL: http://news.webindia123.com/news/Articles/India/20071004/783957.html; accessed last on: 05–08–08.
54. Anand Mohan had parted ways with the JD after Lalu Yadav implemented the Mandal Commission report in Bihar. The Janata Dal nominee was the wife of S.N. Sinha, a big name among the Congress politicians in the state.
55. In the 1991 Parliamentary elections from Madhepura constituency when Anand Mohan was arrested by the BSF for carrying the fire-arms, Chandra Shekhar, the former Prime Minister (who resigned from the post on March 7, 1991) and the national leader of the Samajwadi Janata Party intervened directly and declared Anand Mohan as an SJP-supported candidate from Madhepura. Information gathered during the field trip to Saharsa. Also see Vikas Kumar Jha, (1996). op. cit., pp. 101–175.
56. The only candidate to win on BPP ticket was Vijoy Kumar Mondal from Araria. Anand Mohan contested from Gaighati, Sheohar and Kharagpur, but could not win even at one. For details see Statistical Report on General Election, 1995 to Legislative Assembly of Bihar, prepared by the Election Commission of India. URL:

http://eci.nic.in/StatisticalReports/SE_1995/StatisticalReport-BR95.pdf, Accessed last on: 04–08–08.

57. He was the only candidate to win a seat on the AIRJP ticket in Bihar and also in India. The party had fielded 3 candidates in Bihar and 38 in total in the country. See: www.eci.nic.in
58. See www.eci.nic.in
59. Information collected form the petition filed before the election commission.
60. Information gathered during interviews and group discussions in Purnea.
61. The movie was based on the novel 'Teesri Kasam' of the famous writer Fanishwar Nath Renu of Purnea.
62. See Ajit Sahi, (2009). op. cit.
63. Information gathered during the group discussions with the respondents of Purnea, Gulabbagh, Belori and Kasba. Also see *ST,* 2008, March, Patna, pp. 25–27 and Ajit Sahi, (2009). op. cit.
64. *ST,* 2000, Patna, May pp. 35–39 and July, pp. 44–48.
65. Jaikrishna Mandal was the landlord of the Barhari Estate in the Rupauli area. He was famous for the Dumra caste massacre. For details see Chapter 5. His character will also figure in the discussions ahead.
66. Pappu Singh was the son of Madhuri Singh (she had twice won the Parliamentary elections from Purnea constituency) and grandson of Mole Babu of the Manchand Estate, the biggest landlord of the area.
67. As told by CPM cadre Sudeep Roy and other lawyers who were representing the case for the tribals in the court, in a personal interview in Purnea in June 2009.
68. Ashish Chakrabarti, (1998). op. cit.
69. Some of the local CPM cadres, however, added that 'had Sarkar not taken the enmity with Pappu Yadav and accepted the party's decision, Pappu would not have dared to go to this extent.' It was Sarkar's decision to oppose Pappu in person that annoyed him and he ultimately planned his murder.
70. According to the CBI, Pappu had hired sharp-shooter Rajan Tiwari to eliminate Sarkar on June 14, 1998. CBI investigations revealed that Rajan met an under-trial Surajbhan Singh in Patna jail in January 1998 and Singh reportedly asked Rajan to work for Pappu and DP Yadav. Pappu Yadav later met Rajan in Delhi. CBI sources said Pappu Yadav and Rajan went to Purnea together in April where Rajan put up with one of Pappu's relatives. He introduced himself as Ashok Mehta. After killing Sarkar, Rajan left for Siliguri, the CBI alleged. See *The Telegraph,* URL: http://www.telegraphindia.com/archive/

990728/the_east. htm#head10. Only a day before, on June 13, the RJD MLA from Muzaffarpur Brajbihari Prasad (a dreaded criminal who allegedly had murdered the criminal MLA Devendra Dube, and BPP leader Chhotan Shukla) was also murdered allegedly by Bhupendra Dube (another dreaded criminal and brother of Devendra Dube who also became MLA after the death of his brother), Sriprakash Shukla (rated as No 1 shooter in the world of crime) and Rajan Tiwari (another sharp shooter) in the campus of a hospital where Prasad was under judicial custody. The police suspected that the plan of the murder of both the MLAs Ajit Sarkar and Brajbihari Prasad was made together inside the Beur jail where Pappu Yadav had managed the meeting of Sujan Bhan Singh (another dreaded criminal of the area and also a suspect in the murder of Brajbihari Prasad) and Rajan Tiwari. See *ST,* 2008. March, Patna, pp. 25–27.

71. The victory with the highest record margin in the 1999 Parliamentary elections was that of Sonia Gandhi from the Rai Bareli seat. Source: www.eci.nic.in
72. These landlords with the help of their muscleman Brahmi Mandal, in 1992 had surrounded the area populated by the lower castes and Scheduled Tribes in the Dumra village and burnt their houses, killing nearly 20 of them. The most prominent figure of this massacre was Jaikrishna Mandal, who contested and won the Purnea Parliamentary constituency in 1998 on a BJP ticket.
73. Unfortunately, the Naxals apart from waging violent war against the landlords had become notorious for criminal activities and disturbing common people in the area. Some of the famous names of this group were Jawahar Mandal, Shashi Sah, Yogi Paswan and Gonar Sharma. As expressed by several people in the area during the field work.
74. Avdhesh had gone to Punjab to work as a labourer. Once when Avdhesh Mandal returned home, he was persuaded by Jaikrishna Mandal of Barahri Estate to fight against the Naxals. Avdhesh agreed and successfully created a big and powerful gang. Expressed by several people in the area.
75. Faizan is an Urdu word which means benefactor. Though prima facie it seems that the name might have been given by the people of the backward caste, for which the Faizan Party proclaimed to be fighting for; nobody could either explain its meaning nor could they tell the story behind this nomenclature. Ironically, the upper caste whosoever I asked, replied that Faizan means robber. They further added that the gang was so dangerous that people out of fear started calling it Faizan.
76. As told by 'lower caste' people in Rupauli and Dhamdaha area (names withheld).

77. As told by a member of the NBLA in Jainagar village near Barhara Kothi.
78. For a detailed list of the candidates with criminal record who won the Bihar Assembly election in 2000 see Chapter 4.
79. *ST*, 2000. September, pp. 58–59
80. All the information in this section, unless specified otherwise, is based on interviews with local people, members of the gangs and also some administrative officers. However, names of all the respondents have been withheld.
81. After the murder of Buttan Singh in 2000, the NBLA was taken over by the second in command, Shankar Singh, who recruited many youngsters to maintain its hold over the area. The Faizan Party, too, increased its activities, but unfortunately, it witnessed a split between Avdhesh Mandal (the commander) and Ashok Rai (the second in command). People believe that this divide was scripted by Jai Krishna Mandal who was unhappy with Avdhesh after his defeat in the 1999 Parliamentary elections. Avdhesh had helped Pappu Yadav, instead of his mentor Jai Krishna Mandal. Thus, Jai Krishna Mandal (a Kurmi) played the caste card and supported Ashok Rai (a Kurmi) to revolt against Avdhesh Mandal. Rai joined hands with the NBLA and Shankar Singh, the new NBLA commander made full use of this opportunity. Ashok and Shankar together started attacking the Faizan Party and killed dozens of their members. The Faizan Party although retaliated by attacking villages with Kurmi and Rajput population, he soon began to lose the ground, as the NBLA, with its increased strength, killed several of its supporters in a planned attack on several villages, including that of Avdhesh Mandal. Bima Bharati, the wife of Avdhesh Mandal and the MLA from Rupauli – had a narrow escape in this attack. Ibid.; also see various issues of the magazine *Samkaleen Tapmaan* published in 2000 and 2001.
82. Taslimuddin in the meantime was appointed as the deputy home minister in the Deve Gowda government in 1996. With no restrictions and checks, Taslimuddin after being the deputy home minister, according to reports, had made an attempt to extort money from the owner of a private medical college, Kartar Singh. (as cited in N.K. Singh, 1999. op. cit. p. 88.) He later, introduced his son Sarfarz Ahmed into politics, and also managed to get him included as a minister in the state government. Ahmed too had a glorious criminal record like his father, ranging from beating up the Araria SDO and looting (*The Hindustan Times*, 30 July 1997). On the polling day of Lok Sabha elections in 1996 he knocked out the officer-in-charge of Tehragacha town in Kishanganj and snatched his revolver' (*The Indian Express,* 8 July 1996). Reports also said that there were several gangs being run in this region with Taslimuddin's active

support. One gang with a very unusual name was 'The White Ant Army' involved in the smuggling of cattle from India to Bangladesh (Kanaihya Bhelari, 2002. 'The White Ant Army', *The Week,* October 20; URL: http://www.the-week.com/ 22oct20/events11.htm). An FIR was registered (in December 2008) against the father-son duo for demanding ₹ 2 crore extortion money from B.S. Constructions, a road construction company working in Purnea, Araria and Kishanganj districts (FIR (252/08– Joki Hat Thana), as cited in *Samkaleen Tapman,* Jan. 2009, pp. 28–29.

83. *ST,* 1999. June, Patna, pp. 46–47.
84. As expressed by several people in the area during the field work in Purnea.
85. As told by a member of NBLA during the field trip by the author in August 2008.
86. During the field work in villages, viz., Jaynagar, Sukhsena, Barhara and Bhatotar.
87. As told by the President of the Purnea Merchants Association and many others during the fieldwork between 2006–09.
88. Information collected from the affidavit filed by Shankar Singh before the 2005 Assembly election and also told by some of the lawyers of Purnea during a group discussion.
89. Some such examples collected during the field work were the story of Om Prakash Singh (from Nathpur panchayat) and Ashok Jha (from Sukhsena panchayat). While Om Prakash was threatened with being hanged in full public view, if he contested the election; the NBLA gangmen asked Ashok Jha to pay up ₹ 5 lakh or withdraw. Surprisingly both of them were from the upper castes and both were harassed by the upper caste gang.
90. Some of them such as, Lila Devi (wife of Ashok Rai – initially a member of the Faizan Party but later joined NBLA) from Dobha panchayat in the Rupauli-Dhamdaha area; Geetmala Devi (wife of Gidra Mandal – a member of the Faizan Party) from Bhawanipur panchayat; Archana Singh (widow of Tolva Singh, the NBLA leader) from Barhara Panchayat; Laddu Singh (earlier with Buttan Singh but later started his own ganga) from Sarsi Panchayat were elected uncontested, Numerous other members of the NBLA such as Buchhan Yadav (Dhamdaha), Varun Singh (Bhatotar), Bulla Singh (Sirsia), Nishi Yadav (Munni Balua), Ramnarayan Yadav (Gathia Balua), Pavan Yadav (Kavaiya), Umeash Yadav (Ufrail), Nirbhay Yadav (Chandehi), Ballo Yadav (Kukraun) won the election and became *mukhias*. Pappu Yadav-supported candidates such as Asha Devi (widow of Arjun Yadav, the mentor of Pappu Yadav in his early days) and Dablu Yadav won from Banmankhi and Deepak Yadav and

Raju Yadav won from Maranga and Leela village respectively. See ST, 2001. p. 31, May, pp. 38–39, June, Patna.

91. The Chairman post was won by Saba Zafar – an RJD leader and a relative of Taslimuddin's from Amor and the Vice-Chairman's post was won by Niraj Singh, who also was the vice-chairman of the NBLA. See *ST,* 2001. November, p. 18–22. The NBLA has ultimately finished the domination of Pappu Yadav in Purnea as members of Panchayat Samiti in various parts of the district thus claimed Shankar Singh in an interview with a current affairs magazine *Samkaleen Tapmaan* (published from Patna) in November 2001.
92. 'Massacre in Purnea', Aug 2003. ML Update, A *CPI (ML) Weekly News Magazine*, Vol. 6, No 34, pp. 20–26.
93. Dhiraj Kumar, (2007). "Naxalite, Sunlight, Faijan va Liberation ka Khel", *Purnea Jagaran,* Bhagalpur, December 30.
94. Purnea and Banmankhi assembly seats were won by the BJP; and Kasba was won by the Samajwadi Party.
95. This time all the other three seats Purnea, Banmankhi and Kasba were won by the BJP. This election also saw a change in the guard at the capital and Nitish Kumar was sworn in as the Chief Minister of the state. The JD(U) and the BJP alliance won absolute majority in the Assembly, ending a 15–year reign of Lalu Yadav-Rabri Devi.
96. During a personal interview in April 2008.
97. In a personal interview in June 2009.
98. Another IPS officer in a personal interview in June 2009.
99. The situation in other border districts was also the same. While the average service period of an SP (and also of the DM) in Kishanganj district was 11 months, in district Araria, it was even lesser. In Sitamarhi and East Champaran, the average time period of SPs was 11 and 9 months respectively. In Supaul it was slightly higher at 14 months.
100. As told by people who were part of the incident.

6

The State in Bihar Today

Truth or Myth

The crowning of Nitish Kumar, the leader of the JD(U)-BJP alliance, as the chief minister of Bihar in 2005 was greeted with great optimism. Five years later, he came once again with a 'stormy victory', gaining 63 more seats and nearly 3 per cent more popular votes than that in 2005. While the victory in 2005 was considered as a mandate against the 'Lalu Raj' (details discussed in Part II); the vote of the people in 2010 was being termed as 'vote for economic development and good governance'. In simpler terms, votes for Nitish Kumar transformed from a negative vote (against Lalu Yadav's politics) to a positive support (for Nitish' style of politics).

However, the larger question is what difference did Nitish led JD(U)-BJP government create for such a magnificent change. Most of the answers provided till date, talk in terms of growth and not necessarily in terms of the best indicators of development and 'rule of law', which is the prime concerned of this study. Growth provoked economic development has never been the best measurement tool to analyse the performance of any state, and the case in Bihar where the growth story itself is pretty skewed, is no different. By attempting a critical analysis of current regime's trajectory and concern, this chapter shows how the government's negligence and failure to rectify the wrongs, especially in reference to the most reasoned expectation of the political economy, is not at all praiseworthy. By attaching preference for landowners and powerful over landless and weak, the state continues to maintain its illegitimacy. Serving mere as a conduit which perpetuates the exploitation of the discriminated and the marginalised, it has in fact, reversed the path of democratisation set up by a long struggle of the socialists in the state. The presence of Nitish, yet another socialist leader, at the top is solely acting as a safety-valve against mass anger that may erupt in the days ahead.

Good Governance and Economic Development

In the earlier chapters we have discussed that Lalu Yadav's astute political commitment to 'grass root democracy' by adopting people's language was no doubt a good initiative. But simply by not conforming to the 'rule of law' it actually brought the state closer to a reign of 'participatory autocracy'. He failed to create a 'world of enabling development' even for 'his own political constituency, let alone the state in general'[1] because he succumbed to his self-defined political acumen and did not listen to the demands of the movements from below that actually had shaped his revolutionary élan. The need for building a coalition between people's demand and policy initiatives was never realised even if it was in the best interest of the people (such as land reforms) in general and those of the oppressed and exploited in particular. So the policies initiated, if any, instead of being a 'democratic reconciliation' became 'imposed convictions'.

The results of the 2005 assembly elections, though not different qualitatively (as discussed in Chapter 4), had raised some expectations of change among the people. With Nitish Kumar as the chief minister, the people of Bihar believed that the search for development and growth the government would not be compromised with the hard-earned *ijjat* of the marginalised and the oppressed and their voices and concerns would get proper consideration. In fact, Nitish Kumar responded to this need in his own style of '*Janata Durbar*' (people's court) and tried his best to address all genuine concerns.[2] The Bihar Police Act 2007 seemed to be a good beginning to restrict the unwarranted interference of political influence or pressure on the police and administrative functioning. It enacted a partial separation of the law and order, from the investigative functions of the police and set up a Police Establishment Board to decide all transfers, postings, promotions and other service related matters of police officers of and below the rank of Deputy Superintendent of Police and make recommendations on postings and transfers of officers above that rank. The Act also set up independent Police Complaints Authorities at the state and district levels to look into public complaints against police officers in cases of serious misconduct, including custodial death, grievous hurt, rape in police custody, extortion, land grabbing and serious abuse.[3]

In its early attempt to break the criminal-politician nexus that had transformed Bihar into an anarchic mess, Nitish took other necessary steps, such as appointment or hiring of new judges, pay rise of judges, computerisation of court proceedings, etc., to make the speedy trial of the criminal and civil cases pending for several decades (see Tables 6.1 and 6.2 below), and the fast track courts convicted 56,156 criminals in the initial 5 years.

Table 6.1

Crime Data of Bihar from 2006 to 2010

	2006	*2007*	*2008*	*2009*	*2010*	*Total*
Cognizable	110,716	118,176	130,693	133,525	137,572	630,682
Murder	3,225	2,963	3,029	3,152	3,362	15,731
Dacoity	967	646	640	654	644	3,551
Robbery	2,138	1,729	1,536	1,619	1,538	8,560
Burglary	3,529	3,254	3,343	3,566	3,437	17,399
Theft	13,092	12,306	14,143	15,221	15,544	70,306
Riots	8,541	7,996	8,207	8,554	8,809	42,107
Kidnapping	2,301	2,092	2,735	3,142	3,602	13,872
Kidnapping for Ransom	194	89	66	80	72	501
Rape	1,083	1,122	1,041	929	795	4,970
Road Dacoity	211	151	146	201	207	916
Road Robbery	1,251	1,109	897	962	1051	5,270
Bank Dacoity	15	19	16	7	9	66
Bank Robbery	5	9	7	2	2	25

Source: Data provided on the website of the Police Department, Government of Bihar (accessed at www.biharpolice.bih.nic.in) (Note: the rows marked in red show stagnancy or increase in the crime and the rows marked in green show decrease in the crime in respective categories)

Table 6.2

Conviction of Criminals between 2006 to 2010

Year	*No. of Cases*		*Convicted Criminals*		*Category of Punishment*				
	IPC	*Arms Act*	*IPC*	*Arms Act*	*Hang -ing*	*Life Impri- sonment*	*More than 10 Years*	*Less than 10 Years*	*Total Convi- ction*
2006	2,178	1,156	5,230	1,609	17	1,389	366	5,067	6,839
2007	3,695	800	8,774	1,154	39	2,168	680	6,966	9,853
2008	4,461	706	10,994	1,018	27	2,307	610	9,063	12,007
2009	5,333	482	12,412	704	12	1,824	375	10,935	13,146
2010	6,201	427	13,717	594	37	1,875	640	11,759	14,311
Total	21,868	3,571	51,127	5,079	132	9,563	2,671	43,790	56,156

Source: Data provided on the website of the Police Department, Government of Bihar (accessed at www.biharpolice.bih.nic.in)

The government also ensured that the convicted criminals no longer get lucrative licences for liquor stores and forced them to conceal their weapons, rather than brandishing them out of their cars.[4]

His other significant achievement was in the direction of combating corruption among the government officials. Besieged by tales of corruption during his '*Janata Durbars*' across the state, Nitish Kumar, wasted no time in setting up a Special Vigilance Unit (SVU) under a team of former CBI officials with a separate headquarter. The unit soon made its breakthrough by catching the Police Chief and the State Drug Controller with enough wealth to finance the annual budgets of entire villages. State vigilance squads trapped about 400 government officials in the next four years.[5] The state also passed the Bihar Special Courts Act, 2009, which got the President's assent in March 2010. The Act allows the state to take control of the assets owned by the person being investigated, if the investigating agencies are convinced that an official owns assets in excess of his known sources of income. The vigilance department files a declaration with a special court that the target has amassed unexplained wealth. Bihar has set up six special courts that exclusively deal with this. The special courts then conduct speedy trials and decide within six months whether the property should be confiscated or not. The property would be returned with interest (at 5% annually) if the person is acquitted.[6]

The government also promoted the use and implementation of the RTI law in the state and with the help of the State Information Commission (SIC) established in August 2006, it brought significant achievements to its credit. It even established a call centre, popularly known as *Jaankari* (information) to assist the non-literate masses.[7] However, surprisingly, nothing more substantial have been achieved in cases against corruption than described above as only two officers have been convicted and only five First Information Reports (FIRs) out of these platoons of cases have been filed so far.[8]

In an attempt to adopt best practices of governance and ensure the happy confluence of a democratic political system, a dedicated bureaucracy and generate an atmosphere of professional management of responsibilities and functions with innovative ways of participatory governance, Nitish also moved towards the New Public Management (NPM).[9] The best example of which is Bihar's achievement in the Rural Works Department (RWD) and Road Engineering Organisation (REO) where the state government by hiring new staffs on contract and adopting measures of public-private-partnership (PPP) ensured its smooth functioning. Both the departments together outsourced the preparation of engineering designs for more than 18, 000 km, which led to a successful completion of the projects on time. Similar was experience in health, pathology and radiology services in the health department.[10]

Nitish Kumar's other important initiative towards good governance was through giving proper representation to different caste groups in his cabinet. In fact, moving a step ahead of Lalu Yadav, he constituted the Mahadalit Commission to look into the status of those Scheduled Castes who had remained neglected during the earlier regime. The commission identified 21 out of 22 Dalit sub-castes as Mahadalits and unlike many states that used this sub-classification for creating quotas within quotas, actually invented schemes to target its development.[11] The provisions though meagre brought in accolades for the Nitish's government for targeting the most oppressed and the deprived.[12]

But the most important achievement that seems to have transformed the image of Bihar from a 'lagging state' to a 'booming state' is its growth rate. According to the Bihar Economic Survey Report 2011–12, the state's gross domestic product (GDP) between 2004–05 and 2010–11 has grown at an annual rate of 11.36 per cent, which is much higher to the all-India figure of 8.5 per cent per year, making it the 'nation's fastest growing state' in this period.

While one cannot expect Nitish Kumar to bring Bihar out of the an anarchic mess in just five years, it would also be improper to accept that whatever he did in those years were sufficient or rather real. The popular schemes such as *Mukhya Mantri Balika Cycle Yojna*, in which bicycles were distributed to girls who stayed on in school, no doubt, boosted the female enrolment rate and the confidence among general women to come out of their homes and feel the change taking place; the state on several occasions clearly showed, not only the signs of its non-existence but also of its continued illegitimacy. In the section below, this chapter tries to present an evaluative argument of the state in Bihar today.

The Question of Land

Like Lalu Yadav, Nitish Kumar also realised the fact that Bihar's backwardness lies in the reform of access to land. Thus after coming to power, he promised to carry out land reforms. Indeed, he set up of a Land Reforms Commission (LRC) with D. Bandyopadhyay, the most trusted architect of land reforms in the neighbouring state of West Bengal. The Commission submitted its report to the Chief Minister in April 2008 with some of its prescriptions[13] such as – (1) a ceiling of 15 acres for all types of land per family as well as per religious establishment and per sugar mill; (2) abolition of the distinction between agricultural and nonagricultural land; (3) doing away with the general exemption given to plantations, fisheries, etc.; (4) acceptance of 9 July 1949 as the cut-off date, absentee landlords to be given the option of personal cultivation or through government; (5) enactment of a Bataidari Act to ensure secure and heritable right of cultivation to all tenants/sharecroppers with 60 per cent share of the produce (if the landowner bears the cost of production) or 70 to 75 per cent of the produce (if the bataidar bears the cost of production) and other legal rights to sharecroppers on the land they tilled, so that they could also benefit from institutional loans and crop finance; (6) allotment of between one acre and 0.66 acre of ceiling surplus land to 16.68 lakh households of landless agricultural workers and assignment of 10 decimals of land to each of 5.84 lakh households of homeless non-farm rural workers; (7) redistribution of 2.2 million acres of land, which according to the report was under the illegal possession of big landowners through *benami* (nameless) and other illegal transactions such as fake donations to institutions and religious trusts in the state (evidences of which we have already discussed in Chapter 3, 4 and 5).

However, the Government showed no interest in the report. When the landless rural poor, deprived sharecroppers and tenant cultivators started building up pressure, the Government responded by setting up another committee to study the recommendations of the Commission, only to delay and dilute it further. In fact, few months later, the Government under the veil of Mahadalit commission's recommendation actually diluted the land distribution from 10 decimals to just 3 decimal plots, that too only for those belonging to Mahadalit castes (discussed above). The report had very pointedly marked that the marginal and small farmers that constitute roughly 96.5 per cent of total landowners, own only about 66 per cent of the total land; whereas the medium and large farmers constituting only 3.5 per cent of the landowning community own the rest 33 per cent of the total land.

But all these remained 'a dreaded anathema' to Nitish Kumar's *sushashan* (good governance); who due to the continuous pressure and threat of the big landowners, had explicitly assured them that 'their interests would not be allowed to be affected'.[14] The landowners cutting across the parties and castes, including the dissidents of the JD(U) had spearheaded a campaign that reform of land of any kind would 'lead Bihar towards a civil war'. Joining together to show the unity of big farmer's at a rally held in Patna, ahead of the 2010 Assembly elections in the state, they warned the government of a 'civil strife should the state go ahead with the reforms'. Terming Kumar a "dictator" and an "autocrat", Rajiv Ranjan Singh Lalan, the former Bihar JD-U president and the closest confidant of Nitish said, "We had taken him to be the party bridegroom and helped him to power by sending out Lalu. We can do it again should Kumar go against the wishes of the people." Nagmani, the influential leader of Koeris, said, "We erred in counting him in as chief minister. He needs to be taken down." Such was the pressure that JD(U) spokesperson Shivanand Tiwary had to officially announce that "The government will never take a decision that is inimical to the interests of the landowners".[15] The BJP, in any case had not accepted the proposal at all.

Skewed Economic Development and Intra-State Disparity

There is no denial that the state has been witnessing a record growth rate in the last few years but we need to know where is it coming from? Is it really a 'miracle growth' as some economists and media are projecting,[16] or is it a narrow and unsustainable 'mirage growth' that will disappear at the dusk.[17] This chapter in its attempt to carefully analyse the trend, testimonies for the latter. The growth rate when divided according to the sectors- primary, secondary and tertiary- shows that these reporting good growth such as, registered manufacturing (23.30%), Construction (19.61%), Communications (27.23%) and trade, hotels and restaurant (20.22%) form part of the secondary sector. In particular, as pointed pot by Nagraj and Rahman, thanks to the boom in construction due to its increase in value two and a half times in the initial three years from ₹ 3,100 crore in 2004–05 to ₹ 7,400 crore in 2006–07 – an annual average growth rate of 46 per cent.[18] According to the most recent Economic Survey Report 2011–12, the total road length in Bihar is 112,733.58 kms, an increase of 20 per cent in a year from 94009.42 kms in October 2010.

Nagraj and Rahman further clarified that the growth trend when divided according to the sectors- primary, secondary and tertiary- shows that they were 0.7 per cent, 12.9 per cent and 6.9 per cent per year respectively; the highest in the secondary sector (see Figure 6.2 and 6.3). This also satisfies the reason why state's Per Capita Income even in 2009–10 remains much below the country average of ₹ 46,492 and continues to be at the bottom of the rankings of states with respect to Per Capita Income. The spending on health and education though increased marginally, it is yet far from sufficient.

Manufacturing accounts for less than 5 per cent of Bihar's GSDP. The growth rate has fallen to 4.69 per cent, with registered units growing by only 0.71 per cent and unregistered units accounting for 3.98 per cent. Large and medium enterprises were of course known to be very few, but the Economic Survey 2010 revealed that even the tiny/micro enterprises and artisan sector were on a sharp decline.[19] The combined growth rate of these sectors had fallen from 4.41 per cent in 2007–08 to 3.61 per cent in 2008–09 and only 1.14 per cent up to October 2009. Sugar, despite being the largest agro-based industry in the state had only 10 out of the state's 28 mills functional. All the 18 closed mills of Bihar Sugar Corporation are yet to be revived and re-opened.[20]

Figure 6.1

Bihar's Gross State Domestic Product Growth by Sector 2001–2008

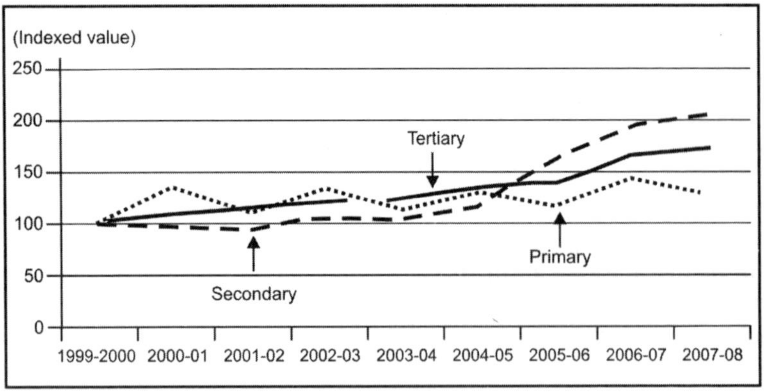

Source: Nagraj and Rahman (2010: op.cit)

Figure 6.2

Bihar's GSDP Growth in Secondary Sector 2000–2008

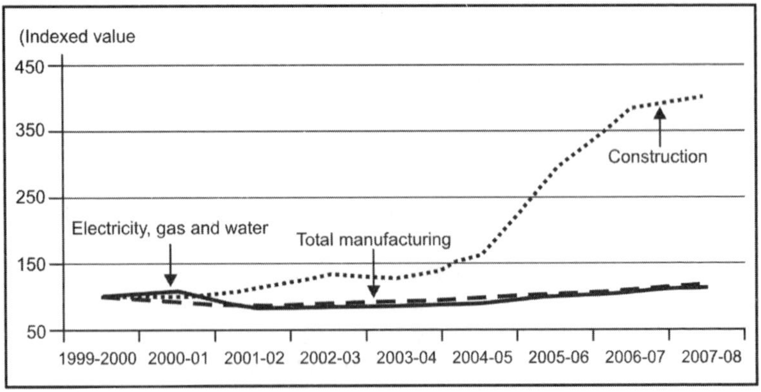

Source: Nagraj and Rahman (2010: op. cit.)

The most serious matter of concern is that agriculture, which accounts for 90 per cent of the State's population living in villages and 74 per cent of total workforce, contributes only 22 per cent of the State's domestic product and has witnessed only a nominal growth rate during the last 5 years.[21] As per the Bihar State Economic Survey 2008–09, the average of the growth rate of primary sector over the period 2005–06 to 2008–09 has been –0.77 per cent, with agriculture in particular doing even worse at an average of –0.87 per cent.[22] Showing negligence towards agriculture, the Nitish Government long back had repealed the Agricultural Produce Marketing Committee Act (APMC Act) in the state, leading to accentuation of the stranglehold of private traders and middlemen over large sections of the peasantry.[23]

Intra-state disparity over the years has also increased, especially in social inequalities stemming from caste, religion and gender. More importantly, the allocation of public expenditures to social and economic development also has been extremely skewed only in favour of one district or two. Evidences show that even at the village, rural development programmes are carried out only at relatively more accessible and developed villages. If one keeps the individuals cases used to showcase in media apart, the fact remains that the distribution of benefits from public investment and development initiatives at village and district level has been so uneven and inefficient that under the present condition Bihar may not rise from being "a mere source of labour supply for the rest of India".[24]

An important point to be noted is that the figure of growth that has been projected so well in the media and that has continuously made Bihar as the 'best-governed state' in the last five years is actually only public investment. A word of praise should also be added to the increased funds from the central government, that has brought Bihar's spending on planned development priorities from just 12 billion in 2002 to a mammoth amount of 160 billion rupees ($3.5 billion) in 2010.[25] The state on its own has not witnessed any significant private investment. For a target growth rate of 8.5 per cent over the 11th Plan period, while the private investment required was estimated at about 1.07 lakh crore; it could, as per the available status attracted only about 1,000 crore, i.e., less than one per cent of the above-noted targeted estimate.[26] Tycoons have visited, and left without showing any signs of big industrial investment. The state is desperately short of electricity (see Figure 6.2 above), which deters private investors. According to the Economic Survey 2010, only 10.3 per cent houses are electrified in the state as compared to the national proportion of 55.8 per cent. The target achieved even in the last two years has been abysmally low at 23.63 per cent and 22.49 respectively keeping the per capita power consumption least in the country.

Thus the growth story of Bihar needs to be seen with more caution. Moreover, this process of movement to a higher growth under Nitish should not be seen, as an observer aptly puts, a 'structural break' from the past. The current economic growth in Bihar is a continuum since 1994–95 which "follows from the diversified patterns of accumulation through the agency of new entrants to accumulation as an outcome of the social justice movement" and can be traced to the "diversification of trade and social empowerment among the backward castes" evident since the late 1970s through land struggles and "the aspirations for social justice that emerged out of caste oppression".[27]

The Secular Credentials

Though there have been no episodes of serious religious riots in the state since 2005, observers feel that the secular credentials of the state have been highly compromised by the alliance of JD(U) – an otherwise a secular force, with the BJP. There is an increasing degree of distrust towards the secular credentials of the state displayed during the turmoil period of the 1990s. The episode of violence perpetrated on the Muslims of Forbesganj in June 2011 over an issue of land acquisition, by the state police in connivance with the state leadership of the BJP is a clear indication in this direction.

Though the mainstream media chose to hide this under Nitish Kumar's teflon-coated suit of the 'best chief-minister', the *Economic and Political Weekly* in its serious editorial note described it as a "wanton act of state violence":

> On the afternoon of 3 June, the police in Forbesganj block of Araria district of Bihar shot, stomped on and beat to death four unarmed villagers and injured at least nine others ... .The dead include a pregnant Shazmeena who received six bullet wounds in her hand, spine and stomach, six-year-old Naushad who was shot twice in his spine, 22–year-old Mukhtar Ansari who was shot in his head, chest, stomach and spine and 18–year-old Mohammad Mustafa, who was shot six times and then when not yet dead, had a policeman repeatedly jump and stomp on his injured body and kick it mercilessly to make sure he died. All the bullet wounds of the dead and injured are in the head, chest, stomach, hands and spine. Not only do these indicate a clear intent to kill in the firing, it also shows that those who were running away or had fallen down were shot by a trigger-happy police.

> ... The villagers of Bhajanpura village, on the outskirts of Forbesganj town, have been protesting against construction of a boundary wall for a proposed factory which is linked to an important leader of the Bharatiya Janata Party (BJP), Ashok Agarwal, who is a lieutenant of Bihar Deputy Chief Minister Sushil Modi. The boundary wall would block Bhajanpura's only access road. On 1 June, representatives of the administration and the factory assured the villagers that the wall would only be built once an alternative road had been provided to them. However, on the morning of 3 June, the residents of the village found that their road had been blocked overnight by a newly constructed factory wall. They gathered in large numbers, broke down the wall and started accessing the road as they had been doing for at least the past six decades. The police arrived a few hours later and, it appears from witnesses, fired randomly at those using this road.[28]

One may not truly believe the claims that conditions were created for a 're-enactment of Gujarat',[29] but ignoring it only as "making a mountain out of a molehill', as Nitish Kumar had alleged was equally worrisome.

The government's intention of not bringing the truth out is clear by its half-hearted attempt of constituting a single member judicial inquiry commission under justice Madhavendra Saran (retired) which has not submitted its report, despite a year's extension in January 2012, till this is being written. In a recent development, the JD(U) led by Nitish Kumar has severed its 17 year old alliance with the BJP due to the elevation of Gujarat's chief Minister, Narendra Modi, as the BJP's Prime Ministerial candidate for the Lok Sabha election 2014. However, the jury is still out whether this is mere symbolic or there is some serious rethinking within the JD(U) to regain its lost secular credentials. Many suspect that this may simply be a vote winning tactic of the JD(U), who due to the incidents discussed above has started fearing to lose its Muslim constituency to the RJD.

The Rule of Law

The description of violence in the case mentioned as 'a wanton act of state violence' is sufficient enough to claim that state in Bihar has once again failed to be a disinterested arbiter and has chosen to be a party of the conspiracy as experienced in the last six decades. Incidents of similar importance that displays state's inability to adhere to the 'rule of law' are many, but some of them are so serious that they cannot be left without mention.

The caste massacre that took place in Khagaria in October 2009 in which 14 Kurmis and 2 Koeris were killed by the Mushahars is one such example. Nitish Kumar without any delay declared the attack as a

Naxalite attack. There was neither an explanation then or even now, as to what led Nitish Kumar to use the old theory of Naxalite violence for explaining the phenomenon which gave no signs of a naxal attack.[30] Three year later, on February 14, 2012, the Khagaria court in its judgement, handed death sentences to 10 accused (all dalits), including the popular mahadalit leader Bodhan Sada, and life sentence to four others. The prosecution had also termed Bodhan Sada as a Maoist. Thousands of mahadalits, reacting to this judgment protested before the Bihar assembly. The protestors also pointed out that Bodhan Sada had no connection with the Maoists. His wife Amla Devi who had been elected the head of the Baraj panchayat was killed by a Maoist squad.[31]

A fact-finding report released by the Joshi-Adhikari Institute of Social Studies in April 2012 stated that those accused and convicted in the case are innocent and were involved in a legal battle to claim the Bhoodan land in the region. The *Mushars* in Amousi and other neighbouring villages who worked as agricultural labourers in the fields were allotted this land in 1998. However, in the absence of implementation of even a single order, many started cultivating the landholdings forcefully. This was resented by the Kurmis of icharwa village, the de facto owners of these lands. There were reports of small skirmishes between Mushars in Amousi and the Kurmis in Icharwa. They were threatened by the goons. They were asked either to surrender their land or face the serious consequences.[32]

On the contrary, when the powerful Yadav leaders of the Phulwari-Korasi and Kareili of the Jamui-Munger belt, who in the name of Naxalism had been continuously unleashing terror on the extremely backward/tribals communities like the Kodas, the Santhals and the Sahs who mostly eke out a living as daily wage labourers and recently (on July 2011) killed six Koda tribals and took 11 others into their hostage; the state government kept mum.[33] Its preference to protect the interests of the landlords became more evident when Brahmeshwar Singh (popularly known as Mukhiya), the chief of the banned private militia, 'Ranvir Sena', was released on bail on July 8th 2011;[34] and few months later all the 23 convicts (including Bramheshwar Singh) of the Bathni Tola massacre in which the marauding Sena took 21 lives, 11 women, 6 children and 3 infants including, were acquitted. The Court cited "defective evidence" for overturning the convictions pronounced by the Arah court in 2010.[35]

Mukhiya accused in 22 criminal cases, including massacres, was given acquittal in 17. The five cases pending against him included a case of murder, a recovery of a mobile phone from his prison cell and three cases under Arms Act. In fact, soon after coming to power in 2006, the JD(U)-BJP government had scrapped the Amir Das commission set up in

1996 to probe the Ranvir Sena's role in the Laxmanpur-Bathe massacre. The commission enquired into 34 massacres committed by the Ranvir Sena and had interrogated deep into the economic and social linkages of politicians with the Sena. It is believed that the Commission had reached the final stage of its report and had named several politicians across the parties, including prominent leaders of the BJP and the JD(U) with links with the Ranvir Sena.[36]

The contrast between the cases of Bodhan Sada, the popular mahadalit leader (discussed above) and Brahmeshwar Singh Mukhiya, the leader of the upper caste militia Ranvir Sena alludes not only to the ineptness of the police and the administration but also to the ever increasing links between the political leadership, the landlords and the mafia. For those who lost their kith and kin at the hands of the Sena, this was clear betrayal by the state.

Brahmeshwar Singh Mukhiya was shot dead by unidentified gunmen outside his home in Bhojpur district on 1 June 2012. This evoked large-scale protests by the still alive thousands of followers of Mukhiya, who called him Gandhi.[37] During Mukhiya's funeral procession in Patna (where he was cremated) his supporters went on a a rampage for more than six hours setting on fire, police outposts, attacking police and media personnel. This was reminiscent of the state of lawlessness that was associated with the Rashtriya Janata Dal's rule in the 1990s in the state. It appeared that the Sena supporters were given free hand in resorting to violence. The event raises two very important questions. Why did the administration allow the supporters of a dreaded criminal organise a procession from Arah to Patna; and if so, why did the police remain a mute spectator to the mayhem caused by the Ranvir Sena supporters? The clarifications issued by the state invite only a mockery of the system. In the words of the state's DGP,

> by not taking action against the irate mob, the police have actually ensured that the violence did not spill over to the rest of the state ... we endured the violence so that it could be contained in Patna. Now we'll take action against the miscreants based on video fottage.[38]

The fact that this murderous incident took place 16 years before and yet no one has been held responsible for committing the murders even after such a long period makes the acquittal more depressing and raises suspicions over the rule of law. It clearly exhibits the sentiment that no regime can book the perpetrators of crime against the most marginalised and dispossessed sections of the population. The apathetic and detrimental approach of the state towards the lives and rights of the most marginalised helps only in claiming the argument more clinically that the existence of the rule of the state in Bihar is still a fallacy.

Even the picture of the prevailing law and order situation in the state is not so rosy. The Table 6.1 presented above shows that the total number of cognisable crimes committed in the state after 2004 has doubled (the annual increase of 1.75 per cent between 1998 and 2004 to 3.79 per cent between 2004 and 2008). The only significant decline has been witnessed in dacoity, robbery and kidnapping for ransom that had once become the 'flourishing industry' during 'Lalu Raj'. But the number of murders, riots, kidnapping in general and burglary has witnessed a substantial increase. The number of rape cases, in particular, went up in the initial years rapidly and has started showing a decreasing trend only in the recent two years.

The most dangerous dimension, however, is the changing social base of crime that is evident by the alarming increase in crime against women, dalits and adivasis. With the annual growth under the first five years under NDA in rape of dalits at 14.5 per cent, kidnapping of women at 18 per cent, arson against dalits and adivasis at 22 per cent and crimes recorded against dalits and/or adivasis under the Prevention of Atrocities Act, 1989, at 24 per cent are clear indication of the "reassertion of the power of Bihar's traditional upper caste feudal patriarchy through the front door of *good governance* under the NDA government" and a distance equal from the rule of law as practiced during the rule of 'swaggering goons' of the RJD period.[39] The propertied and the affluent may have regained their lost sleep, but the state for the most discriminated, oppressed and exploited still remains illegitimate.[40]

Last but not the least, the number of candidates with criminal and serious criminal cases in the Assembly Election 2010 has shown a sharp increase as compared to the Assembly Election in 2005. An analysis presented by Bihar Election Watch and Association for Democratic Reforms put the data as follows:

Table 6.3

Comparison of MLAs with Pending Criminal Cases: Bihar Assembly Election 2005 and 2010

	Bihar Assembly Election, 2005	*Bihar Assembly Election, 2010*	*Increase*	*% Increase*
MLAs with pending criminal cases	117	141	24	21%
Total pending criminal castes	441	440	–1	–0.23%
MLAs with pending serious criminal cases	68	85	17	25%
Total serious IPC sections against MLAs	363	267	–96	–26%

Table 6.4

Party wise Comparison of MLAs with Pending Criminal Cases: Bihar Assembly Election 2005 and 2010

	Bihar 2010 Assembly Election					*Bihar 2005 Assembly Election*				
Party	*Total MLAs analyzed*	*MLAs with pending Criminal cases*	*MLAs with pending Serious Criminal cases*	*% of MLAs with pending Criminal cases*	*% of MLAs with pending Serious Criminal cases*	*Total MLAs analyzed*	*MLAs with pending Criminal cases*	*MLAs with pending Serious Criminal cases*	*% of MLAs with pending Criminal cases*	*% of MLAs with pending Serious Criminal cases*
INC	4	3	2	75%	50%	9	3	2	33%	22%
RJD	22	13	7	59%	32%	48	19	11	40%	23%
JD(U)	114	58	43	51%	38%	86	39	21	45%	24%
BJP	91	58	29	64%	32%	55	32	18	58%	33%
LJP	3	3	2	100%	67%	9	6	5	67%	56%

While the number of criminal cases and serious criminal cases have risen significantly among the Congress and the LJP, the rise in both the BJP and JD(U) is equally dangerous. A summary of all serious violent offences related to murder, kidnapping, extortion, theft, robbery and dacoity shows that JD(U) has 148 serious IPC counts pending against its MLAs and BJP has 88 against its MLAs as compared to 17 of RJD, 7 of INC, 10 of INC and 4 of LJP.[41] Even among the top 20 MLAs with serious pending criminal cases like murder, attempt of murder, extortion, kidnapping, dacoity, etc. BJP comes at the top with 9 followed by the JD(U) with 8 MLAs. Among the top ten only one seat is occupied by a non JD(U), non-BJP MLA.

Concluding Remarks

Thus, attempting at economic development and good governance without rectifying the wrongs of the political economy of the state cannot and has not brought any significant change in the illegitimacy of the state in Bihar. The story of success of the state in Bihar still seems a myth. State's preference for landowners and powerful and negligence for landless and weak continues to be the same and the state still is mere serving as a mechanism by which the perpetuation of the exploitation of the old order continues without any change.

There is a need to check, as an observer aptly remarks, "the internal inconsistency of expenditure priorities and policy rhetoric mismatched under the *sushasan* defined 'development' paradigm" and raise "fundamental questions about the sustainability of political processes and contradictory outcomes" that have been projected under the 'blooming Bihar' campaign by the state.[42] The state needs much more to do than mere showcasing individual success stories as the evidence presented in this chapter belies the 'miracle growth' and proves it rather an uneven and unsustainable 'mirage growth'. There is no doubt that people travel in the state without any fear, but the question of 'rule of law' remains still far from approaching as the state, for the most discriminated, oppressed and exploited, still remains illegitimate.

Notes

1. See Prabhakar Jha (2007), Reviving Culture, *Seminar,* 580, http://www.india-seminar.com/2007/580/580_prabhakara_jha.htm#top
2. Avinash Kumar, (2009). 'Illegitimacy of the State in Bihar', *Economic and Political Weekly,* Vol. XLIV, No. 44, pp. 8–11.
3. The Act ensured that Director General of Police is appointed through a merit based transparent process and he along with other police officers on operational duties (Superintendents of Police in-charge of a district, Station House Officers in-charge of a police station, IGP (zone) and DIG (range)) have a minimum tenure of two years. See Bihar Police Act (Bihar Act 1, 2007).
4. *The Economist,* "The Bihari Enlightenment: India's Most Notorious State is Failing tc Live up to its Reputation", (January 28th 2010); accessed http://www.economist.com/node/15393980
5. K.P. Narayan Kumar, (2011), "Bribeless in Bihar: Bureaucrats in India's most corrupt state are facing the heat from their own chief minister", *Forbes India Magazine,* 11 February, accessed at: http://business.in.com/article/on-assignment/bribeless-in-bihar/220 52/0#ixzz1DKHsnnN9
6. Ibid.
7. For more details on *Jankaari,* see Vikram K. Chand, (2011). 'Transforming Governance in a Lagging State: The Case of Bihar', in Vikram K. Chand, (ed.). *Public Service Delivery in India: Understanding the Reform Process,* New Delhi, Oxford University Press, pp. 36–74; also see Chanchal Kumar, (2007). *Project Report on Jaankari: A Government of Bihar Initiative,* CM Secretariat, Patna.
8. K.P. Narayan Kumar, (2011). Bribeless in Bihar, op. cit.
9. See *Bihar's Exposure to Innovative Governance Practices: A Report of the Special Task Force on Bihar,* Government of India, New Delhi.

10. For more details, see Vikram K. Chand, (2011).op. cit.
11. The state government decided to provide 3 decimal land to each landless mahadalit family for construction of houses under the Mahadalit Development Scheme and also launched a special 'Mahadalit Sauchalaya Nirman Yojana' under which each mahadalit family would receive ₹ 300 from the Bihar Mahadalit Vikash Mission for construction of toilets. See http://www.indianexpress.com/news/actionplanforwelfareofmahadalitsinbih/495634/
12. Avinash Kumar, (2009). op. cit.
13. See 'Riding the Crest of People's Movement', India Country Paper, *Land Watch Asia,* a document prepared by Ekta Parishad, accessed at www.angoc.org/dmdocuments/SRL_India.pdf; Mamman Mathew, (2010). 'Troubled Lands of Bihar' *The Hindustan Times,* May 10. accessed at http://www.hindustantimes.com/Troubled-land-of-Bihar/Article1–541880.aspx; 'Bihar: Implement Bandyopadhyay Commission's Recommendations for Land Reforms' ML Update, a CPI-ML (Liberation) weekly news magazine, also published in *Mainstream,* Vol XLVII, No 33, August 1, 2009.
14. See 'Bihar: Implement Bandyopadhyay Commission's Recommendations for Land Reforms' op. cit.
15. See Mamman Mathew, (2010). 'Troubled Lands of Bihar' op. cit.
16. S.A. Aiyar, (2010). "New Miracle Economies: Bihar, Poor States", *The Times of India*, January 3; (2010). Bihar's Economic Miracle: Real but Fragile, *The Times of India*, February 21; Arvind Panagariya, (2010). "Development is a Tiger", *Times of India*, 11 December.
17. Praveen Jha and Atul Kumar Singh, (2010). 'Deconstructing Bihar's Growth "Miracle"', accessed at http://www.bihartimes.in/Newsbihar/2010/March/Newsbihar12March7.html
18. R. Nagaraj and Andaleeb Rahman, (2010). 'Booming Bihar: Fact or Fiction?' *Economic and Political Weekly,* February 20, Vol. XLV, No. 8, pp. 10–11. In 2003–04 the expenditure was only 51 crore.
19. It is only very recently that signs of upward trend have become visible.
20. Bihar Economic Survey 2012.
21. Ibid.
22. Income in agricultural sector has fell from 21729 crore to 17804 crore. Ibid. also see 'Bihar: Implement Bandyopadhyay Commission's Recommendations for Land Reforms' op. cit.
23. APMC acts were legislated across the country to protect the farmers from the exploitation of intermediaries and traders and also to ensure better prices and timely payment of their produce. Given the fact that 'nearly 80 per cent of the agricultural produce market was

already under control of private traders, if at all, the problem of Bihar's agriculture was not absence of private market, but that of its correction'. The observers opined that 'appropriate guidance and support from the State must not be viewed as a burden on the economy; quite the contrary, it goes to increase efficiency of the system as a whole'. Jha and Singh (2010). op. cit.

24. Yuko Tsujita, Hisaya Oda, Prabhat Ghosh, (2010). 'Development and Intra-State Disparities in Bihar', *Economic and Political Weekly,* December 11, Vol. XLV, No. 50, pp. 13–15.
25. The Economist, 'Bihar's remarkable recovery: On the Move', (January 28, 2010), accessed at http://www.economist.com/node/15393510.
26. See Praveen Jha and Atul Kumar Singh, (2010). op. cit
27. Chirashree Das Gupta (2010). "Unravelling Bihar's 'Growth Miracle'", *Economic and Political Weekly,* December 25, 2010 Vol. XLV No 52, pp. 50–62.
28. Editorial, (2011). 'Silence on the Killings in Bihar', *Economic and Political Weekly,* June 25, Vol. XLVI, Nos. 26 & 27, pp. 7–8.
29. Committee for Justice to Forbesganj Police Firing Victims, Protesting at Bihar Bhavan in New Delhi on 13 June 2011.
30. See Avinash Kumar, (2009). op. cit.
31. Kashi Prasad and Rajiv Kumar, (2012), '10 Get Death for Amausi Massacre', *Times of India,* Feb 15.
32. As cited in Avinash Kumar, (2012). 'Fallacy of the State in Bihar', *Economic and Political Weekly,* November 3, pp. 23-25.
33. See Shoumojit Banerjee, (2011). 'Munger Massacre Undersscores Changing Face of Bihar's Naxal Movement', *The Hindu,* July 26, p. 7.
34. 'Ranvir Sena Chief Released', *The Hindu,* (July 10, 2011). Brahmeshwar Singh has 17 cases registered against him – the most famous being the killing of 61 Dalits in the Laxmanpur-Bathe and Shankarbigha massacre in Jehanabad district on December 1, 1997.
35. Shoumojit Banerjee, (2012) 'For Residents of Bathani, it is a Horror They Cannot Forget', *The Hindu,* April 19, p. 1. The Arah court had sentenced three persons to death and awarded life sentence to another 20.
36. Kavita Krishnan, (2013), Battle for Justice and Democracy: Laxmanpur-Bathe, *Economic and Political Weekly,* November 16, pp. 10–12.
37. Ashwani Kumar, (2012). "No Gentlemen in This Army", *The Hindu,* 6 June.
38. Nirala, (2012). "Old Caste Wars Haunts Nitish Naya Bihar", *Tehalka,* 16 June.

39. Chirashree Das Gupta (2010). op. cit.
40. In fact, to say that even the business class feels a sense of security, would amount to denial of reality. The story, published in *The Economist,* of Husk Power Systems (HPS), a company formed in 2007 by three young Biharis and an American friend, explains this more clearly. The HPS which runs 50 micro power plants in rural areas fired by burning otherwise useless rice husks and employs more than 250 people has not a single word of praise for the government of Bihar and has tried to avoid contact with the Bihar government as much as possible due to several experiences of corruption and criminality. As one of HPS founders describe "A village policeman grabbed a bundle of cables for one of the first plants, demanding a bribe: the company refused, opting to bore him into submission instead. When HPS started building a centre to train its workers near the state capital, Patna, a neighbourhood tough-guy demanded 100,000 rupees ($2,250) in protection money. This was refused, so the builders were threatened, and then beaten, and a mob flattened the construction site." *The Economist,* Bihar's pro-business reforms: Paper tiger, (November 4, 2010); accessed at: http://www.economist.com/node/17419805
41. See 'Analysis of Criminal and Financial details of Candidates and MLAs from Bihar based on 2010 Assembly Election', A report by Bihar Election Watch and Association for Democratic Reforms, accessed at http://adrindia.org/files/Bihar%202010%20v3_0.pdf, Table presented at page 17 and 18.
42. Chirashree Das Gupta (2010). op. cit.

APPENDICES

Appendix 1

Parliamentary by-elections 1980–1988

STATES	Year	PC NO./Name	Winner Party	Winner Votes	Winner Name	Runner Party	Runner Votes	Runner Names	Reason for re-election
BIHAR	1980	13–MADHUBANI	CPI	231874	B.JHA	INC (I)	169648	M.R.Z.AJAZI	DEATH OF SHRI S.ANSARI
						JNP (SC)	71939	A.H.ANSARI	
U.P.	1980	15–KHERI	INC(I)	123640	U.K.VERMA(W)	JNP	55467	J.S.VAJPAI	DEATH OF SHRI B.G.VERMA
						IND	4756	CHURAMANI	
	1980	23–RAEBARELI	INC(I)	176456	A.K.NEHRU	JNP (S)	69166	J.MISHRA	RESIGNATION OF SHRI SMT.I. GANDHI
						IND	4175	K.B.SINGH	
KARNATKA	1980	2–GULBARGA	INC(I)	150665	C.M.STEPHEN	INC (I)	76985	B.R.GOUDA	RESIGNATION OF SHRI D.SINGH
						IND	4224	C.M.SWAMY	
M.P.	1981	5–SAGAR(SC)	BJP	143620	R.P.AHIRWAR	INC	139595	R.L.THAKKAR	DEATH OF SHRI SMT.S.RAI
						JNP	9026	N.P.RAI	
MAHARASHTRA	1981	51–NANDRBAR(ST)	INC	188550	G.M.HODLYA	JNP	61157	A.S.F.JADHAV	RESIGNATION OF SHRI S.S.NAIK
						BJP	47758	P.DILAWARSINGH	

Cont'd…

...Cont'd

ORRISA	1981	6–CUTTACK	INC(I)	156906	J.PATNAIK(W)	LKD	107054	R.RAY	RESIGNATION OF SHRI J.B.PATNAIK
						IND	6727	N.MISRA	
U.P.	1981	12–BARELLY	INC(I)	114231	B.A.AHMAD(W)	BJP	78935	S.K.GANGWAR	DEATH OF SHRI M.Y.KHAN
						INC (I)	27616	MOHD.Y.SALIM	
	1981	25–AMETHI	INC(I)	258884	R.GHANDHI	LKD	21188	S.YADAV	DEATH OF SHRI S.GANDHI
						IND	5690	R.BALI	
	1981	54–MIRZAPUR	INC(I)	92182	UMAKANT	LKD	62012	M.Y.BEG	DEATH OF SHRI A.IMAM
						BJP	26085	R.NATH	
	1981	56–ALLAHABAD	INC(I)	84612	K.P.TIWARI	LKD	37921	M.AHMAD	RESIGNATION OF SHRI V.N.P.SINGH
						JNP	33008	M.M.JOSHI	
W.B.	1981	26–SERAMPORE	CPM	265372	AJIT BEG	INC (I)	168823	S.M.ROY	DEATH OF SHRI D.BHATTACHARYA
						IND	2980	A.N.CHOWDHURY	
BIHAR	1982	53–LOHARDAGA(ST)	INC	134670	S.ORAON(W)	BJP	59221	L.ORAON	DEATH OF SHRI K.ORAON
						IND	13745	J.R.ORAON	
M.P.	1982	25–JABALPUR	BJP	134442	B.PANANJPE	INC	121204	R.K.JIJIBAI(W)	DEATH OF SHRI M.SHARMA
						IND	3348	NARAYANDAS	
MAHARASHTRA	1982	10–THANE	BJP	144458	P.J.SHIAVRAM	INC	99651	P.M.HEGDE	DEATH OF SHRI M.R.KASHINATH
						IND	71885	D.SAMANT	

Cont'd...

...Cont'd

RAJASTHAN	1982	10–BAYANA(SC)	INC	101706	L.R.KEN	IND	45750	B.R.LAHARI	RESIGNATION OF SHRI J.PAHADIA
						BJP	22601	R.L.MAHAMANA	
	1982	18–UDAIPUR	INC	187268	D.VERMA	BJP	143079	S.S.BHANDARI	DEATH OF SHRI M.L.SUKHADIA
						JNP	9083	K.S.KALVI	
T.N.	1982	25–PERIYAKULAM	ADK	252377	JAKKAY.S.T.K	DMK	183117	C.ERAMADDRISHN AN.N	DEATH OF SHRI NATARAJAN C.N.
U.P.	1982	2–GARHWAL	IND	149669	H.N.BAHUGUNA	INC	120645	C.MOHAN	RESIGNATION OF SHRI H.N.BAHUGUNA
						IND	3657	B.SINGH	
W.B.	1982	16–MATHURAPUR (SC)	CPM	254758	N.SINHA	INC (I)	199282	G.NASKAR	DEATH OF SHRI M.MANDAL
						SUC	30414	S.S.NAIYA	
	1982	17–DIAMOND HARBOUR	CPM	296980	A.DATTA	INC	180757	J.ABEDIN	DEATH OF SHRI J.BOSU
						IND	4755	G.C.MUKHERJEE	
BIHAR	1985	23–KISHANGANJ	JNP	212423	S.SHAHABUDDIN	INC	138731	I.HAQUE	DEATH OF SHRI J.RAHAMAN
						IND	14807	K.RAHMAN	
	1985	28–GODDA	INC	197478	SALAUDDIN	BJP	185901	J.YADAV	DEATH OF SHRI SAMINUDDIN
						JNP	17491	P.K.SINGH	
	1985	29–BANKA	INC	162754	C.SINGH	JNP	125659	G.FERNANDES	RESIGNATION OF SMT.M.SINGH
						BJP	74303	J.YADAV	

Cont'd...

...*Cont'd*

MAHARASHTRA	1985	43–BARAMATI	JNP	179507	K.S.SAHEBRAO	INC	130955	P.S.BAJIRAO	RESIGNATION OF SHRI P.S. GOVINDRAO
						LKD	9648	V.P.GUJARATHI	
ORISSA	1985	5–KENDRAPARA	JNP	275105	S.K.DEB	INC	235160	B.K.BISWAL	RESIGNATION OF SHRI B.PATNAIK
						IND	6004	N.MALIK	
RAJASTHAN	1985	3–CHURU	INC	253663	N.BUDNIA	LKD	186016	D.SARAN	DEATH OF SHRI MOHAR SINGH
						IND	4833	B.B.GOSWAMI	
SIKKIM	1985	SIKKIM	SSP	UNCON	D.K.BHANDARI (W)			RESIGNATION OF SHRI N.B.BHANDARI	
T.N.	1985	38–TIRUCHENDUR	INC	169710	R.D.ATHITHAN	JNP	93891	P.VIJAYARAGHAVA N	DEATH OF SHRI K.T.KOSALRAM
						IND	3728	A.D.R.PANDIAN	
U.P.	1985	5–BIJNOR(SC)	INC	128086	M.KUMARI(W)	LKD	122747	R.B.PASWAN	DEATH OF SHRI G.LAL
						IND	61504	M.WATI(W)	
W.B.	1985	41–BOLPUR	CPM	339078	S.CHATTERJEE	INC	240079	S.S.RAY	DEATH OF SHRI S.ROY
						IND	10087	K.K.ROY	
U.T.DELHI	1985	2–SOUTH DELHI	IND	161744	A.SINGH	BJP	121830	V.K.MALHOTRA	DEATH OF SHRI L.MAKEN
						JNP	6004	J.S.PHULL	
BIHAR	1986	29–BANKA	INC	186237	M.SINGH(W)	JNP	156853	G.FERNENDES	DEATH OF SHRI C.SINGH
						IND	5629	S.PATHAK	

Cont'd...

...Cont'd

KARNATAKA	1986	3–RAICHUR	INC	169696	M.Y.CHORPADE	JNP	164014	R.A.NAIK	DEATH OF SHRI B.V. DESAI
						IND	8704	M.S.MUTHUSAMY	
A.P.	1987	31–SECUNDERABAD	INC	182861	T.MANEMMHJA (W)	TDP	90300	B.P.REDDY	DEATH OF SHRI T.ANJAIAH
						BJP	71009	B.DATTARAYA	
HARYANA	1987	5–ROHTAK	LKD	263209	H.LAL	INC	160705	S.SINGH	RESIGNATION OF SHRI H.LAL
						LKD (A)	65340	G.DEVI(W)	
	1987	8–BHIWANI	LKD	312900	R.N.SINGH	INC	223548	D.NAND	RESIGNATION OF SHRI BANSI LAL
						LKD (A)	14419	P.SINGH	
MAHARASHTRA	1987	30–NANDED	INC	283019	C.A.SHANKARRAO	IND	171901	P.Y.AMBEDKAR	RESIGNATION OF SHRI C.S.BHAURAO
						IND	12676	B.T.GANGARAM	
U.P.	1987	85–HARDWAR(SC)	INC	149377	R.SINGH	BSP	125399	MAYAWATI(W)	DEATH OF SHRI SUNDER LAL
						IND	39780	B.RAKESH(W)	
DAMAN&DIU	1987	DAMAN AND DIU	INC	17027	T.G.KALANBHAI	IND	9303	F.N.SRINIVASAN	NEWLY FORMED P.C
						IND	852	M.B.MADHAV BAI	
GUJARAT	1988	18–GODHRA	JNP	141633	P.S.PURSOTTAMB HAI	INC	104796	U.BARIA	DEATH OF SHRI JAIDEEPSINH JI
						IND	11527	S.T.PARAMHANS	

Cont'd...

...Cont'd

HARYANA	1988	6–FARINDABAD	LKD	288123	K.A.CHAUDHRY	INC	186240	J.P.NAGAR	DEATH OF SHRI RAHIM KHAN
						IND	3562	K.N.GULATI	
	1988	10–SIRSA(SC)	LKD	300442	H.RAM	INC	185098	SELJA	DEATH OF SHRI D.SINGH
						IND	13430	A.KUMAR	
J&K	1988	5–UDHAMPUR	INC	133893	MOHD.A.KHAN	JPP	131517	B.SINGH	DEATH OF SHRI G.L.DOGRA
						IND	6356	R.LAL	
MEGHALAYA	1988	2–TURA	INC	106240	W.A.SANGMA	IND	28672	L.SANGMA	RESIGNATION OF SHRI P.A.SANGMA
						HPU	12762	G.MARAK	
RAJASTHAN	1988	21–PALI	INC	202483	S.S/O SOHANLAL	BJP	163278	G.LODHA	DEATH OF SHRI M.C.DAGA
						LKD	73134	S.SONCHA	
U.P.	1988	56–ALLAHABAD	IND	202996	V.P.SINGH	INC	92245	S.SHASTRI	RESIGNATION OF SHRI.A.BACHAN

Source: www.eci.nic.in

Appendix 2

List of the Chief Ministers of Bihar

S.No.	Name	From … to …	Party	Caste
1	Sri Krishna Sinha	2 Apr 1946 to 31 Jan 1961	INC	Bhumihar (UC)
2	Deep Narayan Singh	1 Feb. 1961 to 18 Feb 1961	INC	Rajput (UC)
3	Binodanand Jha	18 Feb1961 to 2 Oct. 1963	INC	Brahmin (UC)
4	Krishana B. Sahay	2 Oct 1963 to 5 Mar 1967	INC	Kayastha (UC)
5	Mahamaya P. Sinha	5 Mar 1967 to 28 Jan 1968	JKD	Kayastha (UC)
6	Satish P. Singh	28 Jan 1968 to 1 Feb 1968	INC	Rajput (UC)
7	B.P. Mandal	1 Feb 1968 to 2 Mar 1968	INC	Kurmi (UBC)
8	Bhola P. Shashtri	22 Mar1968 to 29 Jun 1968	Congress (O)	(SC)
	President's rule	29 Jun 1968 to 26 Feb 1969		
9	Harihar P. Singh	26 Feb 1969 to 22 Jun 1969	INC	Rajput (UC)
10	Bhola P. Shashtri [2]	22 Jun 1969 to 4 Jul 1969	Congress (O)	(SC)
	President's rule	6 Jul 1969 to 16 Feb 1970		
11	Daroga Prasad Rai	16 Feb1970 to 22 Dec 1970	INC	Yadav (UBC)
12	Karpuri Thakur	22 Dec1970 to 2 June 1971	Socialist Party	Nai (LBC)
13	Bhola P. Shashtri [3]	2 Jun1971 to 9 Jan. 1972	INC	SC
	President's rule	9 Jan 1972 to 19 Mar 1972		
14	Kedar Pandey	19 Mar 1972 to 2 Jul 1973	INC	Brahmin (UC)
15	Abdul Gafoor	2 July 1973 to 11 Apr 1975	INC	Muslim
16	Dr Jagannath Mishra	11 Apr 1975 to 30 Apr1977	INC	Brahmin (UC)
	President's rule	30 Apr 1977 to 24Jun 1977		
17	Karpuri Thakur	24 Jun 1977 to 21 Apr1979	Janata Party	Nai (LBC)

Cont'd…

...Cont'd

18	Ram Sunder Das	21 Apr 1979 to 17 Feb1980	Janata Party	SC
	President's rule	17 Feb 1980 to 8 Jun 1980		
19	Dr Jagannath Mishra [2]	8 Jun 1980 to 14 Aug1983	Congress(I)	Brahmin (UC)
20	Chandra S. Singh	14 Aug 1983 to 12Mar1985	Congress(I)	UC
21	Bindeshwari Dubey	12 Mar1985 to 13 Feb 1988	Congress(I)	Bramhin (UC)
22	Bhagwat Jha Azad	14 Feb1988 to 10 Mar 1989	Congress(I)	Brahmin (UC)
23	S.N. Sinha	11 Mar 1989 to 6 Dec 1989	Congress(I)	Rajput (UC)
24	Dr Jagannath Mishra	6 Dec 1989 to 10 Mar 1990	Congress(I)	Brahmin (UC)
25	Laloo Prasad	10 Mar 1990 to 3 Mar 1995	Janata Dal	Yadav (UBC)
26	Laloo Prasad [2]	4 Apr 1995 to 25 Jul 1997	RJD	Yadav (UBC)
27	Rabri Devi	25 Jul 1997 to 11 Feb 1999	RJD	Yadav (UBC)
28	Rabri Devi [2]	9 Mar 1999 to 2 Mar 2000	RJD	Yadav (UBC)
29	Nitish Kumar	3 Mar 2000 to 10 Mar 2000	JD(U)	Kurmi (UBC)
30	Rabri Devi [3]	11 Mar 2000 to 6 Mar 2005	RJD	Yadav (UBC)
	President's rule	7 Mar 2005 to 24 Nov 2005		
31	Nitish Kumar [2&3]	24 Nov 2005 to Present	JD(U)	Kurmi (UBC)

Source: http://cm.bih.nic.in/formercm-bihar.htm

Appendix 3

Chronology of Massacres in Bihar, 1971 to 2005

Year	*Place*	*District*	*Attackers' Caste/Class*	Victims' Caste/Class	*Casualty*
1971	Rupaspur-Chandwa[A]	Purnea	Upper Caste/ landlords	ST/agri. Labourers	14
	Sabdalpur[B]	Purnea	Muslim/Landlords	SC/ST tenants	10
1976	Akodi	Bhojpur	Upper-backward/ landlord	SC/agri. labourers	3
1977	Belchi	Patna	Upper backward/ landlord	SC/agri. labourers	14
	Kargha	Jehanabad	Upper caste/ landlords	SC/agri. labourers	3
	Brahampur	Bhojpur	Upper caste/ landlords	SC/middle peasants	4
1978	Kaila	Jehanabad	Upper backward/ landlord	SC/agri. labourers	3
1979	Samhauta	Rohtas	Upper caste/ landlords	SC/agri. labourers	4
	Bajitpur	Bhojpur	Upper caste/ landlords	SC/agri. labourers	3
1980	Pipra	Patna	Upper backward/ landlords	SC/agri. labourers	14
	Parasbigha	Jehanabad	Upper caste/ landlords	Backward caste/ agri. labourers	11
1981	Mathila	Bhojpur	Police	Liberation cadres	3
1982	Maini Bigha	Aurangabad	Upper caste/ landlords	SC/agri. labourers	6
1983	Panania	Gaya	Police	MCC cadres	5
1984	Gagan Bigha	Rohtas	Upper caste/ landlords	SC/agri. labourers	5
	Ambari	Aurangabad	Upper caste/ landlords	SC/agri. labourers	3
	Danwar-Bihta	Bhojpur	Upper caste/ landlords	SC/agri. labourers	22
	Kharakpura	Aurangabad	Upper caste/ Lorik Sena	SC/agri. labourers	6
	Haldawari Kamat Tola, Dibra[C]	Purnea	Upper Caste/Landlords	ST/agri. Labourers	15
1985	Kaithi Bigha	Aurangabad	Upper caste/landlords	SC/agri. labourers	10
	Kunai	Bhojpur	Police	Liberation cadres	2

Cont'd...

...Cont'd

1986	Neelampur	Gaya	Haare Ram group/ Lorik Sena	SC/agri. labourers	5
	Gaini	Aurangabad	Upper caste/ landlords	SC/agri. labourers	12
	Aminabad	Jehanabad	Upper caste/ Brahmarshi Sena	Muslims/Beedi workers	3
	Jeenpura	Patna	Ramanand Yadav group Lorik Sena	SC/agri. labourers	6
	Arwal	Jehanabad	Police	MKSS cadres	24
	Kansara	Jehanabad	Upper caste/Brahmarshi Sena	Backward caste/agri. labourers	8
	Parasdih	Aurangabad	Upper caste/ Satyanendra Sena	SC/agri. labourers	5
	Darmian	Aurangabad	Upper backward/ middle peasants	Upper-caste landlords	11
1987	Chotki-Chhechani	Aurangabad	Upper caste/ Satyanendra Sena	Upper backward/ Middle peasants	7
	Dalelchak-Bhagaura	Aurangabad	Upper backward/ middle peasants	Upper caste/landlord	52
1988	Narhan	Jehanabad	Upper backward/ dacoits	Upper backward/poor peasants	4
1989	Nonhi-Nagwan	Jehanabad	Ramashish-Rajdev group/Nagwan	Upper backward SC/agri. Labourers	18
	Daumha	Jehanabad	Ramashish-Rajdev group/Nagwan	Upper backward SC/agri. Labourers	9
1991	Tiskhora	Patna	Upper backward/Kisan Sangh	SC/agri. Labourers	15
	DevSahiara	Bhojpur	Upper caste/Jwala Singh group	SC/agri. Labourers	15
	Savanbigha	Jehanabad	Swarna Liberation Front/upper caste	SC/agri. Labourers	7
	Theendiha	Gaya	Sunlight Sena/ upper caste	SC/agri. Labourers	7
	MeinBarsima	Gaya	Swarna Liberation Front/upper caste	SC/agri. Labourers	10
1992	Bara	Gaya	MCC cadres	Upper caste/ Landlords	34
	Chainpur	Rohtas	Police	PU cadres	4
	Ashabigha	Gaya	Police	MCC cadres	6

Cont'd...

...Cont'd

	Dumra D	Purnea	Upper Backward Castes/Landlords	SC/ST/agri. labourers	20
1993	Dadar	Rohtas	Police	Liberation cadres	3
	Ekwari	Bhojpur	Upper caste/landlords	SC/agri. labourers	4
1994	Aghoura	Rohtas	Police	Party Unity	4
	Nadhi	Bhojpur	Police	Liberation cadres	9
	Matgharna	Gaya	Police	MCC	11
1995	Khopira	Bhojpur	Upper caste/ landlords	SC/agri. labourers	3
	Sarathua	Bhojpur	Do	SC/agri. labourers	6
	Gulzarbigha	Aurangabad	Police	PU Cadres	4
1996	Chandi	Bhojpur	Upper caste/landlords	SC/agri. labourers	4
	Pathalpura	Bhojpur	Upper caste/landlords	SC/agri- labourers	3
	Mathanbigha	Aurangabad	Police	MCC cadres	7
	Nanaur	Bhojpur	Upper caste/landlords	SC/agri- labourers	5
	Nadhi	Bhojpur	CPI-ML cadres	Upper caste/landlor	8
	Nadhi	Bhojpur	Upper caste/landlords	SC/agri. labourers	9
	Morath	Bhojpur	Upper caste/landlords	SC/agri. labourers	3
	Bathanitola	Bhojpur	Upper caste/landlords	SC and Muslims/Agr labourers	22
	Purhara	Bhojpur	Upper caste/landlords	SC/agri. labourers	4
	Khanet	Bhojpur	Upper caste/landlords	SC/agri. labourers	5
	Ekwari	Bhojpur	Upper caste/landlords	SC/agri. labourers	6
1997	Khanet	Bhojpur	Upper caste/landlords	SC/agri. labourers	3
	Machil	Bhojpur	Upper caste/landlords	SC/agri. labourers	3
	Haibaspur	Patna	Upper caste/landlords	SC/agri. labourers	10
	Akhopur	Jehanabad	Upper caste/landlords	SC/agri. labourers	4

Cont'd...

...Cont'd

	Jalpura	Patna	PU cadres	Upper caste/landlor	11
	Indo	Patna	Police	PU cadres	6
	Ekwari	Bhojpur	Upper caste/landlords	SC/agri-labourers	10
	Khadasin	Jehanabad	Upper caste/landlords	SC/agri. labourers	8
	Kodihara	Patna	Police	PU cadres	2
	Katesar Nala	Jehanabad	Upper caste/landlords	SC/agri. labourers	6
	Lakshmanpur-Bathe	Jehanabad	Upper caste/landlords	SC/agri. labourers	58
	Chauram	Jehanabad	CPI(ML) Liberation	Upper caste/landlord	9
	Sirsia, Dumra, Kasmara, Mad hukarchak[E]	Purnea	Upper Backward castes/Faijan Party	Upper castes/Rajputs	5
	Bhittha and Parvatta[F]	Purnea	Upper castes/ NBLA	Lower and Upper Backward Castes	10
1998	Nagri	Bhojpur	Upper caste/landlords	SC/agri. labourers	10
	Aiyara	Jehanabad	Upper caste/landlords	SC/agri. labourers	3
	Sigori	Gaya	Police	MCC	6
	Rampur-Aiyara	Jehanabad	PU cadres	Upper caste/landlords	7
	Mahadevbigha	Gaya	Police	MCC cadres	4
1999	Shankarbigha	Jehanabad	Upper caste/landlords	SC/agri. labourers	23
	Narayanpur	Jehanabad	Upper caste/landlords	SC/agri. labourers	11
	Usri Bazar	Jehanabad	Liberation cadres	Upper caste/landlor	7
	Bheempura	Jehanabad	PW cadres	Upper caste/landlor	4
	Senari	Jehanabad	MCC cadres	Upper caste/landlor	35
	Sujathpur	Buxar	Police	Liberation cadres	16
	Sendani	Gaya	Upper caste/landlords	Backward caste and SC	12
2000	Lakhisara[G]	Lakhisarai	Backward caste/Contractors	SC/ST and workers	11

Cont'd...

...Cont'd

	Rajebigha	Nawada	Upper caste/landlords	Backward caste/ Middle farmers	5
	Afsar	Nawada	Backward caste/ Middle farmers	Upper caste landlords	12
	Mianpur	Aurangabad	Upper caste/Ranvir Sena	Backward caste and SC	35
	Dumariyan	Bhojpur	Upper caste/Ranvir Sena	Backward caste and SC	6
2001	Chironichi bigha	Gaya	MCC cadres	Police	6
	Kariambura	Jehanabad	Police	PW cadres	5
2003	Kasmara Jaitola, Dhamdaha[H]	Purnea	Upper Caste and Middle Caste/NBLA and landlord Yadavs	ST/agri. Labourers	12
	Newdhi	Gaya	Upper Caste/Ranvir Sena	Backward caste and SC	2
2004	Berari[I]	Arwal	Upper caste/Ranvir Sena	PWG	11
2005	Bhojpur[J]	Bhojpur	Upper caste/Ranvir Sena	CPI(M-L)Liberation and SCs	5

Source: Unless and otherwise specified, see Prakash Louis, (2002). 'People Power: The Naxalite Movement in Central Bihar', New Delhi, Wordsmiths, pp. 242–6, Table 8.8, URL: http://www.satp.org/satporgtp/countries/india/terroristoutfits/massacres.htm. Last accessed on August 18, 2008.

[A] This was the first ever massacre in the state, source: Anand Chakravarti, (1986). op. cit. p. 1847.

[B,C,D,E,F,G] Information gathered during field work in Purnea;

[I,J] URL: http://ibnlive.in.com/news/what-is-the-ranvir-sena/9046–4.html

[E,F,G,H] These massacres were not related to the agrarian struggle *per se*. [E,F] and [H] These were the fights between the North Bihar Liberation Army (NBLA) of the Rajputs (upper caste) and the Faijan Party of the Kurmis and Gangotas (upper backward castes). For more details see, Chapter 4– Part II; [G] It was an outcome of the struggle for hegemony over sand quarry in the Ganges and Sone riverbeds. In this incident the struggle for supremacy between two contenders for sand quarry—both from the same upper backward caste and supporters of political party currently ruling in Bihar—led to the killing of 11 labourers.

Bibliography

Books and Articles

Adeney, Katherine and Lawrence Saez, 2005. *Coalition Politics and Hindu Nationalism,* London and New York, Routledge.

Advani, L.K. 1998. XII Lok Sabha Debates, *Session III, (Winter)* Monday, December 21.

Ahmad, Faizan. 1992. 'Riot Force Rushed to Sitamarhi' October 10. accessed at URL: http://www.indiarightsonline.com/Sabrang/relipolcom81–90.....pdf

Ahmad, Farzand. 2000. 'CBI: Zzz Files', *India Today,* May 29.

Ahmad, Saroor. 2010. 'BJP caught between Yeddy, Reddys and sleazy Business', *twocircles.net,* July 16.

—— 2000. 'The Cost of an Election in Bihar: Few Score Lives', *Rediff News,* Patna.

Aloysius, G. 1997. *Nationalism without Nation in India,* New Delhi, Oxford University Press

Ananth, V. Krishna. 2001. 'Crime and Politics', *The Hindu,* January 30.

Anderson, R. Michael and Sumit Guha (eds.) 2001. *Changing Concepts of Rights in South Asia,* Delhi, Oxford University Press.

Andhyarujina, T.R. 2006. 'Shibu Soren's Unpunished Crime of Bribery, *The Hindu,* Dec. 16.

Appu, P.S. 1996. *'Land Reforms in India: A Survey of Policy, Legislation and Implementation',* New Delhi, Vikas Publishing House.

—— 1993. 'A Modest Programme for the Nineties', in B.N. Yugandhar and Gopal Iyer (eds.), *Land Reforms in India,* Vol. I, Sage Publications, New Delhi.

Aristotle. 1953. *Ethics,* Book II. Translated by J.A.K. Thomson, Penguin Classics, 1955, Britain.

Austin, Granville. 2005. 'The Expected and the Unintended in Working a Democratic Constitution' in Zoya Hasan, E. Sridharan and R. Sudarshan, (eds.) *India's Living Constitution: Ideas, Practices and Controversies,* London, Anthem Press.

Bailey, John, and Roy Godson. 2000. "Introduction" in their edited book *Organized Crime and Democratic Governability: Mexico and the US-Mexican Borderlands*, Pittsburgh, University of Pittsburgh Press.

Balagopal, K. 1989. 'Rise of Gangsterism in Politics', *Economic and Political Weekly,* February 4.

Banerjee, Shoumojit. 2011. 'Munger Massacre Undersscores Changing Face of Bihar's Naxal Movement', *The Hindu,* July 26.

—— 2012. 'For Residents of Bathani, it is a Horror They Cannot Forget', *The Hindu,* April 19.

Banerjee, Sumanta. 2011. 'Breeding Black Sheep', *Economic and Political Weekly,* January 8, Vol. XLVI No. 2, pp. 10–13.

—— 2009. *The Wicked City—Crime and Punishment in Colonial Calcutta,* Hyderabad, Orient Blackswan.

—— 2006. 'The Underside of a City Divided', *Seminar,* 559.

—— 1990. "West Bengal Today: An Anticipatory Postmortem", *Economic and Political Weekly,* August 18, pp. 1812–1816.

—— 1978. 'Violence of the Rich', *Economic and Political Weekly,* January 7, pp. 11–12.

Bardhan, Pranab.1984. *The Political Economy of Development in India,* New York. Basil Blackwell.

Basu, Amrita. 2001. 'The Dialects of Hindu Nationalism' in Atul Kohli (ed.). *The Success of India's Democracy,* Cambridge, Cambridge University Press.

—— 1997. 'When Local Riots are not merely Local: Bringing the State Back In, Bijnor, 1988–1992'. in Partha Chatterjee, (ed.) *State and Politics in India,* Oxford, Oxford University Press, pp. 390–435.

Benedict, Kay. 1996. 'Crime and Politics Inextricably linked in Bihar', *Indian Express* (Kochi), 23 March.

Bhan, Susheela. (ed.) 1995. *Criminalization of Politics,* New Delhi, Shipra.

Bharati, Indu. 1991a. 'Fighting the Irrigation Mafia in Bihar', *Economic and Political Weekly,* September 21.

—— 1991b. Lok Sabha Elections: Message from Bihar, *Economic and Political Weekly*, August 17.

—— 1991c. 'Survival against Heavy Odds', *Economic and Political Weekly,* January 19.

—— 1990a. 'Bihar: New Government, New Hope', *Economic and Political Weekly* June 30.

—— 1990b. 'Bihar Elections: Violence Inevitable', *Economic and Political Weekly*, March 3.

—— 1990c. 'Election-Eve Promises', *Economic and Political Weekly*, February 17–24.

—— 1989a. 'Rearranged Political Mosaic', *Economic and Political Weekly* December 9.

—— 1989b. 'Making Up with the Mafia', *Economic and Political Weekly* October 14.

—— 1989c. 'Bihar Crisis: Making of a CM', *Economic and Political Weekly*, April 8.

—— 1989d. 'Decay in Gram Panchayat', *Economic and Political Weekly*, January 7.

Bhatia, Bela. 2005a. 'Naxalite Movement in Central Bihar', *Economic and Political Weekly*, April 9.

—— 2005b. 'Jehanabad-I: Jailbreak and the Maoist Movement', *Economic and Political Weekly*, December 17.

Bhatt, Anil. 1975. *Caste, Class and Politics*, New Delhi, Manohar Books.

Bhattacharya, Ajit. (Selected and Introduced), 1975. 'Notes on Bihar Movement' in his *Transforming the Polity-Centenary Readings from Jayaprakash Narayan*, New Delhi, Rupa and Co.

Bhattacharya, Swatantra. 2005, 'One in Every Five Hoping o make it to Bihar House', *The Indian Express*, New Delhi, February 22.

Bhelari, Kanaihya. 2002. 'The White Ant Army', *The Week*, October 20.

—— 1995. 'Blooming Bandits' *The Week*, March 5.

Blair, Harry W. 1980. 'Rising Kulaks and Backward Classes in Bihar: Social Change in the Late 1970s', *Economic and Political Weekly*, Vol. 15, No. 2, January 12.

Block, Fred. 1977. 'The Ruling Class Does Not Rule: Notes on the Marxist Theory of the State', *Socialist Review*, No. 33, pp. 6–28.

Brass, Paul. 2011. *An Indian Political Life: Charan Singh and Congress Politics, 1937–1961*, Sage Publications, New Delhi.

—— 2004. 'National Power and Local Politics in India: A Twenty-year Perspective' in Partha Chatterjee, (ed.) *State and Politics in India*, New Delhi, Oxford University Press.

—— 1980. 'The Politicization of the Peasantry in a North Indian State', *Journal of Peasant Studies*, July and September, pp. 395–426.

Buchanan, Francis. 1928. *An Account of the District of Purnea in 1809–10*, Bihar and Orissa Research Society, Delhi, reprint Usha Publication.

Centre for the Study of Developing Societies, 2008. *State of Democracy in South Asia: A Report*, New Delhi, Oxford University Press.

—— 1999. 'Emerging Pattern', *Frontline*, Volume 16 - Issue 25, November 27–December 10, New Delhi.

Chaitanya, Krishna. 1992. 'Bara Massacre and After', *Economic and Political Weekly,* April 11–18.

—— 1992. 'Emerging Upper Caste Alliance', *Economic and Political Weekly,* July 25.

—— 1991. Social Justice, Bihar Style, *Economic and Political Weekly,* November 16.

Chakravarti, Anand. 2001. *Social Power and Everyday Class Relations: Agrarian Transformations in North Bihar,* New Delhi, Sage Publication.

—— 2001. 'Caste and Agrarian Class: A View from Bihar', in Manoranjan Mohanty (ed.) *Class, Caste and Gender,* New Delhi, Sage Publication.

—— 1986. 'The Unfinished Struggle of Santhal *Bataidars* in Purnea District', *Economic and Political Weekly,* Vol. XX and XXI, No. 42 and 43. October 18 and October 25.

Chakrabarti, Ashish. 1998. 'Here Fight is for Booths, not Votes', *Indian Express,* May 19.

Chakrabarty, Deepesh. 2005. "In the Name of Politics: Sovereignty, Democracy and Multitude in India", *Economic and Political Weekly,* July 23, pp. 3293–3301.

Chakravarti, S.K. 1972. *Final Report on the Revisional Survey and Settlement Operations in the District of Purnea (1952–60),* Government of Bihar.

Chand, Vikram K. (ed.). *Public Service Delivery in India: Understanding the Reform Process,* New Delhi, Oxford University Press.

Chandra, Bipan, Mridula Mukherjee and Aditya Mukherjee, 1999. *India After Independence,* New Delhi, Penguin Books.

Chaterjee, Partha. 2008. 'Democracy and Economic Transformation in India', *Economic and Political Weekly,* April 19, pp. 53–62.

—— 2004 (1997). *State and Politics in India,* New Delhi, Oxford University Press

—— 2002. "On civil and Political Society in postcolonial democracies" in Sudipta Kaviraj and Sunil Khilnani (ed.) *Civil Society,* South Asian edition Cambridge University Press.

—— 1998(a). "Community in the East", *Economic and Political Weekly,* February 7.

—— 1998(b). 'Introduction' in Partha Chatterjee ed. *Wages of Freedom: Fifty Years of the Indian Nation-State,* Delhi. Oxford University Press.

—— 1986. *Nationalist Thought and the Colonial World: A Derivative Discourse?* Zed Books, London.

Choudhary, Ganga Prasad and Ashok Kumar. 1999. 'Seemanchal Rajya Ki Maang Kyon?' *Samkaleen Tapmaan,* May.

Choudhary, Kalyan. 2001. 'Violent Elections in Bihar', *Frontline,* Vol. 18, Issue 10, May 12–25.

Choudhary, P.C. Roy. 1963. *Bihar District Gazetteers—Purnea*, Government of Bihar.

Chaudhary, Prasanna Kumar and Shrikant, 2001. *Bihaar Me Samaajik Parivartan Ke Kuchh Aayaam,* New Delhi, Vani Prakashan.

Choudhary, S.N. 1999. *Power-Dependence Relations: Struggle for Hegemony in Rural Bihar,* New Delhi, Har Anand.

Clements, Paul. 2005. "A Rawlsian Analysis of Plight in Bihar", *Studies in Comparative International Development*, Winter 2005, Vol. 39, No. 4.

Das, Arvind N. 2000. 'Electing Another People in Bihar', *Economic and Political Weekly*, February 19–26.

—— 1992. *The Republic of Bihar,* New Delhi, Penguin Books.

—— 1998. 'India in the Image of Bihar', *Economic and Political Weekly,* December 5.

—— 1998b. 'Para Democracy in Bihar', *Economic and Political Weekly,* November 21.

—— 1986. 'Landowners' Armies Take over 'Law and Order", *Economic and Political Weekly.* January 4.

—— 1982, Agricultural Movements in Twentieth Century Bihar, London, Frank Cass and Company Ltd.

Das Gupta, Chirashree. 2010. 'Unravelling Bihar's 'Growth Miracle", *Economic and Political Weekly,* December 25, 2010 Vol. XLV No. 52, pp. 50–62.

Das, Victor. 1991. 'Bihar Teachers' Struggle for Rights', *Economic and Political Weekly,* January 5–12.

Datar, Abhay. 2004. 'A Vote for Secular Politics', *The Hindu,* 20 May.

Datt, Gaurav and Martin Ravallion. 1998. "Why Have Some Indian States Done Better Than Others in Reducing Rural Poverty?" *Economica*, London School of Economics and Political Science, Vol. 65(257), February, pp. 17–38

Dhanagare, D.N. 1968. 'Violence in the Fourth General Elections: A Study in Political Conflict', *Economic and Political Weekly,* Annual Number, January,

Dhawan, Harish. 1991. 'Letter to the Editor: "Landlord-Police Nexus in Bihar"', *Economic and Political Weekly,* April 20.

Dua, Bhagwan D. 1983. 'A Case in Executive Judicial Conflict: The Indian Case', *Asian Survey,* Vol. 23. No. 4, April.

Durkheim, Emile. 1966, *Rules of Social Method,* New York, Free Press.

Engineer, Asgar Ali. 2003. Communal Riots in 2002: A Survey', *Economic and Political Weekly,* January 25, pp. 280–2.

Evans, Peter, Dietrich Rueschemeyer, and Theda Skocpol. 1985. *Bringing the State Back In,* Cambridge University Press, London.

Fisher, Michael H. 1991. *Indirect Rule in India: Residents and the Residency System 1764–1858,* Delhi, Oxford University Press.

Foucault, Michael. 1991. 'Governmentality' in Graham Burchell, Colin Gordon and Peter Miller, (eds.) *The Foucault Effect: Studies in Governmentality*, London, Toronto, Sydney, Harvester/Wheatsheaf

—— 1977. *Discipline and Punish: The Birth of the Prison*, (translated in English by Alan Sheridan), London, Penguin Press.

Frankel, Francine. 1978. *India's Political Economy, 1947–1977: The Gradual Revolution*. Princeton, Princeton University Press.

Frankel, Francine and M.S.A. Rao (eds.) 1989. *Dominance and State Power in Modern India: The Decline of Social Order*' 2 Vols. New Delhi, Oxford University Press.

Gargan, Edward A. 1993. 'Indian Government Survives Parliament Votes', *The New York Times*, July 29.

George, Varghese K. 2005, 'Paswan's fistful' Indian Express, March 2.

—— 2004. 'Massacres in Bihar never invited TADA until Bara: Killers in this case were Dalits', *Indian Express*, December 2.

Ghosh, S.K. 2000. 'Inside Bihar' in his book *Bihar in Flames*, New Delhi, APH Publications.

Grossman, Mark. 2003. *Political Corruption in America: an Encyclopedia of Scandals, Power, and Greed*, ABC-CLIO publishers, California, USA.

Guha, Ranajit. 1983. *Elementary Aspects of Peasant Insurgency in Colonial India*. Delhi: Oxford University Press.

Gupta, Saibal. 2005. 'What are the priorities for strengthening institutions?' Research Paper presented at Workshop on Bihar's Development Strategy, Government of Bihar, Planning Commission and World Bank, June 18. URL: http://siteresources.worldbank.org/INTINDIA/Resources/BiharWKSHOP_Shaibalgupta.pdf

—— 2002. 'Subaltern Resurgence: A reconnaissance of Panchayat election in Bihar', *Crisis States Programme, Working Paper*, 8. Development Research Centre, London School of Economics, January.

Gupta, Tilak D. 1995. 'Elections with a Difference', *Economic and Political Weekly, April 15*.

Habib, Irfan. 2003. *The Agrarian System of Mughal India 1556–1707*, New Delhi, Oxford University Press.

Hall, Stuart. 1993. 'The State in Question' in Gregor McLenan, David Held and Stuart Hall. (eds.) *The Idea of a Modern State*, Philadelphia, Open University Press.

Hanson, A.H. 1966. *The Process of Planning: A Study of India's Five-Year Plans, 1950–1964*.London, Oxford University Press.

Harasymiw, Bohdan. 2003. 'Putting Organized Crime in its Place …Within Political Science', Paper prepared for presentation at the *annual meetings of the Canadian Political Science Association*, Dalhousie University, Halifax, Nova Scotia, 1 June.

Hardgrave, Robert L. and Stanley A. Kochanek. 1999. *India: Government and Politics in a Developing Nation,* 6th ed. Fort Worth, Texas, Harcourt College Publishers

Hasan, Zoya, E. Sridharan and R. Sudarshan. (eds.) 2005. *India's Living Constitution: Ideas, Practices and Controversies,* London, Anthem Press.

Hauser, Walter. 1997. 'General Elections 1996 in Bihar: Politics, Administrative Atrophy and Anarchy', *Economic and Political Weekly,* October 11, pp. 2599–2607.

Heller, Patrick. 2000. 'Degrees of Democracy: Some Comparative Lessons from India', World Politics, 52, pp. 484–519.

Houlton, Sir John. *Bihar: The Heart of India,* Orient Longman, Calcutta, 1949.

Huber, Evelyne, Dietrich Rueschemeyer, and John D. Stephens, 1999. 'The Paradoxes of Contemporary Democracy: Formal, Participatory, and Social Dimensions, in Lisa Anderson, (ed.) *Transitions to Democracy,* New York, Columbis University Press.

Hunter, W.W. 1877. *A Statistical Account of Bengal, Vol XV. Monghyr and Purnea,* London.

Huntington, Samuel P. 1968. *Political Order in Changing Societies,* New Haven, Yale University Press.

India, 1951. *Census of India, 1951: Livelihood Classes,* Vol. V, Bihar, Patna.

Iyer, K. Gopal. 1993. *Evaluation of Land Ceiling Measures in Bihar,* in B.N. Yugandhar, *Land Reforms in India-Volume 1: Bihar-Institutional Constraints,* New Delhi, Sage Publication.

Iyer, V.R. Krishna. 2001. *Off The Bench,* New Delhi, Universal Law Publishing Co. Pvt. Ltd.

Jaffrelot, Christophe and Sanjay Kumar. (eds.) 2009, *Rise of the Plebians? The Changing Face of Indian Legislative Assemblies,* New Delhi, Routledge.

Jaffrelot, Christophe. 2003. *India's Silent Revolution: The Rise of Lower Castes in North India,* London, Hurst and Co.

—— 2008. *The Uneven Rise of the Marginalized Castes in Indian Politics: Regional Dimensions,* paper presented at Ambedkar Memorial Lecture organised by the Indian Institute of Dalit Studies, November 3, Jawaharlal Nehru University, New Delhi.

Jannuzi, F.T. 1974. *Agrarian Crisis in India: The Case of Bihar,* Austin, Texas University Press.

Jenkins, Philip, and Gary Potter. 1987. "The Politics and Mythology of Organized Crime: A Philadelphia Case-Study", *Journal of Criminal Justice,* 15, pp. 473–84.

Jha, Prabhakar. 2007, Reviving Culture, *Seminar,* 580, http://www.india-seminar.com/2007/580/580_ prabhakara_jha.htm#top

Jha, Pravin. 2004, 'Continuity and Change: Some Observations on the Landscape of Agricultural Labourers in North Bihar, India', *Journal of Agrarian Change,* Vol. 4 No. 4, October.

—— 1994. *Changing Conditions of Agricultural Labourers in Post-Independent India: A Case Study from Bihar*; Ph.D. dissertation, Jawaharlal Nehru University, New Delhi.

Jha, Praveen and Atul Kumar Singh. (2010). 'Deconstructing Bihar's Growth "Miracle"', accessed at http://www.bihartimes.in/Newsbihar/2010/March/News bihar12March7.html

Jha, Hetukar. 1977. 'Lower-Caste Peasants and Upper-Caste Zamindars in Bihar (1921–1925): An Analysis of Sanskritization and Contradiction between the Two Groups', *Indian Economic and Social History Review* 14, no. 4.

Jha, Raj Kamal and Farzand Ahmed. 1995. 'Laloo's Magic', *India Today,* April 30.

Jha, Vikas Kumar. 1996. *Bihar: Criminalization of Politics* (translated by Ruby Roy), Patna, Shristi Prakashan.

Jones, W.H. Morris. 1975. *Parliament in India,* Philadelphia, University of Pennsylvania Press

Joseph, K.P. 1997. 'Lessons from Fodder Scam' *Economic and Political Weekly*, July 12.

Joseph, Manu and S. Anand. 2002. 'A Plot from the Devil's Lair', *Outlook,* June 3.

Joshi, Prabhash 2008. 'The Uncommon Catalyst', *Tehelka Magazine,* Vol. 5, Issue 50, December 20.

Joshi, Rajesh in interview with Lalu Yadav, 1999. 'If Laloo Goes, Naxals Will Surround the Cities', *Outlook*, March 22.

Kaviraj, Sudipta and Sunil Khilnani. 2005. 'On the Enchantment of the State', *European Journal of Sociology,* Vol. 46, pp. 263–96

—— (eds.) 2001. *Civil Society,* South Asian Edition, Cambridge University Press.

—— 1988. 'A Critique of the Passive Revolution', Economic and Political Weekly, Vol. 23, Nos. 45–47, pp 2429–44.

—— 1986. 'Indira Gandhi and Indian Politics', *Economic and Political Weekly,* Vol. XXI, Nos 38 and 39, September 20–27.

—— 1984. 'On the Crisis of Political Institutions inn India', *Contributions to Indian Sociology,* No. 2; Sudipta Kaviraj.

Khan, Imran. 2009. 'Four Criminal-Politicians Out Of Election Fray, Thanks To Courts', *IANS,* Patna, April 7.

Khilnani, Sunil. 2004 (1997). *The Idea of India,* New Delhi, Penguin Books

—— 2005. 'The Indian Constitution and Democracy', in Zoya Hasan et al. *India's Living Constitution: Ideas, Practices and Controversies,* London, Anthem Press.

Kishore, Avinash. 2004. 'Understanding Agrarian Impasse in Bihar', *Economic and Political Weekly,* July 31.

Kohli, Atul. (ed.) 2001. *The Success of India's Democracy,* Cambridge University Press.

—— 1994. 'Centralization and Powerlessness: India's Democracy in a Comparative Perspective' in Joe Migdal et al. (ed.) *'State Power and Social Forces: Domination and Transformation in the Third World,* Cambridge, Cambridge University Press.

—— 1992. *Democracy and Discontent: India's Growing Crisis of Governability,* Cambridge, Cambridge University Press.

—— 1987. The State and Poverty in India: The Politics of Reform, London, Cambridge University Press.

Kothari, Rajni. 1988a. *State against Democracy: In Search of Humane Governance,* New Delhi, Ajanta Publication.

—— 1988b. 'Integration and Exclusion in Indian Politics', *Economic and Political Weekly,* October 22.

—— 1988c. 'Decline of the Modern State', in *State Against Democracy,* New Delhi, Ajanta Publications.

—— 1964. 'The Congress System in India' *Asian Survey,* 4 (12), December.

Krishnan, Kavita. 2013. Battle for Justice and Democracy: Laxmanpur-Bathe, *Economic and Political Weekly,* Vol. XLVIII, No. 45–46, November 16, pp. 10–12.

Kumar, Ashwani. 2012. "No Gentlemen in This Army", *The Hindu,* 6 June.

Kumar, Avinash. 2009. 'Illegitimacy of the State in Bihar', *Economic and Political Weekly,* Vol. XLIV, No. 44, October 31–November 6, pp. 8–11.

—— 2012. 'Fallacy of the State in Bihar', *Economic and Political Weekly,* Vol. XLVII No. 44, November 3, pp. 23–25

Kumar, Dhiraj. 2007. 'Naxalite, Sunlight, Faijan Va Liberation ka Khel', *Purnea Jagaran,* Bhagalpur, December 30.

Kumar, K.P. Narayan. (2011), "Bribeless in Bihar: Bureaucrats in India's most corrupt state are facing the heat from their own chief minister", *Forbes India Magazine,* 11 February,

Kumar, Sanjay. 1999. 'New Phase in Backward Caste Politics in Bihar, 1990–2000', *Economic and Political Weekly,* 34 (34–5), August.

Laclau, Ernesto. 1975. 'The Specificity of the Political: Around the Poulantzas-Miliband Debate', *Economy and Society* 5(1).

Ladejinsky, Wolf. 1969. 'The Green Revolution in Bihar: The Kosi Area: A Field Trip', *Economic and Political Weekly* Vol. 4 (39), 27 September.

—— 1969. The Green Revolution in Punjab: A Field Trip', *Economic and Political Weekly,* Vol. 4 (26), 28 June.

Lal, Neeta. 2008. 'Huge Case Backlog Clogs India's Courts', *Asia Times*, June 28.

Levinson, David. 2002. *Encyclopedia of Crime and Punishment*, Volume 3, California, Thousand Oaks and Sage Publication

Lohia, Rammanohar. 1960. *Guilty Men of India's Partition*, Allahabad, Kitabistan.

Lyngdoh, J.M. 2006. 'Babu Samjho Ishare'," *Tehelka Magazine*, February 11.

Mahajan, Gurpreet and S.S. Jodhka. (2009). "Religions, Democracy and Governance: Spaces for the Marginalised in the Contemporary India", *Religions and Development Research Programme*, Working Paper 26, University of Birmingham, UK

Majumdar, M.L. 2005. *Emerging Grassroots Power: A Critique on Elections to the Panchayats and the Municipalities in Bihar*, New Delhi, Concept Publishing Company.

Manor, James. 2002. 'Changing State, Changing Society in India', *Journal of South Asian Studies*, South Asia, 25, 2.

Mathew, Mammen. 2010. 'Troubled Lands of Bihar' *The Hindustan Times*, May 10.

—— 1995. 'Don-Sayers on Mat' *Hindustan Times*, Patna, April 3, (Monday extra).

McGuire, John, Pater Reeves and Howard Brasted. 1996. *Politics of Violence: From Ayodhya to Behrampada*, New Delhi, Sage Publications.

McLennan, Gregor, David Held and Stuart Hall. (eds.) 1993. *The Idea of the Modern State*, Philadelphia, Open University Press.

McMillan, Alistair. 2005. 'The BJP Coalition: Partnership and Power Sharing in Government', in Adeney and Saez. (eds.). *Coalition Politics and Hindu Nationalism*, Oxon, Routledge.

Mehta, Pratap Bhanu. 2006. 'The Promise of Uncertainty', in Pran Chopra (ed.) *The Supreme Court Versus the Constitution: a Challenge to Federalism*, New Delhi, Sage Publication.

Migdal, Joel S. 2001. *State in Society: Studying How States and Societies Transform and Constitute One another*, Cambridge, Cambridge University Press.

—— 1989. *Strong Societies and Weak States*, Princeton, NJ, Princeton University Press.

—— with Atul Kohli and Vivienne Shue. 1994. (eds.). *State, Power and Social Forces: Domination and Transformation in the Third World*, Cambridge, Cambridge University Press.

Miliband, Ralph. 1973. *Class Power and State Power*. London, Verso.

—— 1969. *State in Capitalist Society*. London: Quartet Books.

—— 1965. 'Marx and the State', *The Socialist Register*. Reprinted in *Class Power and State Power*, London, Verso

Mishra, Dinesh Kumar. 2008. 'Bihar Flood: The Inevitable has Happened', *Economic and Political Weekly,* September 6.

Mishra, Ratneshwar. 2004. 'Land, Labour and Power: Pargana Dharmapur of Raj Darbhanga under the Permanent Settlement', *IHC Proceedings,* 65th Session.

Mishra, Vandita. 2005. 'No Longer Backstage', *The Indian Express,* November 30.

Mishra, Richa. 2010. 'On Your Bikes: Get, Set and Go', *Business Line.*

Misra, Amaresh. 1994. 'Changing Peasant Struggle, *Economic and Political Weekly,* May 7.

Mitchell, Timothy. 1991. 'The Limits of the State: Beyond Statist Approaches and Their Critics', *The American Political Science Review,* Vol. 85, No. 1 (March).

Mitra, Manoshi and T. Vijayendra. 1982. Agricultural Labourers and Peasant Politics: Rural Proletarianisation in Purnea, Bihar' in A.N. Das, (ed.) *Agricultural Movements in Twentieth Century Bihar,* London, Frank Cass and Company Ltd.

Mohanty, Manoranjan (ed.) 2001. *Class, Caste and Gender,* New Delhi, Sage Publications.

—— 2001. 'Land Distribution among Scheduled Castes and Scheduled Tribes', *Economic and Political Weekly,* October 6.

Moore, Barrington Jr. 1978. *Injustice: The Social Bases of Obedience and Revolt,* New York, Sharpe.

Mukherjee, Kalyan. 1979. 'Caste-Class Polarisation in Bihar: A Case Study of Bhojpur, *Public Enterprises Centre for Continuing Education,* New Delhi.

Mukul. 1992. 'Bihar's Land Liberation Struggles', *Economic and Political Weekly* August 22.

Myrdal, Gunnar. 1968. *Asian Drama: An Inquiry into the Poverty of Nations,* New York, Pantheon Books. Vol. 2.

Nagaraj, R. and Andaleeb Rahman, (2010). 'Booming Bihar: Fact or Fiction?' *Economic and Political Weekly,* February 20, Vol. XLV, No. 8.

Naik, S.D. 2001. "Census 2001: Disturbing Inter-State Disparities," *Business Line Internet Edition,* April 3, URL: www.blonnet.com/businessline/2001/04/03/stories/01032001.htm

Naipaul, V.S. 1992. *A Million Mutinies Now,* New Delhi, Penguin Books.

Nair, Harish V. and Satya Prakash. 2007. 'Shibu Soren's Aquittal on Expected Lines', *Hindustan Times,* August 7.

Nandy, Ashis. 2009. 'The Hour of the Untamed Cosmopolitan', *Tehalka Magazine,* May 30

—— 1989. 'The Political Culture of the Indian State', *Daedaulus,* Vol. 118, No.4.

—— 1980. 'Indira Gandhi and the Culture of Indian Politics' in his book *At the Edge of Psychology: Essays in Politics and Culture,* Delhi, Oxford University Press.

Narayanan, K.S. et al. 1998. 'A Commission a Day', *Outlook,* April 13.

National Commission on Agriculture, 1973. 'Working Group on Land Reforms: A Field Study: Agrarian Relations in Two Bihar District', *Mainstream,* 11 (40), June 2.

Nedumpara, Jose J. 2004. *Political Economy and Class Contradictions: A Study,* New Delhi, Anmol Publications

Nigam, Aditya. 2009. 'The Implosion of the Political', *Critical Encounters: A Forum of Critical Thought From Global South,* 14 May, URL: http://criticalencounters.wordpress.com/2009/05/14/the-implosio n-of- %e2%80%98the-political%e2%80 %99/

Nirala, 2012. "Old Caste Wars Haunts Nitish Naya Bihar", *Tehalka,* 16 June.

Noorani, A.G. 2007. "Ninth Schedule and the Supreme Court", *Economic and Political Weekly*, March 3.

—— 2003. 'The Betrayal of India' *Frontline,* Vol. 20, January 18–31.

—— 2000. 'The Law and its Potency', *Frontline,* Volume 17 - Issue 22, October 28–November 10.

—— 1980. 'Judiciary-Transfer of High Court Judges', *Economic and Political Weekly,* September 20.

—— 1976. 'Judiciary- Transfer of High Court Judges', *Economic and Political Weekly,* May 8.

O'Donnell, Guillermo.1993. 'On the State, Democratization and Some Conceptual Problems: A Latin American View with Glances at Some Postcommunist Countries', *World Development,* 21, no. 8.

Offe, Claus. 1974. 'Structural Problems of the Capitalist State: Class Rule and the Political System: On the Selectiveness of Political Institutions', *German Political Studies*, I, pp. 31–57.

Ojha, G. 1977. *Land Problems and Land Reforms,* New Delhi, Sultan Chand.

Pandit, C.S. 1977. *End of an Era: The Rise and Fall of Indira Gandhi,* New Delhi, Allied Publishers

Palonen, Kari, Tuija Pulkkinen, and José María Rosales. 2008. (eds.) *The Ashgate Research Companion to the Politics of Democratization in Europe: Concepts and Histories*, Ashgate, London.

Pankaj, Ashok Kumar and M.P. Singh. 2004. 'The Changing Sociopolitical Profile of Local Political Elites (Mukhias) in Bihar', *Contributions to Indian Sociology,* Vol. 38, No. 1–2.

Pinch, William R. 1996. *Peasants and Monks in British India.* Berkeley, University of California Press.

Potter, David. 1996. *India's Political Administrators: from ICS to IAS,* Oxford University Press, Delhi.

Poulantzas, Nicos. 1973. *Political Power and Social Classes*, London, New Left Books

—— 1976. 'The Capitalist State: A Reply to Miliband and Laclau', *New Left Review* 95, pp. 63–83.

Poulantzas, Nicos and Ralph Miliband. 1969. "The Problem of the Capitalist State" *New Left Review* 58: pp. 67–78

Prasad, Binoy S. 1997. 'General Elections, 1996: Major Role of Caste and Social Factions in Bihar', *Economic and Political Weekly*, November 22.

Prasad, Kashi and Rajiv Kumar. 2012. '10 Get Death for Amausi Massacre', *Times of India,* February 15.

Prasad, Pradhan H. 1987, 'Agrarian Violence in Bihar', *Economic and Political Weekly,* May 30, 22 (22).

—— n.d. 'Neglect of Land Resources: Misfortune of Bihar', available in the archives of Loksahi Hakk Sangathan, URL: http://www.cscsarchive.org:8081/MediaArchive/liberty.nsf/(docid)/65DD3DD45 07BB77E5256AD30013065E.

Prasad, P.H. and G.B. Rodgers. "Class, Caste and Landholding in the Analysis of the Rural Economy," *Population and Labour Policies Programme, Working Paper No. 140, World Employment Programme Research (Working Papers)*, International Labor Office, Geneva, 1983 (unpublished).

Prasad, R.C. 1976. 'Bihar: Social Polarisation and Political Instability', in Iqbal Narain (ed.) *State Politics in India,* Meerut, Meenakshi Prakashan.

Punj, Balbir K. 2003. 'Ojha and the Lord of Misrule' *Pioneer,* December 19, available online at URL: background.

Pye, Lucian W. 1995. 'Political Culture' in S. Lipset. (ed.) *The Encyclopedia of Democracy*, London and New York, Routledge.

Ramachandran, Raju. 2006. 'The Supreme Court and the basic Structure Doctrine', in B.N. Kripal, et al. (eds.) *Supreme but not Infallible: Essays in Honour of the Supreme Court of India,* New Delhi, Oxford University Press.

Raj, K.N. 1970. 'Ownership and Distribution of Land', *Indian Economic Review,* April.

Rajlakshmi, T.K. 2001. Land Rights and Wrongs in Bihar, *Frontline,* Volume 18 - Issue 22, October 27–November 09.

Ramakrishnan, Venkatesh. 2005. 'Canker of Criminalization', *Frontline,* Volume 22 - Issue 04, February 12–25.

Ramalingam, Sudha. 2002. 'Do We Really Adhere to the Rule of Law?' *PUCL Bulletin*, September

Ranade, S.N. 1974. 'Social Work Research: A Trend Report' in *Survey of Research in Sociology and Social Anthropology*, Vol. 2, Bombay: Popular Prakashan.

Rao, C. Rajeswara, Bhowani Sen and Y.V. Krishna Rao. 1970. *Problems of India's Agrarian Sector*, New Delhi, Communist Party Publication

Rawls, John. 1999. *The Law of Peoples*. Cambridge, Harvard University Press.

Reddy, P. Jaganmohan.1999. *The Judiciary I Served,* New Delhi, Orient Blackswan.

Robin, Cyril. 2009. 'Bihar: The New Stronghold of OBC Politics' in Christophe Jaffrelot and Sanjay Kumar, *Rise of the Plebians? The Changing Face of Indian Legislative Assemblies,* New Delhi, Routledge.

Rodgers, Gerry and Jenine Rodgers. 2001.'A Leap Across Time: When Semi Feudalism Met Market Economy in Purnea', *Economic and Political Weekly* June 2.

Roy, A.K. 1995. 'Industrialising Bihar: The Options' *Economic and Political Weekly,* July 29.

Roy, Arundhati. 2002. 'Who's She When She's at Home?' *Outlook,* May 6.

Roy, Ramashray. 1995. 'Bihar' in Sadhna Singh (ed.), *Caste Politics in India,* New Delhi, Mittal Publications.

Rudolph, L.I. and S. Rudolph, 2001. 'Redoing the Constitutional Design', in Atul Kohli (ed.). *The Success of India's Democracy,* Cambridge University Press.

—— 1998 (1987). *In Pursuit of Lakshmi: The Political Economy of the Indian State,* Hyderabad, India, Orient Longman.

—— 1969. *The Modernity of Tradition: Political Development in India*, New Delhi, Orient Longman;

Sanjana. 2009. 'Into The Madding Crown', *Tehelka Magazine,* Vol. 6, Issue 38, September 26.

Skocpol, Theda. 1979. *State and Social Revolutions,* Cambridge University Press, Cambridge.

Sahi, Ajit. 2009. 'The Gangster's Last Gamble', *Tehelka,* Vol 6, Issue 20, May 23.

Sankar, B.L. and Valerian Rodrigues. 2010. *The Indian Parliament: A Democracy at Work,* New Delhi, Oxford University Press.

Saxena, N.C. n.d. '*Tenancy Reforms vs Open Market Leasing – What Would Serve the Poor Better?*' Accessed at http://planningcommission.nic.in/reports/articles/ncsxna/leasing.htm.

Schneider, Jane and Peter Schneider. 2008. 'The Anthropology of Crime and Criminalization', *Annual Review Anthropology,* 37.

Sen, Ashok. 1976. "Bureaucracy a Social Hegemony", in *Essays presented to Professor S.C. Sarkar*, New Delhi, Peoples Publishing House.

Sharma, Alakh Narayan. 1995. 'Policy Economic of Poverty in Bihar', *Economic and Political Weekly,* Vol. 30, No. 41/42, Oct. 14–21.

Sharma, Ram Avtar and Sushma Yadav. 1989. *Political Culture in Post Independent India,* New Delhi, Sharma and Yadav.

Shenoy, TVR. 1997. 'Hypocrisy of the Honest: The Nation's Bugbear', *The Indian Express,* June 7.

Shukla K.S. 1985. 'Sociology of Deviant Behaviour' in *Survey of Research in Sociology and Social Anthropology,* Vol. III, New Delhi, Satvahan.

Singh, D.R. 2000. 'Crime Delinquency and Correctional Methods', in M.S. Gore (ed.),*Third Survey of Sociology and Social Anthropology*, Vol-2, New Delhi, Indian Council of Social Science Research and Manak Publishers Pvt. Ltd.

Singh, N.K. 1999. *'The Politics of Crime and Corruption: A Former CBI Officer Speaks',* New Delhi, Harper Collins.

Singh, Prakash. 2001. "Crime, Politics and Governance', *Seminar,* 502.

Singh, Santosh. 2009. 'Bihar's musclemen suffer blow as wives lose fight', *The Indian Express,* Patna.

Singh, V.P. 'Power and Equality – Changing Grammar of Indian Politics', Lecture delivered at Harvard University USA.

Sinha, Arun. 1978. 'Politics of Panchayat Election', *Economic and Political Weekly,* Vol. XIII, No. 24

—— 1978. 'Bajitpur: Landlord's Violence' *Economic and Political Weekly,* Vol. XIII, No. 50, December 16.

—— 1977. 'Landlords on Rampage in Champaran', *Economic and Political Weekly,* Vol. XII, No. 39, September.

—— 1977. 'Police, Politicians and Hoodlooms', *Economic and Political Weekly,* Vol. XII, No. 40, October,

—— 1977. 'Police to Landlord's Aid', *Economic and Political Weekly,* Vol. XII, No. 49, December 3.

—— 1977. 'Murder of a Peasant Leader', *Economic and Political Weekly,* Vol. XII, No. 31, December 10.

—— 1977. 'The Killing Continues', *Frontier,* October 15–20.

Sinha, Dipankar. 1991. 'V.P. Singh, Chandra Shekhar, and No-Where Politics of India', *Asian Survey,* 31, July.

Sinha, Indradeep. 1970. 'Land Liberation Movement in Bihar', *Mainstream,* October 20.

Sinha, Indu and Arvind Sinha. 1996. 'Setback to Political Arrogance' *Economic and Political Weekly*, June 29.

Sinha, S.K. 1995. 'Bihar, Poll and Seshan' *Hindustan Times,* (Patna), April 3

Skaria, George and Rohit Saran. 1997. 'Reforms 97: The Inside Story', *Business Today,* New Delhi, March 7–21, pp. 74–89.

Smart, Bary. 2002. *Michael Foucault,* London, Routledge.

Skocpol, Theda. 1979 *States and Social Revolution,* Cambridge, Cambridge University Press

Srivastava, Arun. 1998. 'Mob sets 4 tribal women; 2 children ablaze in Purnea', *The Indian Express,* December 15.

Subramanian, T.S.R. 2009. *GovernMint in India: An Inside View,* New Delhi, Rupa and Co.

Thakur, Sankarshan. 2000. *The Making of Lalu Yadav: The Unmaking of Bihar*. New Delhi, Harper Collins Publishers India.

Therborn, Goran. 1978. *What Does the Ruling Class Do When It Rules?* New Left Books, London

Thorner, D. 1980. *The Shaping of Modern India.* New Delhi, Allied Publishers.

Tilly, Charles and Sidney Tarrow, 2006. *Contentious Politics,* London, Paradigm Publishers.

Tocqueville, Alexis de.1955. *Democracy in America,* (ed. Philips Bradley), New York, Knopf.

Trehan, Madhu. 2009. *Tehelka as Metaphor,* Lotus Roli Books, New Delhi

Trimberger, Ellen Kay. 1977. 'State Power and Modes of Production: Implications of the Japanese Transition to Capitalism', *The Insurgent Sociologist,* 7, Spring;

——. 1977. *Revolutions form Above,* New Brunswick, N.J. Transaction Books.

Trivedi, Vibhesh. 2000. 'Vote, Bihar aur Bahubali' (Hindi), *Samkaleen Tapmaan,* March,

Vadlamannati, K.C. 2008. *'Socioeconomic, Institutional and Political Determinants of Human Rights Abuses: A Substantial study of India 1993–2002.* William Davidson Institute Working Paper Number 926, July.

Vanaik, Achin 1990. *The Painful Transition: Bourgeois Democracy in India,* London, Verso.

Varshney, Ashutosh. 1998. 'India Defies the Odds; Why Democracy Survives', *Journal of Democracy,* Vol. 9, No. 3, July.

—— 1995. *Democracy, Development and the Countryside: Urban-Rural Struggles in India,* Cambridge University Press, Cambridge.

Verma, Ravindra Kumar and Nihora Prasad Yadav. 1991. 'Caste and Candidate Selection: Lok Sabha Poll in Bihar', *Economic and Political Weekly*, June 1–8

Weiner, Myron. 1989. *The Indian Paradox: Essays in Indian Politics,* New Delhi, Sage Publication

—— 1967. *Party Building in a New Nation: The Indian National Congress,* Chicago, Chicago University Press.

Weingast, Barry R. 1997. 'The Political Foundations of Democracy and the Rule of Law', *The American Political Science Review,* Vol. 91, No. 2, June, pp. 245–263.

Weyland, Kurt. 1998. 'From Leviathan to Gulliver? The Decline of the Developmental State in Brazil', *Governance,* Volume 11, Issue 1, pp. 51–75, January

—— 1997–1998. 'The Brazilian State in the New Democracy', *Journal of Interamerican Studies and World Affairs,* Vol. 39, No. 4 (winter), pp. 63–94.

Wilkinson, Steven I. 2001. 'Cleansing Political Institutions', *Seminar,* October 20.

Wilson, Kalpana. 1999. 'Patterns of Accumulation and Struggles of Rural Labour: Some Aspects of Agrarian Change in Central Bihar', *Journal of Peasant Studies,* 26 (2–3)

Witsoe, Jeffrey. 2006. 'Social Justice and Stalled Development: Caste Empowerment and the Breakdown of Governance in Bihar', Spring, Philadelphia, Centre for Advance Study of India.

Yadav, N.P. 1990. *Land Reforms and Agricultural Development: A Study of their Impact on Small Farmers,* Delhi, Commonwealth Publishers.

Yadav, R.K. 'Ravi'. 2004. *Bihar Myth and Reality'* Hope India Publications, Gurgaon.

Yadav, Yogendra. 2009. 'Making Sense of the Verdict', *The Hindu,* 18th May. URL: http://www.thehindu.com/2009/05/18/stories/2009051854961100.htm.

—— 2004. 'Reconfiguration in Indian Politics: State Assembly Elections 1993–1995' in Partha Chaterjee (ed.) *State and Politics in India,* New Delhi, Oxford University Press.

Yugandhar, B.N. and Gopal Iyer. (eds.) 1993. *Land Reforms in India-Volume 1: Bihar-Institutional Constraints,* New Delhi, Sage Publication.

Reports

Constituent Assembly Debates, Vol. VII, IX, New Delhi, Lok Sabha Secretariat.

State of Democracy in South Asia: A Report, CSDS, New Delhi, Oxford University Press.

Report of the Punjab Police Commission 1961–62.

Ninth Report of the National Police Commission, Government of India, August 1979

High Court Judgement of the Criminal Appeal No. 64 of 2007 and Criminal Appeal No. 158 of 2007 on August 22, 2007,

Supreme Court Judgement P.V. Narasimha Rao Vs State (CBI) (1998) 4 SCC 626.

Census of India, 2001, 1951.

District Census Handbook Purnea, 1951 and 1961.

Report on the Agrarian Trouble in Dhamdaha and Dharahara Police Stations of Purnea District in PS, F 120 (I), n.10, N.P. Thadani.1940.

ML Update, 2003. 'Massacre in Purnea', A CPI (ML) Weekly News Magazine, August, Vol. 6, No 34.

CPI (ML) Approach Paper, *New Democracy, 'People's democratic Revolution in India and Land Problem',* presented at the convention on July 4th 2007 at Hyderabad.

CPI (ML) Document, 1986. *Report from the Flaming Fields of Bihar,* Kolkata, no 23.

Crime in India, Ministry of Home Affairs, Government of India, 1980–2005.

Project Report on Jaankari: A Government of Bihar Initiative, CM Secretariat, Patna.

Bihar's Exposure to Innovative Governance Practices: A Report of the Special Task Force on Bihar, Government of India, New Delhi.

Index